PRAISE FOR PREVIOUS EDITIONS OF

# Oregon
## Off the Beaten Path ®

"A great little book to keep in the glove compartment."
—*Tri-City Herald* (Pasco, Wash.)

"Oakley has a gift for finding the unusual, the charming and friendly places. Just moseying through the book is a delightful journey around the state."
—*Journeys* magazine

"The author, Myrna Oakley, is a native Oregonian, and her love of this magnificent state is revealed through her writing. Whether it's the varied botanical gardens of the Southern Coast, the spectacular beauty of the Cascades and Columbia Gorge, or the awe-inspiring Southeast desert that piques your interest, you'll find it all in this one book."
—*Inkfish* magazine

## Help Us Keep This Guide Up to Date

Every effort has been made by the author and editors to make this guide as accurate and useful as possible. However, many changes can occur after a guide is published—establishments close, phone numbers change, hiking trails are rerouted, facilities come under new management, etc.

We would love to hear from you concerning your experiences with this guide and how you feel it could be improved and be kept up to date. While we may not be able to respond to all comments and suggestions, we'll take them to heart, and we'll make certain to share them with the author. Please send your comments and suggestions to the following address:

The Globe Pequot Press
Reader Response/Editorial Department
P.O. Box 480
Guilford, CT 06437

Or you may e-mail us at: editorial@GlobePequot.com

Thanks for your input, and happy travels!

INSIDERS' GUIDE®

OFF THE BEATEN PATH® SERIES

# Off the
EIGHTH EDITION
# Beaten Path®

# oregon

## A GUIDE TO UNIQUE PLACES

## MYRNA OAKLEY

INSIDERS' GUIDE®

GUILFORD, CONNECTICUT
AN IMPRINT OF THE GLOBE PEQUOT PRESS

The prices, rates, and hours listed in this guidebook
were confirmed at press time. We recommend,
however, that you call establishments to obtain
current information before traveling.

To buy books in quantity for corporate use
or incentives, call **(800) 962–0973, ext. 4551,**
or e-mail **premiums@GlobePequot.com.**

**INSIDERS'** GUIDE®

Text design by Linda Loiewski
Maps by Equator Graphics © Morris Book Publishing, LLC
Spot photography throughout © Purestock/Getty
Illustrations on pages 29, 117, and 227 by Carole Drong; page 55 by Julie Lynch;
all other illustrations by Elizabeth Neilson Walker.

"Three Ways of Getting to Bandon" on page 7 courtesy *Western World;* quotes from
Jonathan Nicholas on page 139 © 1999 Oregonian Publishing Co. All rights reserved.
Reprinted with permission.

ISSN: 1535-8070
ISBN-13: 978-0-7627-4208-0
ISBN-10: 0-7627-4208-9

Manufactured in the United States of America
Eighth Edition/First Printing

To some very special young people—
Bradford, P.J., and Marisa; Emily and Sam;
Nathan, Douglas, and Brittany—
who will one day, I trust, discover the joys
of traveling off the beaten path.
To some special big people—
"Grandma" Doris,
Peter and Monica, Kenneth Nels, Nanette Marie,
Byron Charles, Maurine and Bill,
Roberta and Chuck, Marla and Jim, and
Robert "Humbert"—
kindred spirits in the joy of "shunpiking,"
finding out what's over there,
just around the bend.
And to those Faubion Elementary School
seventh-graders and their parents
that my fellow teachers and
I hauled all over Oregon
during 1969 and 1970.

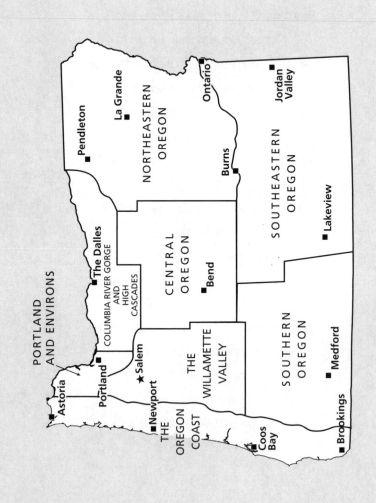

PORTLAND
AND ENVIRONS

Astoria

Portland

★ Salem

Newport
THE
OREGON
COAST

Coos
Bay

Brookings

The Dalles

COLUMBIA RIVER GORGE
AND
HIGH
CASCADES

CENTRAL
OREGON

Bend

THE
WILLAMETTE
VALLEY

SOUTHERN
OREGON

Medford

Pendleton

La Grande

NORTHEASTERN
OREGON

Ontario

Burns

SOUTHEASTERN
OREGON

Lakeview

Jordan
Valley

# Contents

# Acknowledgments

As always, oceans of thanks go to all the folks who help make a writer's life on the road comfortable and fruitful. Special thanks also to those who helped update information for their regions for this eighth edition. These include innkeepers, shopkeepers, historians, writer colleagues, helpful visitor information center staff and their friendly volunteers, and the helpful folks at the offices and ranger districts of the Bureau of Land Management (BLM), the USDA Forest Service, and the Fish and Wildlife Service.

An extra special thank you to hard-working project editors, freelance editors, and to other staff members at Globe Pequot who help get the guidebooks ready to go to the printers and binders. Also, special thanks to Darlene Brown who helped with fact-checking for this eighth edition. And, too, a heartfelt thank you to the traveling book representatives who help get our travel guides into bookstores near and far.

# Introduction

Looking back a number of years ago, I remember fully discovering—and truly appreciating—the vast, diverse character of my native Oregon in the late 1960s and early 1970s, when I traveled with some forty-seven seventh-graders, several fellow teachers, and helpful parents on working field trips throughout the Beaver State. We climbed aboard big yellow school buses and headed west to the Oregon coast to find eons-old seashell fossils. We trekked into the Columbia River Gorge and explored its history and geology. We headed east into the high-desert regions around Bend, camping out and experiencing four days of school under wide blue skies. We learned about life zones and native trees and native vegetation. We snooped into lava caves, lava cast forests, and ancient volcano remnants. It was an unforgettable time.

By now, traveling off the beaten path has become a well-worn habit, one shared by fellow Oregonians as well as visitors. Our wide ocean beaches and spectacular coastline remain a favorite destination—fully preserved for everyone to enjoy. A sense of the mid-1840s pioneer past still permeates much of the state, and sections of the Oregon Trail, including the actual wagon ruts, have been identified and preserved in eastern and central Oregon.

## Exploring 101: My Favorite Oregon Highways and Byways

**Historic Columbia River U.S. Highway 30:** Starting at Troutdale, east of Portland, and continuing in several sections roughly paralleling Interstate 84, to The Dalles

**U.S. Highway 101:** The length of the Oregon coast starting at Astoria in the north (where Lewis and Clark camped) or at Brookings on the south coast

**Highway 126:** From Florence, on the central coast, to Eugene, then east and onto Highway 242 at McKenzie Bridge and winding up and over McKenzie Pass to Sisters and the central Oregon high-desert area

**Highway 138:** From Roseburg winding east along the scenic Umpqua River to Diamond Lake and Crater Lake

**John Fremont Highway 31:** Heading southeast from LaPine (on U.S. Highway 97) and continuing on U.S. Highway 395 to Lakeview

**Highway 205:** From Burns south through the Malheur Wildlife Refuge to Frenchglen

**Highway 82:** From LaGrande to Elgin, Enterprise, Joseph, and into the scenic Wallowa Mountains area

**Highway 86:** From Baker City to Halfway and on to Hells Canyon Dam

## TOP HITS IN THE BEAVER STATE

**Columbia River Gorge**
from Troutdale east to Umatilla

**Crater Lake National Park**
southern Oregon

**Covered bridges**
Willamette Valley and southern Oregon
www.coveredbridges.stateoforegon.com

**Hells Canyon National Recreation Area**
northeastern Oregon

**Historic Columbia River U.S. Highway 30**
from Troutdale to The Dalles

**Klamath Basin Wildlife Refuge**
Klamath Falls

**Lava Lands and Newberry National Volcanic Monument**
central Oregon

**Lewis and Clark Corps of Discovery sites**
Columbia River Gorge, Long Beach Peninsula, and Astoria
www.nps.gov/focl

**Malheur Wildlife Refuge**
south of Burns in southeastern Oregon

**Oregon coast lighthouses**
from Astoria on the north coast to Brookings on the south coast

**Oregon farmers' and Saturday markets**
communities statewide
March through October
www.oregonfarmersmarkets.org

**Oregon Trail sites**
northeastern Oregon to the Willamette Valley

**Public, historic, botanic, and display gardens**
Portland and environs, the Willamette Valley, and the Oregon coast

**Whale Watch Weeks**
Oregon coast
www.whalespoken.org

An even earlier time is reflected in sites you can visit throughout the Columbia River Gorge and at the mouth of this mighty river at the Pacific Ocean. Along this route some thirty-three members of the Lewis and Clark Corps of Discovery, including Clark's Newfoundland dog, Seaman, met and traded with local Indian tribes, collected plant and animal specimens, and camped during 1805–6.

While modern explorers will enjoy more amenities and accommodation choices in Oregon than Lewis and Clark did, it is worthwhile to be mindful of the weather when planning a trip. The Pacific Northwest has four distinct seasons and two distinct weather patterns.

The eastern half of the state, the high desert, at elevations of 3,000 to 5,000 feet and higher, offers crisp, cold winters and hot, dry summers. Destinations east of Bend and east of U.S. Highway 97 offer quieter byways and many undiscovered and less crowded destinations. This is real cowboy and cowgirl country, and you'll find longer distances between towns and cities. In these outback areas, however, are ample visitor information centers as well as friendly locals glad to help travelers with directions. If you enjoy snow and winter sports, plan treks to the Cascade Mountain regions from mid- to late November through February and March. (See these chapters: Southeastern Oregon, Central Oregon, Northeastern Oregon, and Columbia River Gorge and High Cascades.)

The western half of the state, situated between the Cascade Mountain Range and the Pacific Ocean, offers low-elevation, green and lush regions with mild temperatures year-round. Hundreds of public gardens and nurseries, vineyards and wineries, and major metropolitan and coastal areas are here. If you want less traffic and less crowded places, especially along the coast, visit midweek. Or, travel early spring, April through June, and early fall, September (after Labor Day) and October. Autumn in the entire Northwest is sunny and warm. (See these chapters: the Oregon Coast, Southern Oregon, Portland and Environs, and the Willamette Valley.)

At the end of each chapter, places to eat and places to stay are listed, including resorts, inns, historic hotels, RV parks, and bed-and-breakfast inns, along with coffeehouses, bakeries, cafes, and restaurants. Casual, informal, and friendly are the bywords here; however, open hours can change, so it's best to call ahead if possible.

Hundreds of day-use parks and overnight campgrounds located in scenic areas throughout the state are managed by Oregon State Parks, city and county parks, the USDA Forest Service, and the Bureau of Land Management (BLM). You can call the Oregon State Parks reservation line (800–452–5687) up to six months ahead to reserve full-service RV sites and tent sites. (For general information call 800–551–6949.) A number of state parks are open year-round, and many now offer cabins, basic camping yurts, and even deluxe yurts with kitchens. For more information obtain a copy of Oregon Parks and Heritage Guide from any visitor information center.

I hope you enjoy this field trip through the Beaver State—walking in the footsteps of yesterday and today. Happy travels!

## Fast Facts about Oregon

- **Area:** 97,073 square miles
- **Capital:** Salem, located in the central Willamette Valley
- **County names:** Baker, Benton, Clackamas, Clatsop, Columbia, Coos, Crook, Curry, Deschutes, Douglas, Gilliam, Grant, Harney, Hood River, Jackson, Jefferson, Josephine, Klamath, Lake, Lane, Lincoln, Linn, Malheur, Marion, Morrow, Multnomah, Polk, Sherman, Tillamook, Umatilla, Union, Wallowa, Wasco, Washington, Wheeler, and Yamhill

- **Highest point:** Mount Hood (11,235 feet), located approximately 50 miles east of Portland
- **Largest county in Oregon** (and largest county in the United States): Harney, 10,228 square miles, located in the southeastern section of the state
- **Least populated county in the state:** Harney
- **Major rivers:** Columbia River, which flows south then west from its source in the Canadian Rockies and empties into the Pacific Ocean at Astoria on the north coast; the Willamette River, which flows north from its source in the Umpqua National Forest in the southern Cascade Mountains and empties into the Columbia River just north of downtown Portland
- **Mascot and colors, Oregon State University:** Beavers, orange and black (located in Corvallis, central Willamette Valley)
- **Mascot and colors, Portland State University:** Vikings, green and white (located in Portland)
- **Mascot and colors, University of Oregon:** Ducks, green and yellow (located in Eugene, southern Willamette Valley)
- **Nickname:** the Beaver State
- **Population:** 3.3 million
- **State animal:** beaver
- **State bird:** western meadowlark
- **State birthday:** February 14, 1859
- **State fish:** chinook salmon
- **State flower:** Oregon grape
- **State gem:** sunstone
- **State rock:** thunder egg
- **State tree:** Douglas fir

# The Oregon Coast

## Myrtlewoods, Redwoods, Easter Lilies, and Cranberries

With its mild, relatively dry winters, the southern Oregon coast offers many appealing options—clamming, crabbing, hiking, fishing, beachcombing, museum hopping, and just plain solitude beckon visitors to linger awhile.

From late June to early September, fields of lilies, both Easter lilies and Oriental hybrids, nod in colorful profusion, and travelers can detour from coastal U.S. Highway 101 just south of Brookings to see them, at the **Easter Lily Foundation,** 15636 US 101 (541–469–1000) and at **Flora Pacifica,** 15447 Ocean View Drive, Brookings (541–469–9741). Enjoy the viewing garden and several acres of flowers for cutting, such as calla lilies, astilbe, delphinium, lavender, and larkspur. You can see where the flowers are dried and made into gorgeous natural swags and wreaths as well as browse the gift shop Tuesday through Sunday from 10:00 A.M. to 5:00 P.M. Before continuing north, stop at the well-stocked Welcome Center located at 1650 US 101 and near **Harris Beach State Park,** open daily May through October.

# THE OREGON COAST

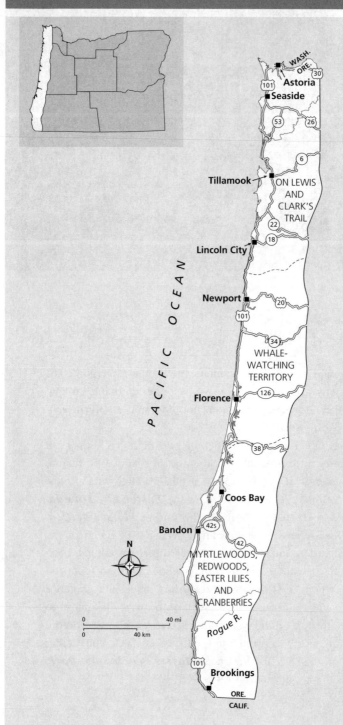

WASH.
ORE.
30
101
**Astoria**
**Seaside**

53
26

6

**Tillamook**
ON LEWIS
AND
CLARK'S
TRAIL

22
18
**Lincoln City**

**Newport**
20
101

34
WHALE-
WATCHING
TERRITORY

**Florence**
126

38

**Coos Bay**

**Bandon**
42s
42

MYRTLEWOODS,
REDWOODS,
EASTER LILIES,
AND
CRANBERRIES

*Rogue R.*

N

0          40 mi
0          40 km

101
**Brookings**
ORE.
CALIF.

P A C I F I C   O C E A N

You can then head out the Chetco River Road and spend an hour or so hiking the 1-mile ***Redwood Grove Nature Trail***, located 8½ miles inland from US 101 and ½ mile north of Alfred A. Loeb State Park, on the north bank of the Chetco River. Aided by the helpful interpretive brochure, you'll pass some fourteen numbered stations and identify trees, shrubs, ferns, and flowers that are characteristic of this coastal region. The centuries-old giant redwoods range between 300 and 800 years in age and may reach heights of 350 feet and girths of 25 feet. To travel into the heart of the awesome redwoods and ***Redwood National Park*** (707–464–6101), continue south from Brookings to Crescent City, California.

## preservingthe redwoods

For information on efforts to preserve and expand the range of Oregon's redwoods, contact Save the Redwoods League, 114 Sansome Street, Room 1200, San Francisco, CA 94104-3823 (415–362–2352; www.savetheredwoods.org).

For other wilderness hiking information, including wilderness cabins, contact the Chetco Ranger Station at 539 Chetco Avenue, Brookings (541–412–6000).

## TOP HITS ON THE OREGON COAST

**Azalea Park Gardens**
Brookings

**Cape Kiwanda and dory fishing fleet**
Pacific City

**The Connie Hansen Garden**
Lincoln City

**Darlingtonia Wayside**
Florence

**Devil's Churn and Cape Perpetua**
Yachats

**Flavel Mansion Museum and Uppertown Firefighters Museum**
Astoria

**Fort Clatsop**
south of Astoria

**Historic Seaside Promenade**
Seaside

**Rogue River mailboat trips**
Gold Beach

**Shore Acres Gardens and Sunset Bay State Park**
Coos Bay–Charleston

**Tillamook County Pioneer Museum**
Tillamook

**Tillamook Naval Air Station Museum and World War II blimp hangar**
Tillamook

**Umpqua Discovery Center**
Reedsport

**Yaquina Head Lighthouse**
Newport

**Coaster Theatre Playhouse**
Cannon Beach

> # Redwood Grove Nature Trail
>
> Along the trail notice the native rhododendron and tanbark oaks that often grow with the tall redwoods. The "rhodies" sport lush blooms in early spring. At one time tannin from the peeled bark of the oaks was used by the Pacific Coast leather industry. You can also spy the bushy perennials—black huckleberry, which has bluish black fruit; and the red huckleberry, which has bright red, tart berries. Both make delicious jelly.

Guided rafting and drift-boat fishing trips are also available on the Chetco River; information about local guides can be obtained from the ranger station or from the Brookings-Harbor Visitor Information Center, 16330 Lower Harbor Road (541–469–3181, www.brookingsor.com).

Consider taking in some live local theater while you're in the area. The *Chetco Pelican Players* in Brookings Harbor (541–469–1857) perform throughout the year and offer contemporary, light comedy and melodrama as well as popular Broadway musicals.

History buffs may want to plan a visit to the *Chetco Valley Historical Society Museum* (541–469–6651) located in the Blake House, the oldest standing house in the Brookings-Harbor area. The vintage red-and-white structure served as a stagecoach station and trading post on the south coast during the early 1800s. The museum is located at 15461 Museum Road in Brookings. It's open mid-March through November, Thursday through Sunday, noon to 4:00 P.M.

If time permits, detour at *Cape Sebastian,* located just north of Brookings and Pistol River, some 5 miles south of Gold Beach. Rising 500 feet from the Pacific Ocean, the cape offers spectacular wide-angle views of the coastline north and south, as well as hiking trails and picnic areas. Don't be deterred by the weather; this sight is not to be missed, even on a blustery day.

For one of the best side trips on the south Curry County coast, take one of the *Rogue River mailboat trips* (800–458–3511) from Gold Beach up the lower Rogue River. Here passengers and mail are transported in open and safe hydrojet-powered launches across ripples and easy rapids about 32 miles upriver, to Agness. Good-natured pilots point out wildlife and geological features along the way, often recounting lively tales of early river life.

A hearty lunch at rustic *Singing Springs Lodge* and the 32-mile return trip to Gold Beach complete this memorable foray into the Rogue River's pioneer past. Information about the mailboat trips and overnight options can be obtained from the Gold Beach–Wedderburn Visitor Information Center, 29279 Ellensburg Avenue, Gold Beach (800–525–2334; www.goldbeach.org). A longer, 102-mile, round-trip excursion up into the federally designated Wild and Scenic section of the Rogue River is also available. You could spend the night at remote ***Lucas Pioneer Ranch & Fishing Lodge*** (541–247–7443) upriver near Agness.

As you head north on US 101, the coastal headlands press close to the ocean, and the highway, once a narrow Indian trail, curves along a shelf high above the waves and around Humbug Mountain to ***Port Orford.*** In 1828 mountain man Jedediah Smith trekked through the area with more than a dozen men and some 250 horses loaded with furs obtained by trapping and trading in California. Crossing the mouth of the Rogue River, Jedediah reported in his journal that twelve horses drowned, but the furs, ferried across in canoes, were saved.

At Port Orford visit the local harbor, a natural deepwater area where fishing boats are hoisted in and out of the churning waters each day with an enormous converted log boom. You'll often see the boats resting high and dry on long trailers atop the pier.

The Visitor Information Center is located at the south end of Port Orford at Battle Rock City Park (541–332–8055; www.discoverportorford.com).

If time allows, drive about 5 miles west of US 101—just north of Port Orford—to ***Cape Blanco State Park*** to see the ***Cape Blanco Lighthouse.*** Constructed in the 1870s, the lighthouse is the oldest still standing on the coast, and its light still shines 21 miles out to sea. The lighthouse is open for tours

## Best Bed-and-Breakfasts on the South Coast

**Brookings South Coast Inn
Bed & Breakfast**
Brookings
(541) 469–5557
www.southcoastinn.com
Sheldon and Gru Lent

**By the Sea Bed and Breakfast**
Brookings
(877) 469–4692
www.brookingsbythesea.com
Carol and Larry Goetze

**Chetco River Inn**
Brookings
(541) 670–1645
www.chetcoriverinn.com
Sandra Brugger

**Holmes Sea Cove Bed & Breakfast**
Brookings
(541) 469–3025
Lorene and Jack Holmes

**Home by the Sea**
Port Orford
(541) 332–2855
www.homebythesea.com
Alan and Brenda Mitchell

## TOP ANNUAL EVENTS ON THE OREGON COAST

**Chocolate Lovers' Festival**
Seaside; late February
(503) 738–3097, (888) 306–2326

**Newport Seafood and Wine Festival**
Newport; late February
(541) 265–8801, (800) 262–7844

**Oregon Dixieland Jubilee**
Seaside; late February
(503) 738–3097, (888) 306–2326

**Astoria Crab & Seafood Festival**
Astoria; late April
(503) 325–6311, (800) 875–6807

**Clam Chowder Festival**
Gold Beach; early May
(541) 247–7526, (800) 525–2334

**Rhododendron Festival**
Florence; mid-May
(541) 997–3128, (800) 524–4864

**Azalea Festival**
Brookings-Harbor; late May
(541) 469–3181, (800) 535–9469

**Scandinavian Midsummer Festival**
Astoria; mid-June
(503) 325–6311, (800) 875–6807

**American Music Festival**
Brookings-Harbor; mid-July
(541) 469–3181, (800) 535–9469

**Oregon Coast Music Festival**
Coos Bay; mid-July
(541) 269–0215, (800) 824–8486

**Blackberry Arts Festival**
Coos Bay; late August
(541) 269–0215, (800) 824–8486

**Cranberry Festival**
Bandon; mid-September
(541) 347–9616

**Glass Floats Coastal Treasure Hunt**
Lincoln City, Florence, Newport, and
Rockaway Beach; October to June
(541) 996–1274, (800) 352–2151

April through October, Thursday through Monday from 10:00 A.M. to 4:00 P.M. Nearby, the restored **Historic Hughes House** (541–332–6774; www.hughes house.org), ca. 1898, sits in a small meadow above the winding Sixes River. It was built by pioneers Patrick and Jane Hughes thirty years after they had bought the land and started a dairy ranch. Now part of the Cape Blanco State Park complex, the house is open from April through October, Thursday through Monday from 10:00 A.M. to 4:00 P.M.

Of the nine original lighthouses on the Oregon coast, light beams from six of them continue to guide mariners, fishing parties, sailors, and pleasure boaters along coastal waters. Although newer technology in marine navigation—radio beacons and such—has retired the other three lighthouses from active service, there is growing interest in preserving these vintage maritime structures as historical sites, interpretive centers, and museums. *NOTE:* See list of Oregon lighthouses on page 24.

The nearby **Sixes River** offers fishing for fall chinook, spring and fall sea-run cutthroat, and winter steelhead. Cape Blanco State Park is open from April to November and has complete facilities for day and overnight use, in addition to a primitive hiker-biker camp. *NOTE:* There are large state campgrounds in each section of the coast that remain open all year, and many offer roomy yurts as an alternative to tent or RV camping (call 800–452–5687 or browse www.oregonstateparks.org).

Located at the mouth of the Coquille River, where the river surges into the Pacific Ocean, the community of **Bandon** is known for its cheese and its cranberries. Milk for the original Bandon Cheese and Produce Company, founded in 1927, was hauled from nearby Coquille Valley dairies by stern-wheel river-boats, and both cheddar cheese and butter were shipped to San Francisco by steamboat.

Some 900 acres of cranberry bogs are under cultivation near Bandon. The original vines were brought from Cape Cod, Massachusetts, in 1879 by pioneer grower Charles McFarlin. In those days the Coos Indians helped pick the bright red berries with wooden-toothed scoops each autumn. The Bandon community celebrates a cranberry festival each September. You can take a cranberry-bog tour at **Faber Farms** (541–347–4300; www.faberfarms.com), 519 Morrison Road, and also browse through a small gift shop that offers cranberry coffee-cake mix and brandied cranberries, among other specialty items. During the fall harvest, shop hours are 9:00 A.M. to 5:00 P.M., Monday through Saturday.

Displays of Indian artifacts and old photos of the cranberry harvest, as well as exhibits of local history—the town burned to the ground twice, in 1914 and 1936—can be seen at the **Bandon Historical Museum** (541–347–

## Three Ways of Getting to Bandon
from *Western World,* December 16, 1915

Take the steamer *Elizabeth* from San Francisco, fare $10;

Take either the *Alliance* or the *Breakwater* from Portland to Marshfield, then take a train to Coquille at 9 o'clock connecting with the Coquille River boat, landing you at noon the same day in Bandon; combined fare, not counting lodgings, is approximately $12;

Over stage from Roseburg to Myrtle Point from which place you take the river boat to Bandon as before, fare being $5 for stage and $1 for boat.

We recommend boat clear through, in the winter time at least. It is quicker and pleasanter for those not afflicted with seasickness.

## One of My Favorite Places

Regardless of how many times I head south from Portland to Bandon, the scenic route along the coast never fails to halt me in my tracks. I pull off at all the viewpoints along US 101, grab my camera and film, pull on my windbreaker, and head for the closest view of the water, the rocky headlands, the lighthouses, and the offshore seabird rookeries. I breathe in the salt air, turn my face to the afternoon sun as it shimmers on the Pacific Ocean, and thank my lucky stars that I live so close to the edge of the world. One of my favorite innkeepers in Bandon used to call me and say, "Don't you think it's time that you came down to the ocean for a while, get out of the rat race for a while?" I would smile and say, "Yes, it's definitely time." I would drive to Bandon, stay at the bed-and-breakfast inn with its 200-degree view of the water, the beach, and the seabirds. I would walk on the beach among the rugged sea stacks, on the dry sand or on the wet sand; I would photograph the small shore birds skittering along at the edge of the surf; I would sit on a chunk of driftwood and contemplate the day. My favorite innkeeper passed away several years ago, but I still feel the warmth of her hospitality and her special telephone calls that urged me to the ocean.

2164; www.bandonhistoricalmuseum.org), located at 270 Fillmore Avenue and US 101 and near the harbor and **Old Town** shops and eateries. The museum is open Tuesday through Sunday from 10:00 A.M. to 4:00 P.M. and is well worth a stop. If time allows, from here drive a couple of blocks up to the bluff top and turn onto **Beach Loop Drive;** wind along the ocean to see enormous sea stacks—giant rock formations left over from eons-old underwater volcanoes—and large rocks filled with colonies of seabirds. There are several places to park and walk down to the beach, one being **Face Rock State Scenic Viewpoint.** This is one of the best beach walks on the south coast. For ocean view sleeps call the **Sunset Motel** at 1865 Beach Loop Drive (800–842–2407).

Within walking distance of the museum, you can enjoy a stroll through Old Town shops and galleries. For tasty espresso drinks and deli sandwiches pop into **RayJen's Internet Cafe** (541–347–1144) on Third Street or **2 Loons Cafe & Deli** on Second Street. For current information call the Bandon Visitor Center (541–347–9616). Ask too about the **Bandon Playhouse** (541–347–2383; www.bandonplayhouse.com)—they do several productions each year, including a musical, a mystery, even a reader's theater.

Nestled alongside the Coquille River, just north of Bandon's Old Town marina, the **Coquille River Lighthouse,** now a museum, celebrated its centennial in 1996. You can access the historic structure from **Bullards Beach State Park,** off US 101 just north of Bandon. Walk out the jetty trail to see spectacular ocean waves crash on the rocks that edge both sides of the Coquille River as it surges into the Pacific. The large state park offers RV sites, tent sites, and space for hiker-bicycle parties and for horse campers. Contact the state reservation number (800–452–5687) weekdays 8:00 A.M. to 5:00 P.M. Bullards Beach is open year-round.

For a pleasant side trip from Bandon, head east on Highway 42 for about 15 miles to Coquille. There you can take in an old-fashioned melodrama, such as *Sweet, Sweet Revenge* or *Live Women in the Mines,* at the **Sawdust Theatre** (541–396–3414) on Saturday evening at 8:00 during June and on Friday and Saturday from July through Labor Day. The community's annual Gay Nineties Celebration on the first Saturday of June launches the summer season.

To experience some of the most magnificent scenery on the south coast, detour from US 101 about 10 miles north of Bandon to Charleston and then double back to Sunset Bay, Shore Acres, and Cape Arago. This area can also be accessed from Coos Bay–North Bend.

Sandstone cliffs curve around picturesque, half-moon **Sunset Bay.** Atop the cliffs are easy hiking trails. At low tide walk out along the rocks on the south side to explore tide pools filled with sea anemones, tiny crabs, oblong chitons, and purple sea urchins. Keep close supervision of children and wear sturdy shoes for this trek so as not to take a spill on wet rocks and slippery seaweed.

There are shady picnic areas, a large overnight campground, and a safe, sandy beach at Sunset Bay. For state campsite reservations call (800) 452–5687. Plan to spend couple of hours visiting nearby **Shore Acres State Park and Gardens,** once the grand turn-of-the-twentieth-century estate of a wealthy south coast lumberman, Louis J. Simpson, whose prospering business had been built by his father, Asa Meade Simpson, in the late 1800s. The garden is just a mile beyond Sunset Bay State Park Campground.

## OTHER ATTRACTIONS WORTH SEEING ON THE COAST

**Fort Stevens Historic Area**
near Astoria in Hammond; *Peter Iredale* shipwreck on beach

**Port Orford Head State Park and Nautical Museum**
Port Orford

**South Slough National Estuarine Reserve and Interpretive Center**
near Charleston

**Tillamook Forest Center**
Highway 6 (milepost 22)
www.tillamookforest.org

A wooded walkway invites visitors past a display illustrating the history of Shore Acres and the Simpson family, researched by Oregon historian Stephen Dow Beckham. The beautifully restored garden features enormous beds of elegant roses, lush plantings of dahlias, exotic tree species, and a lovely sunken Japanese garden. Along the nearby sea cliff is an enclosed gazebo where the mansion once perched—an excellent place to watch for whales and to safely view the crashing waves of winter storms. You'll notice, too, many uptilted ledges and massive outcroppings—ancient geology at its best on the south coast!

Easy hiking trails and picnic areas are also available on the grounds. The park is open year-round from dawn to dusk and is decorated with thousands of lights from the second week in December through New Year's Eve. Call Shore Acres or visit the Web site for spring and summer bloom times (541–888–3732; www.shoreacres.net). Don't miss a visit to this stunning coastal garden.

Drive on to **Cape Arago,** at the end of the road, for another panorama of wave-sculpted bluffs, for ocean breezes, and, often, for the cacophony of barking Steller's sea lions, harbor seals, and elephant seals, on Simpson's Reef. You'll find secluded picnic tables and hiking trails here as well. Year-round camping is also available at nearby **Bastendorff Beach County Park,** along with a wide sandy beach and good views of the ocean. This less-crowded spot is excellent for flying kites and for walking along the beach.

Heading past the county park back toward Coos Bay–North Bend, notice the colorful boat harbor at **Charleston;** here visitors can go crabbing from the dock area. A small visitor center near the bridge is open May to September and can provide information about crab nets and bait (541–888–2311). Charter fishing excursions are also available at the Charleston Marina; for current information call the friendly folks at Betty Kay Charters (541–888–9021). Stop at one of the many cafes and restaurants in the boat basin for specialty coffees, sandwiches, soups, fresh fish dishes, and fresh bagels.

## Early Coastal Explorers

The journals of early 1800s mountain man Jedediah Smith and explorer Alexander McLeod often reported traveling less than 5 miles a day on horseback through thick coastal forests, over rugged ravines and valleys, and across rushing streams, rivers, and bays. Later, a stage-line route along the beach was established and remained in use until 1916. The stage operated on a "flexible" schedule—determined by the incoming or outgoing tide.

On US 101 South pop into **Kaffe 101** at 171 South Broadway (541–267–4894) for steaming lattes and great pastries from Early to Rise Bakery. If your taste buds cater to natural foods, try the **Blue Heron Bistro,** which is well known for home-baked breads, tasty soups, delicious entrees, freshly made desserts, and gourmet coffee. The bistro, located at the corner of Commercial Street and US 101, is open daily from 9:00 A.M. to 9:00 P.M.

For a tour through one of the south coast's myrtlewood factories, stop at **The Oregon Connection** (800–255–5318; www.oregonconnection.com), at the south edge of Coos Bay. You can tour the factory, watch the production process, and see local artisans create polished bowls, trays, cups, golf putters, and other handcrafted gift items from the rough myrtlewood logs.

As an added treat, more than twelve varieties of cream and butter fudge are made here—be sure to ask for a taste of your favorite. The gift shop also stocks many Northwest wines and an assortment of local and regional gourmet foods. The factory and gift shop are open daily from 8:00 A.M. to 5:00 P.M.

For a visit to a historic newspaper and job-printing shop on the National Register of Historic Places, plan a summertime stop at the **Marshfield Sun Printing Museum,** located at the corner of Front Street and Bayshore Drive (US 101) in Coos Bay. The *Marshfield Sun* newspaper was edited and published by Jesse Allen Luse from 1891 until 1944. You'll see a Washington handpress, a Chandler and Price platen press, and nearly 200 type cases and fonts of type on the main floor of the museum. On the upper level see exhibits on the history of printing and on early Marshfield, which was Coos Bay's former name, as well as a collection of old U.S. newspapers. The museum is open during the summer Tuesday through Saturday from 1:00 to 4:00 P.M. Visits during winter months can be arranged by calling the Bay Area Visitor Information Center (541–269–0215).

On Tuesday through Saturday history buffs can stop at the **Coos County Historical Society Museum** at Simpson Park on the outskirts of North Bend, 1220 Sherman Street (541–756–6320), for a look at south coast Indian and pioneer displays, exhibits, and vintage books and scrapbooks. On the grounds you'll see an old-time railroad steam engine and antique logging equipment. The museum is open Tuesday through Saturday from 10:00 A.M. to 4:00 P.M.; closed holidays. Just next door is the well-stocked North Bend Visitor Information Center (800–472–9176) along with a shady picnic area and public restrooms. Ask the staff at the visitor center which plays are currently running at **Little Theatre on the Bay** (541–756–4336; www.ltob.net) in North Bend or at **On Broadway Theater** (541–269–2501; www.onbroadwaytheater.com) in Coos Bay. Little Theatre is the second-oldest community theater in the state, having begun in 1948. For a spot of tea or coffee in North Bend, stop at **Sozo's,** 1955 Union Street (541–756–4634). For seafood, great pita sandwiches, and

## Live Theater on the Oregon Coast

Theater lovers who live and perform in Oregon's coastal towns and communities enthusiastically welcome visitors and invite them to take in the season's offerings, from Broadway musicals old and new, favorite comedies, and chilling mysteries to lively dinner theater and old-fashioned melodramas. Call ahead for currently scheduled plays and to order tickets. Sampling from years past: *Blithe Spirit, Arsenic and Old Lace, Steel Magnolias, Greater Tuna, South Pacific, H.M.S. Pinafore, Gypsy, Pajama Game, Hello, Dolly!* and *The Music Man.*

### SOUTH COAST

**Bandon Playhouse**
Bandon
(541) 347–2383
www.bandonplayhouse.com

**Chetco Pelican Players**
Brookings
(541) 469–1857

**On Broadway Theater**
Coos Bay
(541) 269–2501
www.onbroadwaytheater.com

**Sawdust Theatre**
**Melodrama Players**
Coquille
(541) 396–3414

### CENTRAL COAST

**Last Resort Players**
Florence
(541) 997–3128
www.lastresortplayers.tripod.com/

**Porthole Players and Coastal Act Productions**
Newport
(888) 701–7123

**Red Octopus Theatre Company**
Newport
(888) 701–7123

**Theatre West Players**
Lincoln City
(541) 994–5663
www.theatrewest.com

### NORTH COAST

**Arts on Stage**
Astoria
www.clatsopcollege.com

**Astor Street Opry Company**
Astoria
(503) 325–6104

**Coaster Theatre Playhouse**
Cannon Beach
(503) 436–1242
www.coastertheatre.com

tasty Greek and Italian favorites, try ***Café Mediterranean,*** 1860 Union Street (541–756–2299).

Heading north from Coos Bay–North Bend, you'll drive high above the bay via ***McCullough Bridge,*** one of the longest bridges constructed by the Works Progress Administration (WPA) along the Oregon coast. Signed into law by President Franklin D. Roosevelt, the WPA provided much-needed work for thousands of Americans during the Great Depression. McCullough Bridge is nearly a mile in length and was dedicated on June 5, 1936. The channel spans rise 150 feet to accommodate ships entering and leaving Coos Bay's large, protected harbor.

Motoring on scenic US 101, with its many bridges spanning numerous rivers, it's easy to forget this was once a windswept wilderness laced with deer and Indian trails. In the 1800s Indians, explorers, and pioneers traveled on foot, on horseback, by canoe, and, later, by ferry. During the late 1800s and early 1900s, the stagecoach lines traveled on sections of the sandy beach.

Much of **North** as well as **South Tenmile Lake** is still accessible only by boat, its many arms reaching into Coastal Range forests. Anglers return year after year to stalk the black bass, bluegill, trout, and catfish in the lake's waters. Good boat ramps, a marina, art boutiques, motels, and campgrounds are found in and about **Lakeside** and the **Tenmile Lakes** area. For current information about boat rentals and the bass-fishing contest held each spring, call Lakeside Marina (541–759–3312, www.lakesidemarina.net).

## Whale-Watching Territory

Travel north again on US 101 to **Winchester Bay,** the largest salmon-fishing harbor on the Oregon coast, and discover bustling **Salmon Harbor**—where the Umpqua River meets the Pacific Ocean—by turning west toward **Windy Cove Campground.** You'll find facilities here for launching seaworthy boats and for renting crabbing and fishing equipment; you'll also find custom canning, bait, fuel, and ice, as well as information about appropriate fishing licenses.

Charter deep-sea fishing trips are available throughout most of the year at Salmon Harbor; call the Reedsport–Winchester Bay Visitor Center (800–247–2155, www.reedsportcc.org) for information.

Continue on the loop drive, following the south shore of Salmon Harbor, to discover **Umpqua Lighthouse.** From the impressive 65-foot tower, a bright red flash is seen some 16 miles at sea, the only colored signal on the Oregon coast. You can visit the Lighthouse Museum May 1 through September 30, Wednesday to Saturday from 10:00 A.M. to 5:00 P.M.; to arrange a guided tour limited to groups of six, call Douglas County Parks and Recreation, (541) 271–4631. Camping options include **Umpqua Lighthouse State Park** or nearby **Windy Cove** (800–452–5687 for reservations); or, for RV spaces and cottages on Half Moon Bay, call the folks at **Discovery Point Resort & RV Park** (541–271–3443). This is a popular spot for dune-buggy enthusiasts.

At **Reedsport** you can walk along reconstructed boardwalks that are reminiscent of the industrial area that housed canneries and sawmill sheds in earlier days and learn about the small coastal town's history at the splendid **Umpqua**

Salmon Harbor

**Discovery Center.** It is located near the boardwalk at 409 Riverfront Way in Old Town, just off US 101 (541–271–4816). The kids will enjoy peeking through the center's periscope for a 360-degree view of the Umpqua River, nearby railroad swing bridge, and jet-boat dock. The center is open 9:00 A.M. to 5:00 P.M. from June to September 30; winter hours are 10:00 A.M. to 4:00 P.M. Snacks are available nearby at the **Schooner Inn Cafe** (541–271–3945) and at the **Sugar Shack Bakery** (541–271–3514).

If you decide to drive east toward Roseburg and Interstate 5 via Highway 38, be sure to pull off at the **Dean Creek Elk Viewing Area** just 3 miles east of Reedsport and near the Umpqua River. Pause at Hinsdale Interpretive Center for helpful displays and to peek through the viewing scope, then gaze out over nearly 500 acres of bottomland and 600 acres of hilly woodlands, where the mammoth elk roam free. Depending on the time of day, you may also see a parade of other wildlife, such as porcupine, coyote, and raccoon, as well as many bird species.

Just south of Florence, detour at the **Oregon Dunes Overlook,** a scenic pullout area whose wheelchair-accessible observation decks offer good views of the ocean and dunes. In the Oregon Dunes are twelve developed trails, ranging from a ¾-mile stroll along a small lagoon to a 6-mile hike through Douglas fir forests and rugged sand dunes. Maps and information about other accessible sand-dune areas can be obtained from the well-stocked Oregon Dunes National Recreation Area Headquarters, 855 US 101, Reedsport (541–271–3611; www.fs.fed.us/r6/siuslaw).

At the junction of US 101 and Highway 126, near the mouth of the Siuslaw River, stop and explore Florence, a thriving community of some 5,000 coast dwellers. *Old Town Florence,* along the river near Bay Street, is a pleasant place to stroll and poke into charming shops, galleries, and eateries housed in some of the town's most historic buildings.

Along Bay Street, in Old Town, stop and eat at *Waterfront Depot* (541–902–9100); enjoy great sundaes and cones at *BJ's Ice Cream,* or stop in for a steaming cup of espresso at *Old Town Coffee Company* (541–997–1786). It's just east a few blocks from the Kite Shop and near the port of Siuslaw. An old-fashioned gazebo in tiny *Old Town Park* offers a cozy spot where you can sit with a view of the Siuslaw River and its graceful drawbridge, ca. 1936, constructed by the WPA.

If you haven't time to try catching your own crabs but would like to see how it's done, drive a couple of miles out to the *South Jetty,* walk out on the large wooden pier, and watch folks lower bait-filled crab rings into the churning waters. Here you're on the Siuslaw River estuary, where the river meets the Pacific Ocean—surging mightily against the oncoming tides.

If you visit from November through February, look for the squadron of some 200 snowy white tundra swans that winter on the Siuslaw River's marshes near South Jetty. *NOTE:* It's a good idea to bring rain gear, waterproof boots, and binoculars.

## trivia

*Siuslaw* is an Indian word meaning "faraway waters." Most of the lakes in this area have special Indian names: *Cleawox,* meaning "paddle wood"; *Siltcoos,* meaning "plenty elk"; and *Tahkenitch,* meaning "many arms."

After this invigorating trek head back to Old Town in Florence to *Siuslaw River Coffee Roasters* at 1240 Bay Street (541–997–3443) for bagels and fresh-brewed coffee, or to *Lovejoy Tea Room* at 195 Nopal Street (541–902–0502) for sumptuous pastries and tasty soups and sandwiches. Or you could stop at nearby *Mo's Restaurant,* for tasty clam chowder or fish-and-chips, located at the east end of Bay Street (541–997–2185). For comfortable overnight lodgings and great breakfasts, check with the *Blue Heron Bed & Breakfast,* overlooking the Siuslaw River (541–997–4091 or 800–997–7780) or with the *Edwin K Bed & Breakfast,* close to Old Town (541–997–8360).

If you'd just as soon ride a horse, check with the friendly folks at *C and M Stables* (541–997–7540; www.oregonhorsebackriding.com), located 8 miles north of Florence at 90241 US 101 North, to reserve a gentle steed for beach and sunset rides, dune trail rides, or winter rides. The stables are open daily from June through October but closed on Monday and Tuesday during winter months. For other lodging alternatives stop at the Florence Area Visitor Center, 270 US 101 (541–997–3128; www.florencechamber.com).

Next, turn off US 101 at the **Darlingtonia Wayside** sign, pull into the visitor parking area, and follow the shaded trail to the sturdy boardwalk that takes you out onto a marshy bog. This is one of the few small nature preserves in the United States set aside for conserving a single native species. *Darlingtonia californica* is often called cobra lily because it captures and actually digests insects. You can see the unusual greenish-speckled tubular-shaped plants here from spring through summer and into early fall.

Your next stop is **Devil's Elbow State Park,** just beyond Cape Creek Bridge. The park's sheltered beach offers a lovely spot to picnic and to beachcomb for shells and driftwood. Offshore, the large rock "islands," part of the **Oregon Islands National Wildlife Refuge,** are transient nesting grounds for tufted puffin, cormorants, pigeon guillemots, and numerous kinds of seagulls. From here you can walk the forested trail over to the ca. 1894 **Heceta Head Lighthouse.** The lighthouse is open for touring May through September, noon to 5:00 P.M. daily.

By now, midway on your coastal trek, you have surely felt the magic of the ocean seeping into your bones. Even words like *magnificent, incredible,* and *awesome* seem inadequate to describe the wide-angle views along this stretch of the Oregon coast. It's a panoramic showstopper of the first order, and nearly every inch of it is open to the public. One such dramatic encounter is found by walking down the short trail at **Devil's Churn Wayside** to watch incoming waves as they thunder and foam into a narrow basalt fissure. *NOTE:* Wear sturdy walking shoes and use caution here, especially with children.

For another spectacular view drive up to **Cape Perpetua** and its visitor center, just a short distance off US 101, perched atop a jagged chunk of forty-million-year-old volcanic basalt. The Forest Service staff offers lots to see and do at Cape Perpetua, including six nature trails, campfire talks at Tillicum Beach, and naturalist-led hikes down to the tide pools, together with interpretive nature exhibits and films. The visitor center (541–547–3289; www.orcoast.com/capeperpetua) is open daily all summer from 9:00 A.M. to 6:00 P.M. Also within the **Cape Perpetua Scenic Area** are group picnic areas, a campground, and a 22-mile self-guided auto tour.

For pleasant oceanside lodgings and good eateries on the central coast, there are several possibilities near Waldport and Yachats. **Sea Quest Bed & Breakfast,** 95354 US 101 (541–547–3782), offers five splendid guest rooms, all within 100 feet of the sandy beach and the melodious ocean surf. **Cape Cod Cottages** (541–563–2106), 4150 SW US 101 near Waldport, offers fireplaces, kichens, ocean views, and miles of sandy beach.

Try *Joe's Town Center Cafe* (541–547–4244) on US 101 at Fourth Street in Yachats for soups and sandwiches. *The Drift Inn* (541–547–4477), a historic restaurant and bar at 124 US 101 North, offers seafood, chowder, and home-made breads and desserts. You can also pop into *Rain Dogs Gift Shop* (541–547–3000) or *Grand Occasions Deli* at 162 Beach Street (541–547–4409), both across from the Post Office. *Toad Hall* on Second Street (541–547–4044) offers great coffee, espresso, and pastries. *Leroy's,* on US 101 near Seventh Street, has simply delicious fish-and-chips (541–547–3399). For additional information contact the Yachats Area Visitor Center (800–929–0477; www.yachats.org).

Continue north again on US 101 for about 20 miles to Newport, where two more lighthouses await—the *Yaquina Bay Lighthouse* in Yaquina Bay State Park (541–265–5679), and the *Yaquina Head Lighthouse* and *Yaquina Head Outstanding Natural Area* (541–574–3100; www.yaquinalights.org), 3 miles north and 1 mile west of the highway. Both lighthouses are open for touring usually from noon to 5:00 P.M. Yaquina Head's tower, rising 93 feet, is especially dramatic; you can view from the tower watch room between 9:00 A.M. and noon from mid-June to mid-September. Its light has remained active since 1873. Be sure to notice the colonies of seabirds on the offshore island here.

Most everyone who travels through this part of the coast will plan a stop at the *Oregon Coast Aquarium* (541–867–3474; www.aquarium.org) to see where *Keiko* the orca whale lived for two years before being returned to his home waters off the coast of Iceland.

Both the aquarium and the *Hatfield Marine Science Center* (541–867–0100; www.hmsc.orst.edu) are located just beneath the Yaquina Bay Bridge at the south edge of Newport. Hours are 9:00 A.M. to 6:00 P.M. daily during summer months and 10:00 A.M. to 4:30 P.M. the rest of the year.

To immerse yourself in central coast history, plan to stop at the *Burrows House Museum* and the *Log Cabin Museum* at 545 SW Ninth Street in Newport (541–265–7509). Both museums are open June through September from 10:00 A.M. to 5:00 P.M. daily and October through May from 11:00 A.M. to 4:00 P.M. each day but Monday.

Yaquina Head Lighthouse

## Golfing on the Oregon Coast

Since earlier times when golf had its beginnings on Scotland's windswept dunes, folks of all ages still enjoy walking the fairways, swinging the clubs, and aiming those elusive putts on the greens. Stow the golf clubs and golf shoes in the trunk and take in a gaggle of scenic links on your travels along the central coast. Call for current rates, tee times, and enjoy.

**Agate Beach Golf Course**
Newport
9 holes, 6,004 yards, par 72
(541) 265–7331

**Alderbrook Golf Course**
Tillamook
18 holes, 5,692 yards, par 69
(503) 842–6413

**Bay Breeze Golf Course**
Tillamook
9 holes, 1,061 yards, par 27
(503) 842–1166

**Cedar Bend Golf Course**
Gold Beach
9 holes, RV park nearby
(541) 247–6911

**Crestview Hills Golf Course**
Waldport
9 holes, 6,124 yards, par 72
(541) 563–3020

**Hawk Creek Hills Golf Course**
Newkowin
9 holes, 4,882 yards, par 68
(503) 392–4120

**The Highlands Golf Course**
Gearhart
9 holes, 2,000 yards, par 30
(503) 738–5248

**Sandpines Golf Links**
Florence
18 holes, 6,085 yards, par 72
(800) 917–4653

Before leaving the Newport area, you can refill your picnic basket or cooler from the carry-out section at *Canyon Way Restaurant,* 1216 SW Canyon Way (541–265–8319), which features homemade pastas, delicious breads, meat- or seafood-filled croissants, and delectable pastries.

In Newport's historic Nye Beach area, the intimate *Nye Beach Hotel* sits on a bluff above the ocean at 219 NW Cliff Street (541–265–3334; www.nye beach.com). In your cozy room you may find a gas fireplace, a whirlpool tub, and a down comforter on the bed. On the main floor you might hunker down in the funky 1930s-style cafe for a meal from the bistro menu. Or, call for dinner reservations and walk across the street to trendy *April's Restaurant at Nye Beach,* 749 NW Third Street (541–265–6855). The inviting space features splendid watercolors done in country floral and nostalgic still-life designs. Enjoy poking into other shops and eateries in Nye Beach along NW Beach Street off Coast Drive. You could also gather goodies at nearby *Village Market Bistro & Deli* (541–574–9393). At *The Tea Party,* 716 NW Beach Drive (877–872–7897), consider reserving a table for an English tea luncheon Tuesday through Saturday. For yummy baked goods, lunch fare, and espresso drinks check out *Panini's,* also in Nye Beach, at 232 NW Coast Street (541–265–5033).

Pleasant inns in the Newport area, most offering great ocean views, include *Newport Belle Bed & Breakfast,* aboard a large stern-wheel–style riverboat (541–867–6290); *Tyee Lodge Oceanfront Bed & Breakfast* (541–265–8953); and *Agate Beach Motel* (800–755–5674) just north of Newport and overlooking the beach.

The Newport Visitor Information Center (800–262–7844) offers current information about lodgings and the variety of goings-on in the area. For live theater offerings by *Coastal Act Productions, Porthole Players,* and *Red Octopus Theatre Company,* call (888) 701–7123 for current playbills.

Heading north again on US 101, you can access *Otter Crest Scenic Loop Drive,* at Otter Rock. First drive out to the bluff to peer down into *Devil's Punch Bowl,* a rounded outcropping into which the ocean thunders. The tiny Mo's Restaurant here offers clam chowder and fish-and-chips. The loop drive reconnects with US 101 within a couple of miles.

If you're driving through the area at low tide—you can pick up current tide tables for a nominal cost at most visitor centers—stop at the *Inn at Otter Crest,* parking close to the ocean, just beyond the Flying Dutchman Restaurant. Walk a short path down to the beach, where you can see a fascinating array of *tide pools* formed by rounded depressions in the large volcanic rocks. Bathed by tidal currents twice each day, coastal tide pools may house a variety of species, such as sea anemones, sea urchins, goose barnacles, sea stars, sea slugs, limpets, jellyfish, and tiny crabs. *NOTE:* Do not disturb live sea creatures.

If your picnic basket and cooler are full of goodies and cold beverages, consider a lunch stop at one of the most charming coastal day parks, *Fogarty Creek Wayside,* just north of Depoe Bay and Pirate's Cove. Here you can walk a path that meanders through the day-use park, alongside a small creek,

## Precautions from the Naturalists

A few precautions from the naturalists: Seaweed is slippery, wear deck shoes, and avoid jumping from rock to rock; keep a wary eye on the incoming tide; watch for large "sneaker" waves, which can appear out of the regular wave pattern; stay away from rolling logs, which can move quickly onto an unsuspecting tidepooler, particularly a small child; don't remove live marine creatures from the tide pools or take any live specimens with you. Other beach treasures you and the kids *can* collect and take home: limpet and barnacle shells, sand-dollar and sea-urchin shells, Japanese glass floats, dried kelp, driftwood, beach rocks, and translucent agates.

and through a tunnel under the highway to a small sandy cove right on the edge of the ocean. Weather permitting, you can have your picnic with seagulls and sandpipers for company. In the park are picnic tables and restrooms. It's a great place for families with small children.

If, however, you're driving through this section of the central coast early in the day and the ocean is flat and shimmering in the morning sun, stop at the seawall in **Depoe Bay,** just south of Fogarty Creek, to see whether the gray whales are swimming past. Of the seven different kinds of whales plying the Pacific Ocean, the grays maneuver closest to the shoreline. Some 15,000 of the mammoth creatures migrate south from November to January and return north from March to May. This 12,000-mile round-trip is the longest known for any mammal. You could also hole up near Depoe Bay at the cozy **Inn at Arch Rock** (800–767–1835; www.innatarchrock.com) or at **Troller's Lodge,** 355 SW Highway 101 (800–472–9335).

Equipment for **whale watching** is minimal—helpful are good binoculars, a camera and tripod, and warm clothing. Or just shade your eyes and squint, gazing west toward the horizon. You might be rewarded for your patience by seeing one of the grays "breach," that is, leap high out of the water and then fall back with a spectacular splash.

During one week in January and another week in March, some 200 volunteers at whale-watching sites all along the coast offer helpful information, brochures, maps, and assistance with spotting the gray whales. Look for the familiar logo WHALE WATCHING SPOKEN HERE and for the volunteers, ranging from

## Best Whale-Watching Sites along the Coast

**Cape Meares State Park**
near Tillamook

**Cape Perpetua overlook**
south of Yachats

**D River State Wayside**
Lincoln City

**Depoe Bay seawall**
Depoe Bay

**Ecola State Park**
Cannon Beach

**Fort Stevens State Park**
Astoria

**Rocky Creek Wayside and Cape Foulweather**
south of Depoe Bay

**Shore Acres State Park**
Coos Bay–Charleston

**Umpqua Lighthouse State Park**
Winchester Bay

**Yaquina Head**
Newport

school kids to oldsters. For more information check the helpful Web site www.whalespoken.org.

Both at Shore Acres, located west of Coos Bay–North Bend, and at Cape Perpetua, north of Florence, you can view whales from glassed-in areas and stay dry to boot.

Just south of Lincoln City, in Gleneden Beach, tucked away at 6675 Gleneden Beach Loop Road, is a good dinner stop, the **Side Door Cafe** (541–764–3825). Sitting at tables amid colorful stage props and stage sets, you may feel like an actor in a Broadway show. Ask about current music and live theater offerings.

Nestled in a hillside setting of coast pine and Douglas fir, **Westin Salishan Lodge** (800–452–2300) offers spacious and comfortable guest suites, an art gallery, a golf course, indoor tennis courts, an indoor swimming pool, and gourmet dining in the inn's three restaurants. The wine cellar is exemplary. Directly across US 101 from the lodge, you'll find the lively **MarketPlace** of small boutiques, bookshops, and eateries, and, at the north end, a pleasant **nature trail** that skirts tiny **Siletz Bay.**

Following all this whale-spying and gourmet eating, stop by **Catch the Wind Kite Shop** at 266 SE Highway 101 in Lincoln City for a look at kites of all sizes, shapes, colors, and prices. It's located just across the highway from the D River Wayside beach, where, on a particularly windy day, you can watch kites being flown by kids of all ages. Try friendly **Wildflower Grill** at 4250 NE Highway 101 (541–994–9663) for homestyle soups and chowder, great seafood dishes, and homemade desserts. Also at the north end of Lincoln City, the legendary **Barnacle Bill's** at 2174 NE Highway 101 (541–994–3022) is a good stop for fresh seafood and deli items. **Pacific Grind Coffee Shop** at 4741 SW Highway 101 (541–994–8314) offers great coffee, espresso, sandwiches, and soups.

For helpful information about the entire area, stop at the Lincoln City Visitor Center at the far north end of town, at 801 SW Highway 101 (800–452–2151). Ask, too, for directions to the nearby **Connie Hansen Garden**—a true plantswoman's botanical paradise. On two city lots, at 1931 NW Thirty-third Avenue, the splendid garden is cared for and staffed by a group of dedicated volunteers on Tuesday and Thursday from 10:00 A.M. to 2:00 P.M. and is also open for visitors daily (541–994–6338; www.conniehansengarden.com).

## On Lewis and Clark's Trail

Leaving the bustling Lincoln City area, travelers notice a quieter, more pastoral ambience along US 101, which winds north from Otis toward Neskowin, Sandlake, Cape Lookout, Netarts, and Tillamook. Those who travel through this region in the early spring will see dairy cows munching lush green grass inside

## The Honeymooners

Lincoln City has been a favorite spot for honeymooning couples for more than a century. In 1837, traveling by horseback on the Old Elk Trail along the Salmon River, missionary Jason Lee brought his bride, Anna Marie Pittman, together with Cyrus Shepard and *his* bride, and a guide, Joe Gervais. The two couples set up camp at nearby Oceanlake and evangelized the Salmon River Indians. The Jason Lee Campsite can be seen at 1333 NW Seventeenth Street in Lincoln City.

white-fenced fields, clumps of skunk cabbage blooming in bright yellows, and old apple trees bursting with pale pink blossoms on gnarled limbs.

Native Oregon grape—an evergreen shrub related to barberry—crowds along the roadside, with tight clusters of bright yellow blooms; low-lying salal, with its pink flowers, carpets forested areas; and gangly salmonberry bushes show pale white blossoms. This is clearly the time to slow the pace and enjoy a kaleidoscope of springtime colors.

If your sweetheart is along, you might want to spend a night in Neskowin near Proposal Rock, at **Proposal Rock Inn** (503–392–3115). Located nearby, popular **Hawk Creek Cafe** (503–392–3838) offers fresh-baked pizza, great sandwiches, seafood, and awesome espresso and coffee drinks.

Heading north on US 101, detour onto **Three Capes Scenic Drive,** heading toward **Pacific City** so that you can watch the launching of the **Dory Fleet,** one of the coast's most unusual fishing fleets. In the shadow of **Cape Kiwanda,** a towering sandstone headland, salmon-fishers from the Pacific City area launch flat-bottomed dories from the sandy beach into the protected waters near the large, offshore rock islands where those ever-present seabirds congregate.

You could also arrive in the late afternoon to see the dories return with the day's catch, skimming across the water and right onto the beach. The boats are then loaded onto large trailers for the night. Then, too, keep watch for those hardy souls who can often be spotted hang gliding from Cape Kiwanda. If you're hungry, stop at **Pelican Pub & Brewery** (503–965–7007) for eats and locally brewed ales along with views of Cape Kiwanda and the beach, or, nearby, pop into **Grateful Bread Bakery,** at 34805 Brooten Road (503–965–7337), any day except Wednesday for scrumptious baked goods and some of the coast's best breads, as well as deli sandwiches. For information about the dory fleet and about dory fishing trips, contact the Pacific City–Woods Visitors' Information Center (503–965–6161).

Just north of Sandlake, nature trails at *Cape Lookout* offer a close-up view of a typical coastal rain forest that includes such species as Sitka spruce, western hemlock, western red cedar, and red alder. The ca. 1894 *Sandlake Country Inn Bed & Breakfast,* at 8505 Galloway Road, Cloverdale (877–726–3525), offers cozy rooms, and a romantic cottage, among tall Douglas fir and native rhododendron.

Then dig out the binoculars and stop far off the beaten path, at the tiny community of *Oceanside,* to walk on the beach and see *Three Arch Rocks.* These offshore islands, set aside in 1907 by President Theodore Roosevelt as the first wildlife preserve on the Pacific Coast, are home to thousands of black petrels, colorful tufted puffins, and penguinlike murres, along with several varieties of gulls and cormorants. The bellow of resident Steller's sea lions and sea pups can often be heard as well. From 500-foot Maxwell Point to the north, you'll often see those hang gliders taking off into the wind. The glider pilots say that curious eagles sometimes fly along with them. (*NOTE:* Restrooms are located near the public parking area.) There are small eateries here and overnight accommodations, some overlooking the ocean. For specific information contact the Tillamook Visitor Center, 3705 US 101 North (503–842–7525; www.tillamookchamber.org).

From Oceanside continue north to the third cape, Cape Meares, which lies about 10 miles northwest of the thriving dairy community of *Tillamook.* Stop to visit the *Cape Meares Lighthouse* (503–842–2244), and also walk the short trail to see the *Octopus Tree,* an unusual Sitka spruce with six trunks. Bordering the paved path to the lighthouse are thick tangles of ruby rugosa roses with large burgundy blossoms; they're especially suited to salt air and coastal mists. You may well see folks sketching or photographing the picturesque, ca. 1890s

## Helpful Resources for Lighthouse Lovers

**Friends of Cape Meares**
www.capemeareslighthouse.org

**Friends of Yaquina Lighthouses**
(541) 574–3129
www.yaquinalights.org

**Historic lighthouses**
www.lighthousegetaway.com

**Lightship *Columbia,* Columbia River Maritime Museum**
Astoria; (503) 325–2323
www.crmm.org

**Oregon Chapter U.S. Lighthouse Society**
www.oregonlighthousesociety.org

## Lighthouses on the Coast

**Cape Arago Lighthouse**
near North Bend and Coos Bay;
illuminated in 1934. It's not open to the
public, but good views are available from
the trail at Sunset Bay State Park.

**Cape Blanco Lighthouse**
near Port Orford; commissioned in 1870
to aid shipping generated by gold mining
and the lumber industry. Visitor programs;
(541) 756–0100

**Cape Meares Lighthouse**
west of Tillamook; illuminated in 1890.
Trails lead to the lighthouse and
viewpoints overlooking offshore islets that
are home to Steller's sea lions and
seabirds. Gift shop and visitor programs;
(503) 842–2244

**Coquille River Lighthouse**
near Bandon; commissioned in 1896 to
guide mariners across the dangerous
river bar. Decommissioned in 1939 and
restored in 1979 as an interpretive
center; open year-round.

**Heceta Head Lighthouse**
north of Florence; illuminated in 1894. Its
automated beacon is rated as the
strongest light on the Oregon coast.
Tours May through September; (541)
547–3416

**Tillamook Rock Lighthouse**
between Cannon Beach and Seaside.
Commissioned in 1881 to help guide
ships entering the Columbia River near
Astoria, it was replaced by a whistle
buoy in 1957. No public access.

**Umpqua River Lighthouse**
near Reedsport; illuminated in 1894.
The structure and museum are
maintained by the Douglas County
Parks and Recreation Department;
(541) 271–4631

**Yaquina Bay Lighthouse**
at Newport; in service from 1871 to
1874. Open daily as a museum May
through September. For information on
tours and special events; (541) 574–
3129, www.yaquinalights.org

**Yaquina Head Lighthouse (and
Yaquina Head Outstanding
Natural Area)**
north of Newport; illuminated in 1873. It
aids navigation along the seacoast and
at the entrance to Yaquina Bay. Open to
the public; (541) 574–3100

structure that was deactivated in 1963. You can learn about Tillamook County's history at the incredibly well-stocked **Tillamook County Pioneer Museum** (503–842–4553, www.tcpm.org), located in the old courthouse building at 2106 Second Street in Tillamook. You'll see the stagecoach that carried mail in the county's early days, vintage horseless carriages, logging memorabilia, the replica of a fire lookout, and a kitchen of yesteryear. Hours are Monday through Saturday from 8:30 A.M. to 5:00 P.M. and Sunday from noon to 5:00 P.M. (closed Monday during winter months). Also stop to see costumes, textiles, and historic and contemporary quilt exhibits at *Latimer Quilt & Textile Center,* 2105 Wilson River Loop Road (503–842–8622). Hours are 10:00 A.M. to 4:00 P.M. Tuesday through Saturday and noon to 4:00 P.M. Sunday.

Linger a while longer on this less-populated section of the coast to visit the world's largest clear-span wooden structure at the *Tillamook Naval Air Station Museum* (503–842–1130; www.tillamookair.com) along with its collection of historic photographs, memorabilia, and vintage airplanes. The building, more than twenty stories high and ⅕ mile long, was the site of a World War II blimp hangar; it was in commission until 1948. Avid airplane buffs are restoring a number of vintage aircraft, such as an F4U Corsair and a 1942 Stinson V-77 Reliant. Operated by the Port of Tillamook Bay, the museum is open daily 10:00 A.M. to 5:00 P.M. (except major holidays). It's located 2 miles south of Tillamook, just off US 101, at 6030 Hangar Road. Needless to say, you can't miss spotting it! Amenities at the museum include a theater, gift shop, and the 1940s-style *Air Base Cafe.*

You could also linger to ride the Port of Tillamook Bay's *Oregon Coast Explorer* (800–685–1719; www.potb.org/oregoncoastexplorer), which includes a 1910 Heisler steam locomotive, a 1953 BUDD Rail Diesel Car (RDC), and the SunSet Supper Train. Call for current schedules that take visitors railroading through the scenic Salmonberry Canyon.

Just a mile north of Tillamook, in a converted dairy barn, the *Blue Heron French Cheese Factory* (503–842–8281) offers visitors a gaggle of small farm animals and delicious French-style cheeses. You can sample not only the cheeses but a selection of Oregon wines and can purchase other international cheeses and deli foods. Open daily at 2001 Blue Heron Drive, just off US 101; hours are 8:00 A.M. to 8:00 P.M. during summer and 9:00 A.M. to 5:00 P.M. during winter.

If you're itching to do a bit of shopping for coastal antiques, stop first in the tiny hamlet of Wheeler and find *Wheeler Station Antique Mall* (503–368–5677) just across from the small Waterfront Park and waterside *Sea Shack Restaurant* (503–368–7897). The mall is filled with an eclectic mix of vintage furniture and collectibles. Hours are 10:00 A.M. to 5:00 P.M. daily.

You want to try camping on the coast, but you don't have a tent? Well, not to worry, both *Cape Lookout* and *Nehalem Bay State Campgrounds* near Tillamook offer a fun alternative to setting up a tent. Try *yurt camping* in a stationary circular domed tent with a wood floor, structural wall supports, electricity, and a skylight. Your yurt is furnished with a bunk bed, fold-out couch, small table, and space heater; bring your own sleeping bags or bedding and your own food and cooking gear. You'd like your digs a bit more plush? Ask about the state parks that now offer three-room cabins and extra-deluxe yurts that come with small kitchens. (Call Oregon State Parks at 800–551–6949 for general information on these accommodations.)

US 101 soon skirts Nehalem Bay and wends through the villages of **Nehalem** and **Wheeler,** known for crabbing and clamming and for fine fishing. Angling for silver and chinook salmon, cutthroat, native, and steelhead trout is among the best along the Nehalem River and bay area; there's a marina here with both free boat launches and private moorages. For good eats in the Nehalem-Wheeler area, try the **Sea Shack Restaurant** (503–368–7897) and **Nina's Italian Restaurant** (503–368–6592), located on US 101, and **Nehalem Currents Restaurant** on the dock at 35815 Seventh Street (503–368–5557).

For a second antiques shopping foray, trundle into **Nehalem Antique Mall** (503–368–7190), where you can browse among an array of antique oak furniture, old books, excellent glassware, and a plethora of intriguing collectibles offered by fifty aficionados of vintage stuff. For information about fishing and crabbing, bicycle and horse trails, and annual festivals, contact the Nehalem Bay Area Visitor Center (877–368–5100) at 495 Nehalem Boulevard (across from Waterfront Park).

US 101 now winds north past Manzanita, where you could detour for tasty scones, muffins, and coffee at cozy **Manzanita News and Espresso** (500 Laneda Avenue, 503–368–7450) or for dinner at **Manzanita Seafood & Chowder House,** 519 Laneda Avenue (503–368–2722). For awesome Chicago-style hot dogs stop at Jim Mudd's outdoor stand on Laneda Avenue, **Manzanita Mudd Dogs.** Then, drive north high atop Neahkahnie Mountain and proceed down to one of the north coast's most hidden coves and beach areas, **Short Sand Beach** and **Oswald West Park.**

Here you can explore the agate- and driftwood-strewn cove, snoop into shallow caves and caverns, fish or wade in an icy creek or shallow streams, peer at delicate tide pools, and let the sounds of the surf lull you to sleep on a blanket or, in good weather, in a tent with the moon and stars casting shimmering bands of light across the water.

The particulars: Park in the large designated parking area along US 101 and walk the ½-mile trail to the beach, through old-growth Douglas fir, coast pines, salal, salmonberry, and ferns growing in lush profusion along the way. Wheelbarrows are available at the parking area for hauling in camping gear; the thirty-six primitive campsites are reached by a ¼-mile trail from the picnic area. A section of the **Oregon Coast Hiking Trail** passes through the area as well.

Sleeping in a tent on the sand is not your thing? Well, not to worry, there are dozens of motels, cozy bed-and-breakfast inns, and hostelries in Cannon Beach, just a few miles north via US 101. For current lodging information contact the Cannon Beach Visitor Center, located at Second and Spruce Streets (503–436–2623; www.cannonbeach.org).

Park the car in downtown Cannon Beach and pull on tennis shoes and warm windbreakers for a walk on the beach to nearby **Haystack Rock**, the north coast's venerable landmark that houses colonies of seabirds and myriad tide pools. Then you could browse through Cannon Beach's main-street art galleries, boutiques, and bookshops, or sip hot coffee and enjoy clam chowder at cozy eateries along the main street such as **Driftwood Inn Cafe**, 179 North Hemlock (503–436–2439), and **Morris' Fireside Restaurant**, 207 North Hemlock (503–436–2917). Pause at **Icefire Glassworks**, at the corner of Hemlock and Gower (503–436–2359) Thursday through Monday to watch the glass-blowing process. Check, too, to see if a chilling mystery, rousing comedy, or serious drama is being offered by local thespians at **Coaster Theatre Playhouse** (503–436–1242; www.coastertheatre.com). Curtain is at 8:00 P.M.

At the north edge of Cannon Beach, drive the shaded winding road up to **Ecola State Park** for one of the most dramatic seascape panoramas on the north coast. In the lush 1,300-acre park, you'll see splendid examples of old-growth Sitka spruce, western hemlock forest, native shrubs, and wildflower species. Picnic tables are tucked here and there, many sheltered from coastal breezes. The views are spectacular, particularly on blue-sky days; walk the trails along the ledges and remain safely behind the fenced areas. You can spy migrating whales during winter months and ask questions of whale-watching volunteers stationed on the bluff during mid-March (www.whalespoken.org).

For those who want to plan hikes along the **Oregon Coast Trail**, some of which passes through scenic Ecola State Park and **Indian Beach**, maps and current information can be obtained from the State Parks and Recreation Division, www.oregonstateparks.org.

Follow US 101 north to one of Oregon's oldest resort towns, **Seaside**, where families have vacationed since the turn of the twentieth century. For a nostalgic experience park the car on any side street near the ocean and walk as far as you like on the **Historic Seaside Promenade**—a 2-mile-long sidewalk, with its old-fashioned railing and lampposts restored—that skirts the wide sandy beach. Benches are available here and there for sitting, and about the only discordant note in this pleasant reminiscence—folks have walked "the Prom" since the 1920s—may be an occasional bevy of youngsters sailing by on roller skates.

The Lewis and Clark expedition reached the Pacific Ocean in 1804, near the Seaside area, and you can see the original salt cairn—just off the south section of the Prom on Lewis and Clark Avenue—where the company boiled seawater to make salt during the rainy winter of 1805.

## Lewis and Clark at the "Ocian"

On November 7, 1805, some 554 days after departing Camp DuBois in Illinois, William Clark wrote in his journal: "Great joy in camp we are in view of the Ocian . . ." Actually, they didn't reach the mouth of the Columbia River and the Pacific Ocean until November 15 due to lashing storms. By December 7 the party of thirty-one, including Clark's Newfoundland dog, Seaman, had crossed the Columbia River from the Long Beach Peninsula area and arrived at the Fort Clatsop site. By December 26 they had built winter headquarters, several log cabins that protected them from one of the wettest winters on record for the north coast.

Standing regally on the corner of Beach Drive and Avenue A is one of Seaside's historic homes, ca. 1890, now the elegant **Gilbert Inn Bed and Breakfast,** 341 Beach Drive (503–738–9770). The old dowager has been transformed into a bed-and-breakfast inn and offers travelers ten spacious guest suites. In the Turrett Room on the second floor, for example, you can sleep in a queen-size four-poster amid romantic, country French–style decor.

Also in Seaside, at **10th Avenue Inn Bed & Breakfast,** 125 Tenth Avenue (503–738–0643, www.10aveinn.com), innkeepers Jack and Lesle Palmeri offer comfy guest rooms on the second floor, all with cozy sitting areas and private baths. For good eats ask about **Norma's Ocean Diner** (503–738–4331) and **McKeown's** (503–738–5232). For steaming espresso drinks pop into **Seaside Coffee Roasting Company,** 5 North Holladay Drive (503–717–8300), located across from **Lil' Bayou Cajun Cafe.**

For a close-up look at Lewis and Clark's 1805–6 winter headquarters, visit **Fort Clatsop National Monument** (503–861–2471), about 10 miles north of Seaside, near Astoria. Walk the winding path from the interpretive center to the log replica of the encampment. Here, from June to September, you can see a living-history program that includes buckskin-clad park rangers, live musket firing, boat carving, tanning, and map making—all frontier skills used by the company during that first, very rainy winter. Within 25 miles are several sites described in the Lewis and Clark journals. The Fort Clatsop brochure, available at the visitor center, gives all the details and a helpful map.

Not far from the Lewis and Clark encampment, enterprising John Jacob Astor founded **Astoria**—just six years later, in 1811. Settled for the purpose of fur trading, the bustling seaport at the mouth of the Columbia River grew into a respectable city during the late 1800s. You can take a walking or a driving tour and see some of the 400 historic structures still remaining, including the historic *Astoria Column* high atop Coxcomb Hill, and restored Victorian homes, many of them now open as comfortable bed-and-breakfast inns.

For helpful maps, brochures, and current lodging information, stop at either of the Astoria-Warrenton Visitor Centers, located at 111 West Marine Drive in downtown Astoria (503–325–6311; www.oldoregon.com) and just off US 101 at the shopping center in nearby Warrenton (503–861–1031, open daily 9:00 A.M. to 5:00 P.M.).

Built in 1883 by Capt. George Flavel, the *Flavel Mansion Museum* is one of the finest examples of Victorian architecture in the state. Located at 441 Eighth Street, between Exchange and Duane Streets, this impressive structure, with its columned porches, carved gingerbread detailing, and tall cupola, is worth a visit. The mansion is open daily. For further information contact the Clatsop County Historical Society (503–325–2203; www.clatsophistoricalsociety .org). Ask, too, about visiting *Uppertown Firefighters Museum* (503–325–2203) on Thirtieth and Marine Drive, open Wednesday through Sunday 10:00 A.M. to 2:00 P.M. Its fine collection of firefighting equipment dates from the 1870s.

*Fort Astoria,* on Exchange Street, is a partially restored fort, originally built by Astor's Pacific Fur Company in 1811. Nearby is the site of the first U.S. post office west of the Rocky Mountains, established in 1847. Pick up a copy of *An Explorer's Guide to Historic Astoria* at the Visitor Center at 111 West Marine Drive. Also check out the splendid *Columbia River Maritime Museum* at 1792 Marine Drive (503–325–2323; www.crmm.org).

If you travel along the north coast during winter and early spring, visit the *Twilight Eagle Sanctuary,* located just 8 miles east of Astoria and ½ mile north of U.S. Highway 30 on Burnside Road. The protected area offers prime feeding and roosting for about forty-eight bald eagles. You can identify the noble birds by their

Astoria Column

white heads and tails, large beaks, and yellow legs. Then, too, during all four seasons, bird lovers far and wide find that one of the best places on the coast to watch an enormous variety of bird species is from the viewing platform at **Fort Stevens State Park,** located 10 miles west of Astoria near Hammond. Be sure to take along your binoculars or cameras with telephoto lenses. Call (800) 452–5687 to inquire about yurts, RV sites, and campsites at Fort Stevens.

And, to complete your tour of the coast, you can do as many families did at the turn of the twentieth century—cross the Columbia River via the graceful, 4⅒-mile-long Astoria-Megler Bridge and drive a few miles north to the historic **Long Beach Peninsula** in Washington State. Take in the **World Kite Museum** at Pacific Avenue and Third Street NW (360–642–4020) and see fascinating exhibits that show the history of kites and kite-flying; fly kites or dig for clams on the wide sandy beach; take in annual music festivals; visit Lewis and Clark sites and walk the wheelchair-accessible **Discovery Trail;** and find a great place to stay the night, such as **Lion's Paw Inn Bed & Breakfast,** 3310 Pacific Highway South in Seaview (800–972–1046), or the comfortable **Boreas Bed & Breakfast,** 607 North Boulevard in Long Beach (888–642–8069). The Long Beach Peninsula Visitors' Bureau (800–451–2542; www.funbeach.com) can provide information about upcoming events in Ilwaco, Seaview, Long Beach, Nahcotta, Oysterville, and Ocean Park.

If you're looking for a way to enjoy a day at the beach and do a good deed at the same time, you can participate in one of the twice-yearly **Great Oregon Beach Cleanup** events. It's work, it's great fun, and it happens along the entire coast, from Brookings in the south to Astoria in the north. Several years ago, beach cleanup volunteers found a plethora of stuff from a shipping accident in which forty-nine containers had washed overboard some 2,000 miles off the coast—such items as hockey gear, athletic shoes, sandals, and even Spiderman toys. Scientists tracked ocean currents for months by following the journey of thousands of tennis shoes! For current information and dates, call the friendly beach cleanup staff at (800) 322–3326 or log onto www .solv.org.

# Places to Stay on the Oregon Coast

## ASTORIA

Clementine's
Bed & Breakfast
847 Exchange Street
(800) 521–6801

## BANDON

Harbor View Motel
355 US 101
(800) 526–0209

## CANNON BEACH

Best Western Inn at
Cannon Beach
3215 South Hemlock Street
(800) 321–6304

## DEPOE BAY

Surfrider
3315 NW US 101
(541) 764–2311

## FLORENCE

Blue Heron
Bed & Breakfast
6563 Highway 126
(800) 997–7780

## GEARHEART

Gearhart Ocean Inn
67 North Cottage Avenue
(800) 352–8034

## GOLD BEACH

Gold Beach Resort
29232 Ellensburg on
US 101
(541) 247–7066

## LINCOLN CITY

The Sea Gypsy Motel
145 NW Inlet Avenue
(541) 994–5266

## NEWPORT

Agate Beach Motel
175 NW Gilbert Way
(800) 755–5674

## ROCKAWAY BEACH

Silver Sands Motel
215 Pacific Street
(800) 457–8972

## SEASIDE

Seashore Inn
60 North Prom
(888) 738–6368

10th Avenue Inn
Bed & Breakfast
125 Tenth Avenue
(503) 738–0643

## SOUTH BEACH

Newport Belle Riverboat
Bed & Breakfast
H Dock, Newport Marina
(800) 348–1922

## YACHATS-WALDPORT

Cape Cod Cottages
4150 US 101
(541) 563–2106

Shamrock Lodgettes
US 101 South
(541) 547–3312

# Places to Eat on the Oregon Coast

## ASTORIA

Baked Alaska Restaurant
No. 1, Twelfth Street Dock
(503) 325–7414

Columbian Cafe
1114 Marine Drive
(503) 325–2233

Danish Maid Bakery &
Coffeehouse
1132 Commerical Street
(503) 325–3657

Gunderson's Cannery Cafe
One Sixth Street
(503) 325–8642

Wet Dog Cafe
144 Eleventh Street
(503) 325–6975

## BANDON

RayJen's Internet Cafe &
Coffeehouse
365 Second Street
(541) 347–1144

## BROOKINGS-HARBOR

Home Port Bagels
& Sandwiches
1011 US 101
(541) 469–6611

Oceanside Diner
16403 Lower Harbor Road
(541) 469–7971

## CANNON BEACH

Morris' Fireside
Restaurant
207 North Hemlock
(503) 436–2917

## DEPOE BAY

Kadi's Kitchen
22 Bay Street
(541) 765–8999

## FLORENCE

Bridgewater Restaurant
1295 Bay Street
(541) 997–9405

## GEARHEART

Pacific Way Bakery
and Cafe
601 Pacific Way
(503) 738–0245

## GLENEDEN BEACH

Side Door Cafe
6675 Gleneden Beach
Loop Road
(541) 764–3825

## GOLD BEACH

Gold Beach Books &
Biscuit Coffehouse
29707 US 101
(541) 247–2495

Port Hole Cafe
29975 Harbor Way
(541) 247–7411

## LINCOLN CITY

Shucker's Oyster Bar
4814 SW Highway 101
(541) 996–9800

## MANZANITA

Manzanita News &
Espresso
500 Laneda Avenue
(503) 368–7450

## NESKOWIN

Hawk Creek Cafe
4505 Salem Avenue
(503) 392–3838

## NEWPORT

La Maison Bakery & Cafe
315 SW Ninth Street
(541) 265–8812

Shark's Seafood Bar &
Steamer Co.
852 SW Bay Front
(541) 574–0590

## NORTH BEND

Cafe Mediterranean
1860 Union Street
(541) 756–2299

## PACIFIC CITY

Pelican Pub & Brewery
Cape Kiwanda Drive
(503) 965–7007

## PORT ORFORD

Port Orford Breadworks
Cafe
190 Sixth Street
(541) 332–4022

## SEASIDE

Corpeny's Cafe
2281 Beach Drive
(503) 738–7353

Lil' Bayou Cajun Cafe
20 North Holladay Drive
(503) 717–0624

Seaside Coffee Roasting
Company
5 North Holladay Drive
(503) 717–8300

## TILLAMOOK

Air Base Cafe
Tillamook Air Museum
(503) 842–1130

## YACHATS

The Drift Inn Restaurant
& Pub
124 US 101 North
(541) 547–4477

Toad Hall Coffee House
Second Street
(541) 547–4044

# HELPFUL TELEPHONE NUMBERS AND WEB SITES FOR THE OREGON COAST

**Astoria/Warrenton Area Visitor Center**
(503) 861–1031
www.oldoregon.com

**Bandon Visitor Center**
(541) 347–9616
www.bandonbythesea.com

**Bay Area Visitor Center**
Coos Bay
(800) 824–8486

**Brookings-Harbor Visitor Center**
(800) 535–9469
www.brookingsor.com

**Cannon Beach Visitor Center**
(503) 436–2623
www.cannonbeach.org

**Cape Perpetua Scenic Area**
(541) 547–3289
www.orcoast.com/capeperpetua/

**Columbia River Maritime Museum and lightship** *Columbia*
Astoria
(503) 325–2323
www.crmm.org

**Florence Area Visitor Center**
(800) 524–4864
www.florencechamber.com

**Fort Clatsop and Lewis and Clark National Historic Park**
(503) 861–2471
www.nps.gov/focl

**Friends of Yaquina Lighthouses**
www.yaquinalights.org

**Gold Beach Visitor Center**
(541) 247–7526
www.goldbeach.com

**Greater Newport Visitor Center**
(800) 262–7844
www.discovernewport.com

**Lincoln City Visitor Bureau**
(800) 452–2151
www.oregoncoast.org

**North Bend–Coos Bay Area**
(800) 472–9176

**Oregon Coast National Wildlife Refuges**
(541) 867–4550
www.oregoncoast.fws.gov

**Oregon State Parks Campground Reservations**
(800) 452–5687

**Port Orford Visitor Center**
(541) 332–8055
www.portorfordoregon.com

**Reedsport–Winchester Bay Visitors' Center**
(800) 247–2155
www.reedsportcc.org

**Seaside Visitor Bureau**
(888) 306–2326
www.seasideor.com

**Tillamook Visitor Center**
(503) 842–7525
www.tillamookchamber.org

**Yachats Visitor Center**
(800) 929–0477
www.yachats.org

# Southern Oregon

## Crater Lake and Southern Cascades

Southern Oregon is a curious mixture of old ghost towns and historic landmarks combined with white-water rivers, wildlife refuges, colorful caverns, a high-altitude volcanic lake, and national forests and mountain ranges containing some of the least-known wilderness areas in the Beaver State. In Oregon's only full-fledged national park, *Crater Lake* shimmers like a crystal blue jewel in the enormous caldera of 12,000-foot Mount Mazama. More than 6,000 years ago this peak in the southern Cascade Mountains collapsed with a fiery roar, some forty times greater than the Mount Saint Helens eruption of 1980 in nearby Washington State, and formed a deep basin of 20 square miles; the lake is more than 1,500 feet deep in places, and because of numerous underground thermal springs, it rarely freezes.

The 33-mile-long *Crater Lake Rim Drive,* encircling the lake at an invigorating elevation of 6,177 feet, can be done in an hour or so, but to savor the 360-degree panorama and succession of splendid changing views, you'll want to plan a longer outing: Spend the whole day there, and then stay

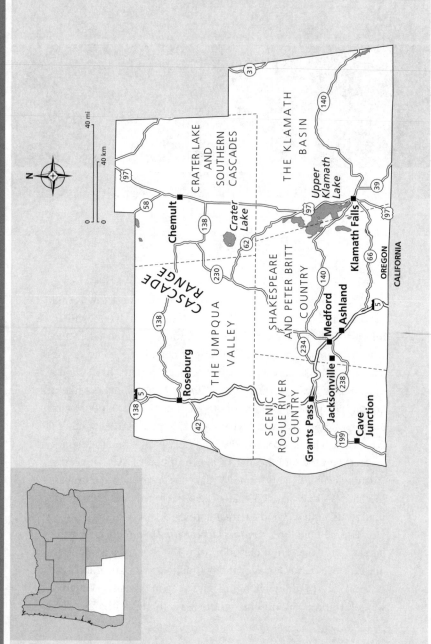

SOUTHERN OREGON

overnight in one of the several campgrounds in the area or in the venerable *Crater Lake Lodge* perched on the south rim.

You can also take a 6-mile side road from *Kerr Notch,* at the southeast corner of the rim, down to the Pinnacles, 200-foot spires of pumice and tuff (layers of volcanic ash). A 4-mile, one-way auto tour traverses Greyback Ridge, allowing a sit-down look at rock formations, native trees, and wildflowers. Within the park are some 85 miles of hiking and nature trails.

For another panoramic view take the two-hour boat trip around Crater Lake's 25-mile shoreline, accompanied by a Park Service interpreter. *NOTE:* The Cleetwood Trail down to the dock at Cleetwood Cove is a very steep, 1⅒-mile hike. For an easier scenic trek, try the 1-mile day hike on *Castle Crest Wildflower Trail* near Rim Village. You can hang out later at Watchman Restaurant or at Llao Rock Cafe, both at Rim Village.

Winter brings a sparkling snowy beauty to the lake, along with outdoor activities such as cross-country skiing, snowshoeing, and ski touring. For information about renting snowshoes or cross-country skis, or about winter tours—reservations are required—contact Crater Lake park staff, Crater Lake (541– 594–3000; www.nps.gov/crla).

Built in the early 1900s and opened in 1915, historic Crater Lake Lodge has undergone complete renovation and reopened in 1995. Accommodations are available from June to mid-October. Call (541) 830–8700 for room reservations. For information about the more than 900 camping sites available in the Forest Service campgrounds, call the Forest Service ranger station at (541) 594–2211 or log onto www.fs.fed.us/r6/rogue.

## TOP HITS IN SOUTHERN OREGON

**Bed-and-breakfast inns**

**Britt Festivals**
Jacksonville

**Butte Creek Mill**
Eagle Point

**Crater Lake National Park**
Highway 138

**Grants Pass Grower's Market**
Grants Pass

**Jacksonville Pioneer Cemetery**
Jacksonville

**Klamath Basin Wildlife Refuge**
Klamath Falls

**Oregon Caves National Monument**
Cave Junction

**Oregon Shakespeare Festival**
Ashland

**Volcanic Legacy Scenic Byway**
Highway 62

**Wildlife Safari**
Winston

## Fast Facts about Crater Lake and Crater Lake Lodge

Discovered by white settlers in 1853, Crater Lake is the second-deepest lake in North America behind Canada's Great Slave Lake.

**Maximum depth:** 1,932 feet

**Average depth:** 1,500 feet

**Elevation at lake's surface:** 6,176 feet above sea level

**Elevation at Rim Village:** 7,100 feet above sea level

**Average snowfall:** 545 inches

The 33-mile Rim Drive is usually clear of snow by July

**Tourists:** 500,000 annually

The seventy-one-room lodge originally opened in 1915; closed in 1989 for a $15 million rehabilitation; reopened in May 1995

**Lodge decor:** 1920s mood with Craftsman- and mission-style furnishings; bent-twig chairs and hickory rockers; and an original stone fireplace in the Great Hall

**Best time to visit:** August and September

Mazama Village, located 7 miles south of Rim Village, is also a good alternative for overnight accommodations. The Mazama Village Motor Inn offers forty units with private baths and showers (541–830–8700 for reservations). The nearby Mazama Campground offers 200 tent and RV spaces on a first-come, first-served basis; there are public showers, laundry facilities, a convenience store, and a gas station.

Access the Crater Lake area via U.S. Highway 97 from Bend (about 80 miles); US 97 and Highway 62 from Klamath Falls (about 60 miles); Highway 62 from Medford (about 70 miles); or Highway 138 from Roseburg (about 80 miles). This last entrance closes with the first heavy snowstorm, usually in mid-October, and reopens by mid-June or July; the south entrance via Highway 62 remains open year-round.

Just north of Crater Lake National Park, at a lower elevation, is **Diamond Lake,** a smaller jewel nestled within Umpqua National Forest. Rainbow-trout season opens here the third weekend of April, and sailboats, motorboats, and canoes can be rented in advance. Moorage space is available throughout the summer and early fall, and fishing and hunting licenses can be purchased at the tackle shop.

Many campground sites, open from May through October, are found on the lakeshore; Diamond Lake and Broken Arrow Campgrounds have trailer dump stations. At **Diamond Lake Resort** (800–733–7593; www.diamond lake.net), lakeshore cabins are available as well as motel-style units—call well ahead of time to reserve one of the cabins with a fireplace and kitchen.

During winter, snow lovers can take a guided snowmobile tour—ask about the special tour, including lunch, to Crater Lake—or arrange for snowcat skiing. Often space is available, but it's wise to call ahead for reservations. There's also a good inner-tube sledding hill for families with small children. During summer visitors enjoy horseback riding— special group rates can be arranged, and guides are also available.

## trivia

"We have two seasons here," says one Crater Lake Park staff member, "winter and August, and you can't always count on August."

Serious snowmobilers can obtain information about the annual **Snowmobile Jamboree,** in mid-February, from the **High Desert Storm-troopers Snowmobile Club** (www.oregonsnow .org) or via the Lake County Visitor Center in Lakeview (541–947–6040). Or, ever dreamed about whisking across a frozen lake or snow-covered trail on a dogsled? At the **Trail of Dreams Training Camp** near Bend, huskies train for the famous Iditarod Trail Race in Alaska by taking visitors on day trips. Reservations for a 7-mile sled-dog ride on trails near Mount Bachelor can be arranged through Mount Bachelor Reservations Department, (800) 829–2442; www.sled dogrides.com. The season is generally from late November until April, snow conditions permitting. In January you can hear the cries of "mush, you

## Crater Lake: Establishing a National Park

A Portland mountain climber and transplanted Kansan, William G. Steel visited the lake in 1885 some thirty years after it was first discovered by white settlers; he then helped lead the crusade to save the area from homesteading. He battled to have the area designated a national park, a measure approved by President Theodore Roosevelt on May 22, 1902. It was the seventh such park to be established in the United States. In 1913 Steel was appointed the second superintendent of Crater Lake National Park; the restored 1934 visitor center near the main headquarters building, open year-round, is named in his honor.

A smaller visitor center, located between the lodge and the cafeteria and gift shop, is open daily during the summer season.

## Early Travels to Crater Lake Park

The first horseless carriage motored up to Crater Lake in 1905, and by 1919 the spectacular Rim Drive, though just a bumpy dirt road, was a standard stop on sight-seeing rambles around the state. In July 1920 the steamer *Klamath* began transporting passengers from Klamath Falls to Rocky Point, at the northern end of Klamath Lake, to meet the Crater Lake Stage Line. This new improved service— steamboat and automobile—deposited travelers at Crater Lake (a total of about 65 miles) in the record time of twelve hours!

huskies!" at the annual *Chemult Invitational Sled Dog Races.* Chemult is located on US 97 south of Bend and north of Crater Lake.

More events have been added each year, including a mid-distance race; a weight pull; four-, six-, and eight-dog team sprint races; novice-class races; and a peewee race for the kids. The races start and finish at the Walt Haring Snopark just north of Chemult; the weight pull is held in downtown Chemult. Other fun events may include a chili cook-off, a dad-sled race, a beard-growing contest, and a beer-barrel race. The Chemult Rural Fire Department usually operates a food-and-beverage stand at the race and also sponsors a mushers banquet at the Chemult Fire Hall. A number of local snowmobile clubs, such as Walker Rim Riders, Chiloquin Ridge Riders, and Bohemia SnoSledders, help to groom the snowy trails for the event. For current information call Forest Service staff at the Chemult Ranger District, (541) 365–7001. The first sled-dog event was organized in 1995.

To bed down in the southern Oregon Cascades near the *Willamette Pass Ski Area,* consider *Odell Lake Lodge and Resort* off Highway 58 just north and west of Chemult (541–433–2540; www.odelllakeresort.com). Rustic and comfortable, the lodge has welcomed travelers for more than seventy-five years. Facilities include a small cafe, boat docks, boat rentals, and housekeeping cabins. You're breathing crisp mountain air above 4,000 feet elevation in the company of tall firs, soft breezes, and ground critters like squirrels and chipmunks. During snowy winter months families bring their cross-country skis, sleds, and inner tubes, and they pack hearty lunches along with thermoses of hot coffee and hot chocolate.

Another historic retreat within driving distance of Chemult, *Union Creek Lodge* (541–560–3565) was built in the early 1900s and is on the National Register of Historic Places. Located on Highway 62 between Crater Lake and Medford are rustic cabins, rooms in the main lodge, a country store, and gift shop.

Directly across the highway, **Beckie's Restaurant** (541–560–3563) is known for home-style cooking and tasty pies (open 9:00 A.M. to 5:00 P.M. Friday through Monday during the winter and daily during the summer). While you're in the area, ask for directions to see where the **Rogue River** has its frothy beginnings—it's definitely worth a stop and several frames of film. *NOTE:* Pack plenty of woolens, warm parkas and coats, stocking caps, and warm boots if you travel into the Cascade Mountains during the winter months. Take along extra blankets, sleeping bags, and extra food and beverages as well. Traction devices may be required from November through March on snowy mountain passes—many of them more than 5,000 feet in elevation—depending on current weather conditions. (To check conditions, log onto www.tripcheck.com or call 800–977–6368.)

Wilderness seekers, backpackers, and hikers can try climbing 8,363-foot Mount Bailey—strenuous but worth the sweat—or the 4-mile trail to 9,182-foot Mount Thielson. Both offer superb views of the southern Cascades, Crater Lake, and Diamond Lake. Rangers caution that summer is quite short at these alpine elevations and urge folks to dress adequately and bring the proper gear, including sufficient food, water, and emergency shelter. For information about the **Pacific Crest National Scenic Trail,** which crosses the west side of the area and winds south through the wooded ridges and plateaus of Mountain Lakes Wilderness, contact the Diamond Lake Ranger District (541–498–2531) 59 miles east of Roseburg via Highway 138 and near Toketee Falls.

# The Klamath Basin

Continuing your exploration of southern Oregon, head south via Highway 62 or US 97 toward **Klamath Falls** to see another region of diversity, including one of the largest wildlife and wildfowl refuges in the Northwest. Many of the roads in this area, particularly Highway 66 from "K Falls" to Ashland, were used by early mail and freight stagecoach lines between the Klamath Basin and settlements along the Rogue River, to the west.

When it was the land of the ancient Ouxkanee, or "people of the marsh," the million-acre Klamath Basin contained a vast expanse of lakes and marshes ideal for waterfowl courtship and nesting. White settlers nearly drained the area dry for farmland, but beginning in 1908, in an effort aided by the emerging conservation ethic, portions of the Klamath Basin were set aside as wildlife refuges, secure from further encroachment. With the last of the area reserved in 1958, the entire region is now known as the **Klamath Basin National Wildlife Refuge.** Though their domain is much smaller than in the days of the Ouxkanee, birds

## TOP ANNUAL EVENTS IN SOUTHERN OREGON

**Winter Wings Festival**
Klamath Falls; February
(541) 884–0666

**Oregon Shakespeare Festival**
Ashland; February–October
(541) 482–4331

**Umpqua Valley Roundup**
Roseburg; mid-June
(800) 444–9584

**Britt Festivals**
Jacksonville; June–August
(800) 882–7488

**Northwest Cutting Horse
Association events**
Fort Klamath; July

**Rogue Valley Model Railroad Show**
Medford; late November
(541) 535–7952
www.rvmrc.railfan.net

**Annual Glide Wildflower Show**
Glide-Roseburg; late April
(541) 677–3797
www.glidewildflowershow.org

and waterfowl of all species crowd enthusiastically into what remains: some 83,000 acres of marsh and shallow lakes near Klamath Falls.

For the visitor there are countless opportunities for close-up, nondisturbing viewing of waterfowl, marsh birds, shorebirds, and upland species—along lakes and marshes, near grassy meadows and farms, among the sagebrush and juniper, near ancient lava flows, and in nearby coniferous forests.

The great thrill is seeing the early spring or fall migrations, when the sky is dark with wings and the silence pierced by much cacophonous honking—climaxing to some seven million birds en route along the **Pacific Flyway,** which extends the entire length of North and South America. First the ducks—pintails, ruddies, mallards, shovelers, and wigeons; then the geese—Canada, snow, white-fronted, and cackling—to mention just a few of the more than 270 species recorded here.

In March visitors can welcome the return of the white pelicans, Klamath Falls's feathery mascot; they nest and remain here until November. Link River and Lake Ewauna at **Veteran's Memorial Park** in Klamath Falls are among the most accessible places to see these large, curious birds, with their pouched beaks. And during winter some 500 bald eagles visit from the frozen north, attracting naturalists and bird lovers from all over to count and observe their nesting habits at the annual **Winter Wings Festival** during mid-February (www.greatbasinvisitor.info).

For current information about the Klamath Basin Wildlife Refuge, including maps, bird species lists, viewing sites, interpretive sites, canoe trails, and self-guided auto tours on the refuge, drive 25 miles south of Klamath Falls to refuge headquarters at 4009 Hill Road just east of Tule Lake, California; (530) 667–2231; also browse the refuge Web site at klamathbasinrefuges.fws.gov. Additional information about the Klamath Falls area, including overnight accommodations, can be obtained from the Great Basin Visitor Center at 507 Main Street in Klamath Falls (800–445–6728; www.greatbasinvisitor.info).

The **Klamath County Museum,** at 1451 Main Street (541–883–4208), offers exhibits and displays on the history, geology, anthropology, and wildlife of the Klamath Basin; it's open Tuesday through Saturday from 11:00 A.M. to 5:00 P.M. Also part of the museum complex, the four-story **Baldwin Hotel Museum,** a noted hostelry built in 1906 by state senator George Baldwin, offers a look at the hotel's opulent original furnishings and early history. Located at 31 Main Street, the brick building is open for tours from June to September, Tuesday through Saturday from 10:00 A.M. to 4:00 P.M.

## geothermalarea

Klamath Falls, named Linkville when founded in 1876, sits atop a geothermal area, and in those early days many businesses and homes were heated by the hot water; the early native peoples used it for cooking. A number of businesses and the local hospital still use this source for heating.

Maud Baldwin, a well-known photographer at the turn of the twentieth century, followed her father, George, around the county and into the marshes to record on film the area's early farmland reclamation project. More than 2,000 of her vintage photographs are housed at the Klamath County Museum.

For good eats, Klamath Falls offers a number of great options, including **Mr. B's Steakhouse** at 3927 South Sixth Street (541–883–8719) for steak and seafood. **Gino's Italian Cafe** at 149 East Main Street (541–884–6474) offers traditional Italian dishes for lunch and dinner Tuesday through Saturday. For great soups, tasty sandwiches and bagels, and specialty coffees and fresh pastries, try **The Daily Bagel** at 636 Main Street (541–850–0744); **Quackenbush Coffee Co.** at 2117 South Sixth Street (541–884–1927); or **Nibbley's Cafe** at 2560 Washburn Way (541–883–2314). And for local ales and tasty pub fare pop into the **Klamath Creamery Micro Brewery Pub & Grill** at 1320 Main Street (541–273–5222).

Galleries to visit in Klamath Falls include **Gallery 803** on Main Street (541–883–2814) and **Favell Museum of Indian Artifacts & Western Art,** 125 West Main Street (541–882–9996).

If time allows, call and check out the current play or concert offerings at the **Ross Ragland Theater** (541–884–5483), housed in an elegant and historic art deco–style building at 218 North Seventh Street. The **Linkville The-**

## Historic Logging Trivia

Both steam-powered machinery and railroads were important to logging. Portable "donkey" steam engines provided power for skidding logs to loading areas; colorful jargon like "high lead," "choker," and "whistle punk" came from this era. Railroads hauled timber from the woods to mills. Four large pieces of railroad equipment can be seen near Chiloquin off US 97 at Collier State Park, including a stiff-boom loader, a log buncher, a swing-boom loader, and a track-laying car; these are mounted on sections of railroad track. Samples of Oregon's commercial tree species can also be seen— Douglas fir, sugar pine, and ponderosa pine, each more than 6 feet in diameter.

*atre Players* (541–884–6782) offers a season of live theater each year at 201 Main Street; call Shaw Stationery for tickets (541–882–2586).

Just 30 miles north of Klamath Falls via US 97 is *Collier State Park and Logging Museum* (541–783–2471), where you can take a gander at the largest collection of logging equipment in the United States. Look for the huge steam locomotive—it ran on roads rather than on tracks. Stop at the Ouxkanee Lookout for a panoramic view of Spring Creek Valley and for historical information about the region. Collier State Park offers both RV and tent campsites. Take in the park's annual *Living History Day* in mid-June.

You could also head northwest on Highway 140 for about 30 miles to find lakeside cabins and RV spaces at *Lake of the Woods* (541–949–8300).

For a special outdoor experience, consider the *Upper Klamath Canoe Trail,* particularly the northern section, where you can canoe gently along the 50-foot-wide water trail and often see families of beavers and muskrats. Families of ducks, geese, cormorants, and swans may protest a bit as you paddle along the 10-mile water trail. For canoe and kayak rentals, contact *Rocky Point Resort,* 28121 Rocky Point Road, Klamath Falls (541–356–2287). Take Highway 140 along the west side of Upper Klamath Lake about 28 miles and turn at the signs to the resort; the put-in spot is nearby.

Covering an area of 133 miles, Upper Klamath Lake is Oregon's largest freshwater lake. Located on the Pacific Flyway, the area hosts more than 500 wildlife and bird species, including red-winged blackbirds, bald eagles, beavers, otters, mink, raccoons, deer, Canada geese, trumpeter swans, white pelicans, white-faced ibis, and sandhill cranes. For additional information and maps, contact the U.S. Fish and Wildlife Service, 1850 Miller Island Road West, Klamath Falls, 97603 (541–883–5732). Canoers can also find good floating and paddling on Crystal Creek and on Lake Ewauna in Klamath Falls.

If you decide to stay overnight in the area, check out the resort and RV accommodations at *Rocky Point Resort* (541–356–2287) located on Upper Klamath Lake near Fort Klamath. Here you can commune with gaggles of wildlife and bird species (www.klamathbirdingtrails.com) as well as go canoeing or fishing. Guests can explore hundreds of miles of nearby forest trails and backcountry roads, in the winter by clamping on cross-country skis and in the summer atop mountain bikes or on guided horseback rides.

For nearby campgrounds, hiking trails, places to fish, helpful maps, and general visitor information, stop by the Klamath Ranger District office at 1936 California Avenue in Klamath Falls (541–885–3400), or the Tule Lake Ranger District (530–667–2246) just across the border in Tule Lake, California. Both are open Monday through Friday from 8:00 A.M. to 4:30 P.M.

If you'd like to venture farther off the beaten path, consider trekking east into the Gearhart Mountain Wilderness environs and arranging a couple of days at *Aspen Ridge Resort* (541–884–8685; www.aspenrr.com), located northeast of Klamath Falls. This 14,000-acre working cattle ranch, owned by former Californians Steve and Karen Simmons, is accessed via Chiloquin, Sprague River Road, Highway 140, and, finally, Fish-hole Creek Road just east of Bly. But what's there to do here, you ask? Well, go horseback riding with the cowboys and learn how to manage a herd of cattle; hole up and read; go trout fishing or mountain biking; inhale fresh air and aromatic high desert smells of sagebrush and juniper; eat hearty meals prepared by the ranch cook; then listen to evening sounds, like the howl of coyotes or the bawl of cattle, and gaze at a wide sky jam-packed with glittering stars.

By this time your senses will have become saturated with the wonder of Crater Lake's crystalline waters; the quietness and mystery of the southern Cascade Mountains wilderness areas will have seeped into your bones. Having experienced the breathtaking sight of a half million or so ducks, geese, swans,

## OTHER ATTRACTIONS WORTH SEEING IN SOUTHERN OREGON

**Dogs for the Deaf**
Central Point–Medford

**Jacksonville Museum**
Jacksonville

**Lava Beds National Monument**
40 miles south of Klamath Falls

white pelicans, and other waterfowl and wildlife congregating along the Pacific Flyway near Klamath Falls, you can now head farther east, via Highway 140, into Oregon's Old West country; north on US 97, into Oregon's high desert country; or west on Highway 66, toward Ashland, Medford, and Jacksonville.

# Shakespeare and Peter Britt Country

Heading west on Highway 66 from Klamath Falls toward Ashland, stock up on groceries and consider holing up in one of the rustic cabins (all have kitchens) at **Green Springs Box R Ranch,** located at 16799 Highway 66 (541–482–1873; www.boxrranch.com) along the historic Applegate Trail. Those weary pioneers who detoured from the Oregon Trail along this southern route in the mid-1840s often rested in this place at the 3,600-foot elevation level, near the springs and lush meadow. The ranch house, built in 1904, sits alongside the meadow, which in late spring and summer bursts with blooming wildflowers.

The ranch served originally as a stagecoach stop. Today it is a guest ranch and working cattle ranch of more than 1,000 acres, a place where you can help gather eggs from the henhouse, feed woolly spring lambs, or just relax and do nothing but soak in those marvelous southern Cascade Mountain sunrises and sunsets. You can also enjoy a sleigh ride during a winter visit or a wagon ride during the rest of the year, both activities involving a friendly pair of large roan Belgian horses, Kitty and Katie, harnessed and hitched and ready to go. A teamster-guide will share lively tales about the historic Applegate Trail as you tour a small pioneer village containing some of the oldest structures in southern Oregon.

Another option is to stay at one of the five cozy bed-and-breakfast guest rooms at **Pinehurst Inn at Jenny Creek** (17250 Highway 66, Ashland; 541–488–1002; www.pinehurstinn.us), a handsomely restored, 1920s-style roadhouse located just across the highway from the Box R ranch house. Lunch and dinner are available in the inn's sunny dining room on the main level; guests are served a full breakfast. Jenny Creek, well known for its brown trout fishing, bubbles alongside the inn, and you may even spy oddly shaped beaver lodges along its banks as well.

To rest one's travel-weary body at a century-old mineral springs resort at an invigorating elevation of about 4,000 feet, contact the folks at **Buckhorn Springs,** also located off Highway 66, about twenty minutes east of Ashland at 2200 Buckhorn Springs Road (541–488–2200; www.buckhornsprings.org). Here you'll find seven cabins to choose from located near Emigrant Creek. Bring your own food for cooking and your hiking shoes for walking the trails in the nearby *Cascade-Siskiyou National Monument* region. *Green Springs Inn Restaurant* (541–482–0614), located at 11470 Highway 66 (toward Ashland and about 10 miles east of Emigrant Lake), offers breakfast, lunch, and dinner daily year-round in a rustic lodge setting at a 4,500-foot elevation. The inn also offers eight guest rooms. *NOTE:* Highway 66 between Klamath Falls and Ashland is narrow and winding and is kept open all year; travelers should be prepared for snow conditions during winter months.

Highway 66 intersects with busy Interstate 5 near *Ashland,* just north of Mount Ashland and the Siskiyou Pass, which takes travelers to and from the Oregon-California border. Detour at this intersection into the bustling community of Ashland, where you can take in a southern Oregon Shakespeare tradition that dates from 1935.

In that year young professor Angus Bowmer of Southern Oregon Normal School—later renamed Southern Oregon State College—conceived the idea of producing Shakespeare's plays by reworking the walls of the town's old Chautauqua Building into an outdoor theater reminiscent of those of Elizabethan England. Convincing Ashland's city leaders took some time, but with their conditional blessing the first productions—*Twelfth Night* and *The Merchant of Venice*—took place over the Fourth of July in 1935.

The deficits from a boxing match that was scheduled to satisfy the Shakespeare skeptics were covered by the resounding success and bulging receipts from the two plays. In 1937 the *Oregon Shakespeare Festival* Association was organized as a nonprofit corporation, and in 1941 the first scholarships for actors were offered. The festival celebrated its seventieth year in 2005.

## The Applegate Trail

While motoring along Highway 66 between Klamath Falls and Ashland, you're following the path of early pioneers Jesse and Lindsay Applegate. In 1845 the brothers carved a route through the rugged mountains here as an alternative to the Oregon Trail and the treacherous Columbia River to the north. The Applegates' route, which crossed northern Nevada and California before reaching Oregon, was well traveled, but pioneer families suffered many hardships, including battles with the Modoc Indians who lived in the area. From Ashland the Applegate Trail continues along the route of I–5 north toward Roseburg and Oakland. The Southern Oregon History Center (541–773–6536, www.sohs.org) offers more history, journals and diaries, and maps for retracing the pioneers' footsteps.

To complement the splendid outdoor Elizabethan Theatre, the indoor Angus Bowmer Theatre was built in 1970, the intimate Black Swan Theatre was constructed in 1977, and the New Theatre, incorporating the former Black Swan, was inaugurated in 2002. The three theaters anchor a large outdoor plaza, a gift shop, and ticket offices. Visitors can also poke into interesting shops and eateries along nearby Main Street.

For information about the current repertoire of traditional as well as contemporary offerings—eleven or more plays are staged from mid-February through October; past fare included *Hamlet, Romeo and Juliet, The Merry Wives of Windsor, Two Sisters and a Piano, Blithe Spirit,* and *Cyrano deBergerac*—contact the Oregon Shakespeare Festival (541–482–4331; www.osfashland.org). *NOTE:* The plays staged at the outdoor Elizabethan Theatre run from June through October.

Ask for a complete schedule, including information about the Backstage Tour; the Exhibit Center, where you can try on a bevy of costumes, ranging

## Crazy for Live Local Theater

Regardless where in Oregon I'm traveling and researching, I always check out the local theater offerings. I love live theater, and it's fun to meet local folks and find out what's happening in their part of the state. The first time I saw *The Merry Wives of Windsor* in Ashland, the play was done in the traditional way, and it was wonderful. The second time I saw it there, several years later, *Wives* was done with a Roaring Twenties theme. It was marvelously fun, and the 1920s costumes were fabulous. One of my Ashland all-time favorites, though, was *Blithe Spirit,* done in the 1980s. The female ghost character was gowned in yards and yards of soft gray chiffon that twirled and swirled in the most enchanting way when she cavorted about the stage.

As a sophomore in high school in Portland (years ago!), I auditioned for our spring musical and was chosen to play the role of Molly in George Gershwin's *Girl Crazy* (now renamed *Crazy for You*). I could sing, but I was shy and soft-spoken then. The drama coaches called me in after school one day and plunked me in the middle of the stage. From their seats in the very back row of the auditorium they bellowed, "We have to be able to hear you from the back row, Myrna—now let's practice!" Well, from that shaky beginning I've nurtured a love of live local theater as an enthusiastic member of the audience. From Ashland to Brookings, from Eugene to Cannon Beach, and from Monmouth to Lake Oswego, I've enjoyed seeing such plays as *Greater Tuna, Ten Little Indians, Laughter from the 23rd Floor, Chapter Two, Crimes of the Heart, Pump Boys and Dinettes, Brigadoon, The Music Man, South Pacific,* and a host of others. Mmmm. . . . I wonder, how about two of my favorite roles—Mitzi Gaynor's character, Nellie Forbush, in *South Pacific,* or Marsha Mason's role in *Chapter Two?* Do I dare audition?

from the garb of queens, kings, courtesans, and heroes to that of villains, monsters, madmen, and fools; and special festival events held throughout the nearly year-round season. A traditional, summertime feast officially opens the Shakespeare Festival season in mid-June. It's held, amid much music and colorful heraldry, in Ashland's lovely **Lithia Park.** The park includes acres of lawn, shade trees, and mature rhododendrons along with bubbling Ashland Creek and a band shell.

For a quiet respite visit the **Japanese Garden,** located on a gentle slope across from the Butler-Perozzi Fountain (access from Granite Street, which skirts Lithia Park's perimeter). Stroll graveled paths and giant stepping-stones, perhaps pausing to sit at one of several benches placed to catch the best views of native shrubs, many tree species, and a gently flowing stream.

You've had your fill of William Shakespeare for a day or so? Well, not to worry, you can enjoy lots of smiles and laughs at **Oregon Caberet Theatre.** Built in 1911, the historic Baptist Church building, including its lovely stained-glass windows, was renovated as a caberet-style theater in 1982 and is located at First and Hargadine Streets (541–488–2902; www.oregoncaberet.com). Past musicals have included Guys on Ice, Pump Boys and Dinettes, Nunsense Jamboree, and The Bachelors. Call ahead for dinner reservations and for tickets to this popular theater; dinner seating is an hour and a half before curtain time. Other theaters to check out are **Camelot Theatre Company** (541–535–5250; www.camelottheatre.org), also near Ashland, which presents contemporary and classic plays such as One Flew Over the Cuckoo's Nest, The Ukrainians Are Coming, and The Member of the Wedding; and, one of the oldest theater groups in southern Oregon, founded in 1952, **Barnstormers Little Theatre,** 112 NE Evelyn Avenue, Grants Pass (541–479–3557). This all-volunteer community theater offers such plays as Neil Simon's Jake's Women, Thornton Wilder's The Skin of Our Teeth, Arthur Miller's Death of a Salesman, and Bernard Slade's Romantic Comedy.

You will find some forty fine bed-and-breakfast inns in the Ashland area. Here is a brief sampling: **Country Willows Bed and Breakfast Inn,** 1313 Clay Street (541–488–1590), located on five acres just south of downtown, offers elegantly decorated rooms in the two-story balconied farmhouse, as well as private havens in the redecorated barn (including a lodgepole-pine king bed facing a rock fireplace in one of the suites). At **Cowslip's Belle Bed & Breakfast,** 149 North Main Street (541–488–2901), guests are greeted by teddy bears and chocolates, homemade cookies, sherry and homemade biscotti, and three sumptuous rooms that have outside decks; a separate carriage house has two small suites.

At **The Iris Inn,** 59 Manzanita Street (541–488–2286), **Oak Hill Bed &**

*Breakfast,* 2190 Siskiyou Boulevard (541–482–1554), and *Coolidge House Bed & Breakfast,* 137 North Main Street (541–482–4721), guests find lovely gardens and landscaped grounds, comfortable guest rooms, waist-bulging breakfasts, and innkeepers who enjoy sharing Shakespeare town with out-of-towners.

Travelers can also enjoy cozy rooms at *The Peerless Hotel,* 243 Fourth Street (541–488–1082), where, until the late 1920s, rooms were rented to Southern Pacific railroad workers. In Ashland's Historic Railroad District, these once-meager lodgings have been upgraded to a classy European-style hostelry of the first order, and there is a lovely, intimate restaurant on the premises as well. Other comfortable bed-and-breakfasts in the downtown area include *Chanticleer Inn,* 120 Gresham Street (541–482–1919); *Romeo Inn,* 295 Idaho Street (541–488–0884); *Ashland's Tudor House,* 271 Beach Street (541–488–4428); and *Lithia Springs Inn,* not far from downtown Ashland at 2165 West Jackson Road (800–482–7128).

Because of the busy theater season, it's best to make lodging reservations early. For helpful brochures contact the Ashland Visitor Information Center, 110 East Main Street (541–482–3486; www.ashlandchamber.com). When you stop by the visitor center—located near the Festival Center—ask about the self-guided walking tour brochure and map of historic buildings and homes, the *Inside and Outdoor Activities* guide, and winter sports information for nearby Mount Ashland.

If the notion of sleeping in a 4,200-square-foot, handcrafted mountain log lodge sounds appealing, consider *Mount Ashland Inn Bed & Breakfast,* 550 Mount Ashland Road (541–482–8707; www.mtashlandinn.com), just off the beaten path—about 16 miles south of town, on the road up to 7,528-foot Mount Ashland. Climb up log steps to the large deck and stop for a

## Lithia Springs

The area surrounding Ashland has long been known for its mineral waters, with native families using the springs to care for their sick and aged. In 1911 the city began developing lithia water fountains; the lithia spring that presently serves the city is located about 3 miles east. Early pipelines of wood were replaced with cast iron, and this 2-inch line serves public fountains on the downtown plaza, in Lithia Park, and at the library. The water, which has a decidedly mineral-salty taste (try at least one sip!), contains more than twenty different kinds of minerals and acids, including lithium (Li), calcium (Ca), magnesium (Mg), barium (Ba), potassium (K), sulfuric acid ($H_2SO_4$), and phosphoric acid ($H_3PO_4$).

moment to savor the wide-angle view past tall pines to the verdant slopes of the Siskiyou mountain range, the valley floor, and 14,162-foot, snowy Mount Shasta, looming some 50 miles to the south in northern California.

A large stone fireplace dominates the inviting common area, beckoning guests to the cheerful fire with a good book or a glass of hot spiced cider. The aroma of fresh-baked cookies may tempt a peek into the cozy kitchen just beyond the dining area. Choose from comfortable guest rooms on the third level, each with a private bath.

Work off your delicious breakfast with an outdoor stroll or a hike along a section of the *Pacific Crest National Scenic Trail,* which crosses the inn's parking area. The trail angles through groves of ponderosa pine and red-barked manzanita up to lush alpine meadows that burst with colorful wild-flowers in mid- to late summer. The wild larkspur, blue lupine, and white bear grass usually peak in August at the higher elevations.

During winter clamp on cross-country skis and enjoy a trek right from the inn's door, on the old logging roads located nearby—or try the snowshoes and sledding equipment kept handy for guests. You'd prefer to bed down at a lower elevation? Call the friendly folks at comfy *A-Dome Studio Bed & Breakfast* at an elevation of about 3,200 feet, located at 8550 Dead Indian Memorial Road (541–482–1755; www.adomestudio.com), about fifteen minutes east of downtown Ashland.

Right next door to Ashland is *Medford,* the Rogue River Valley's industrious timber-processing and pear-packing center. Once the home of the Takelma tribe, the region changed drastically when gold was discovered near Jacksonville, just west of Medford, in 1852. Miners invaded the valley in search of fortunes in gold nuggets and were followed by early settlers lured to the valley by its fertile soil and favorable growing conditions. The fortune hunters panned and claimed, the farmers cleared and planted—and both groups displaced the peace-loving Takelma tribe. Of course, in addition to all these events, railroad tracks were laid, and the clatter and whistles of trains were heard.

To recapture some of the nostalgia and history connected with the railroad's reaching into the Rogue River Valley at Medford, visit *Medford Railroad Park* (541–535–7952; www.rvmrc.railfan.net), where you and the kids can take a short train ride on the second and fourth Sunday of the month from 11:00 A.M. to 3:00 P.M. The historic park and its vintage train are located near Berrydale Avenue and Table Rock Road.

The *Southern Oregon Historical Society Center* also contains exhibits and historical collections and is a worthwhile addition to your travel itinerary. The center is located at 106 North Central Avenue in downtown Medford

(541–773–6536; www.sohs.org), and it's open from 9:00 A.M. to 5:00 P.M. Tuesday through Friday and from 10:00 A.M. to 4:00 P.M. Saturday. For additional information about the area contact the Medford Visitor Information Center, 1314 Center Drive (541–776–4021; www.visitmedford.org).

Medford is loved by bicyclists for its **Bear Creek Nature and Bicycling National Recreation Trail,** which meanders through town along the banks of Bear Creek. Walkers and joggers are also welcome to use the paved trail. The Old Stage Road to Jacksonville, though heavily used by automobiles, is also popular with bicyclists.

Detour just 10 miles north of Medford on Highway 62 to visit the ca. 1872 **Butte Creek Mill** at 402 Royal North in Eagle Point (541–826–3531; www.butte creekmill.com). From the long wooden loading dock, step into the dim, coolish interior, where you and the kids can watch the miller at work. The tangy fragrance of wheat, rye, and corn will tantalize your nostrils, and you'll hear the faint bubbling sound of the creek, whose waters are turning two enormous millstones, 1,400 pounds each.

These giant stones were quarried in France; milled in Illinois; shipped around Cape Horn to Crescent City, on the northern California coast; and carried over the Coast Range by wagon. Water diverted from Butte Creek activates the turbine that turns the wheels, generating power for the mill; the spent water then reenters the stream through the tailrace, located below the waterwheel.

In addition to the freshly ground flours, meals, and cracked grains, you'll find old-fashioned peanut butter, nuts, dried fruits, seeds, granolas, yeasts, raw honey, molasses, teas, and bulk spices in the adjoining **Country Store.** Butte Creek Mill and its old-fashioned Country Store is open year-round Monday through Saturday from 9:00 A.M. to 6:00 P.M. The small **Eagle Point History Museum** next door is generally open on Saturday from 11:00 A.M. to 4:00 P.M. For a tasty breakfast or lunch in Eagle Point, locals suggest **Barbwire Cafe & Grill** (541–830–0560).

## 1885: Middle Ford Becomes Medford

In 1883, when the Oregon and California Railroad reached southern Oregon, a railroad station was built at Middle Ford on Bear Creek. Later a town site was platted here and the name shortened to Medford. Incorporated in 1885, the town took up its first order of business: to establish an ordinance that discouraged disorderly conduct. A second ordinance prohibited minors from loitering at the railroad depot, and a third solemnly outlawed hogs from running loose within the town.

In nearby Shady Cove browse a collection of western memorabilia and dive into baby back pork and beef ribs at *Two Pines Smokehouse & Carlotta's Dining,* Highway 62 (541–878–7463; www.twopines.com). From here you could continue north to Crater Lake National Park or backtrack to the Medford-Jacksonville area.

In Medford you can take exit 27 from I–5 and browse another pleasant country store and gift shop, *Harry & David's Country Village,* 1314 Center Drive (541–864–2278), which offers treats from dried fruit and nuts to chocolates and cheesecakes. Not too far away,

Butte Creek Mill

stop and stroll through the fine Rose Display Garden at *Jackson & Perkins,* 2518 South Pacific Highway. The folks here have been developing new and old rose varieties since 1872. You can also see a splendid display of J&P roses, including the elegant tree roses, at *McCully House Bed & Breakfast Inn, Restaurant and Gardens* at 240 East California Street (541–899–1942), in nearby Jacksonville. Those who are into common and rare alpine plants, like species and colors of creeping phlox, sedum, creeping thyme, alyssum, dianthus, and fern, can visit the display gardens at *Siskiyou Rare Plant Nursery,* 2825 Cummings Road, Medford (541–772–6846; www.siskiyourareplant nursery.com) Monday through Friday from 9:00 A.M. to 5:00 P.M. March through November.

A pleasant option is to take the scenic route to the National Historic Landmark community of Jacksonville—the *Old Stage Road* off Highway 99 from the Central Point–Medford area—for a close-up view of tidy pear orchards, open-air fruit stands, and old farmsteads. During early spring the whole valley seems a canopy of luscious white pear blossoms. This eye-catching spectacle takes place from mid- to late April; call ahead to one of the visitor information centers for current weather and bloom times.

Among the amenable bed-and-breakfast inns in the area is the historic *Under the Greenwood Tree Bed and Breakfast,* formerly a weigh station for hay and grain in the 1870s and 1880s. Situated comfortably amid enormous old oak trees and lush green lawns and gardens, the large square farmhouse was renovated in the mid 1980s.

Four lovely guest rooms, all with private baths, offer views of the grounds from the second floor. Breakfast is a tempting gourmet affair, cooked fresh each morning. For further information and reservations, contact the innkeepers at 3045 Bellinger Lane, Medford (541–776–0000). The inn is about midway between Medford and Jacksonville.

Designated a National Historic Landmark in 1966, the town of Jacksonville diligently works to preserve the atmosphere of the mid-1800s. Park on any side street and stroll down California Street for a glimpse into the colorful past. Did I just hear the clump of miners' boots, the crunch of wagon wheels pulled by mules or horses, the laughter of the saloon and dance hall queens, and the wind echoing around the old iron town-water pump next to the 1863 Beekman Bank Building?

To further savor Jacksonville's colorful history, trek from the old depot on C Street up E Street to the *Jacksonville Pioneer Cemetery.* Situated on a small hill shaded by tall oak and madrona trees, the historic cemetery offers quiet paths into the past. Pick up a map and self-guided walking tour and history guide of the cemetery at the visitor information center. Don't miss this lovely spot, especially from April to June.

## A Pioneer Cemetery I Have Known and Loved

I never entertained the notion of falling in love with a cemetery. But every time I visit Jacksonville I head for the Pioneer Cemetery on the small bluff just outside of town. I always take my camera. Only the rustle of leaves or soft breezes blowing through the tall oak and madrona trees disturbs the reverent hush. Its many pathways and byways lead me to stories of the past. I notice the granite headstones often drift or lean to one side. Weathered and yellowed, they are carved with intricate patterns of leaves, roses, drapery, and scrolls. I read names of loved ones, dates, and fond farewells that are etched into the stones. Many headstones date from 1859, when the cemetery was first platted. In the spring I walk among carpets of colorful wildflowers— the heart-shaped leaves, lavender blossoms, and tendrils of wax yrtle trail about; shooting stars, fawn lilies, and columbine poke up in shady nooks and crannies. Unexpected steps lead me to terraced areas throughout the grounds. I love the jumble of tall trees and undergrowth and wildflowers. The old headstones urge me to stay longer and read their poignant stories again. I wouldn't miss a visit to this special place, one of the quintessential outdoor scrapbooks of southern Oregon's pioneer past.

Jacksonville Pioneer Cemetery

The large white Courthouse Building, constructed in 1883, is home to the *Jackson County Historical Society Museum.* Plan a visit to this fine museum Wednesday through Saturday from 11:00 A.M. to 4:00 P.M.; it's just off California Street at 206 North Fifth (541–773–6536; www.sohs.org), with its collections of photographs, vintage clothing, books, and other pioneer memorabilia. Picnic tables are set on the grounds under tall, old-fashioned locust trees during summer months.

Living-history programs are offered afternoons during summer at *Beekman House,* located on California Street near the restored, ca. 1854 Methodist church. Then stroll along the side streets to see more than eighty restored homes and other structures, many dating from the early 1800s, and all labeled; some have their own private gardens, which can be enjoyed from the sidewalk.

For information about other living-history exhibits and programs, contact the Jacksonville Visitor Information Center, 185 North Oregon Street (541–899–8118; www.jacksonvilleoregon.org).

Other old buildings, now restored, house specialty shops and boutiques, ice-cream parlors, bakeries, cafes, tea rooms, and bed-and-breakfast inns. The 1863 *Jacksonville Inn* (541–899–1900) offers a good restaurant, as does the *Bella Union* (541–899–1770); both are on California Street.

Walk up First Street to the Britt Gardens, founded in 1852 by pioneer photographer, horticulturist, and vintner Peter Britt. Named in his honor, the *Peter Britt Music and Arts Festival* offers a wide variety of classical, bluegrass, jazz, and dance music, the events all taking place outdoors under the stars during June, July, and August. Collect a picnic, blankets, lap robes, pillows, or lawn chairs and find just the right spot on the wide sloping lawn (or on wooden benches) under tall Douglas fir trees for the evening's concert.

The festival has hosted such notables as Kenny Rogers, Dan Fogelberg, Diane Schuur, the Manhattan Transfer, Les Brown's band, and the Dave Brubeck Quartet, as well as classical pianist Lorin Hollander. Several evenings are devoted to bluegrass concerts, and you can also enjoy family concerts as well as participate in a wide variety of music and dance workshops.

For a helpful booklet listing the schedule and for ticket information, contact Britt Festivals, (800) 822–7488 or www.brittfest.org.

For overnight stays in the Jacksonville area, try the **McCully House Inn,** an 1860 Gothic-Revival mansion at 240 East California Street (541–899–1942); **Historic Orth House,** a "teddy bear" inn at 105 West Main Street (541–899–8665; www.orthbnb.com); the spendid **Bybee's Historic Inn Bed & Breakfast** at 883 Old Stage Road (541–899–0106); and **Stage Lodge,** at 830 North Fifth Street (541–899–3953; www.stagelodge.com). To avoid being disappointed, call by February or March to make reservations if you plan to attend summer Britt Festival events.

# Scenic Rogue River Country

If time allows, take winding old Highway 99 and U.S. Highway 199 for a leisurely, 25-mile drive along the upper Rogue River to Grants Pass. You can also detour at Gold Hill to visit the **Gold Hill Historical Museum,** located at 504 First Avenue (541–855–1182). Containing a collection of southern Oregon mining and historical memorabilia, the museum is generally open Thursday through Saturday, noon to 4:00 P.M. from April to mid-October.

If you love old covered bridges, plan to visit **Wimer Covered Bridge,** the only one in Jackson County open to vehicular traffic. The original bridge was constructed in 1892; the current covered structure, often called "a barn over water," was built in 1927 by Jason Hartman, a county bridge superintendent. To find the bridge, detour from the town of Rogue River about 7 miles north on East Evans Creek Road. For information on other covered bridges in the area, call the Southern Oregon Historical Society library in Medford, (541) 773–6536.

For an alternate route from Jacksonville to Grants Pass, take Highway 238, which winds along the Applegate River, passes the hamlet of Ruch (where you'll see **Valley View Winery**—small tasting room here, open afternoons), and continues past **McKee Covered Bridge.** Pause for lunch or dinner at **McKee Bridge Restaurant,** 9045 Upper Applegate Road (541–899–1101); open daily from 7:00 A.M. to 9:00 P.M. Continue another 6 miles west of Ruch to reach **Applegate River Lodge & Restaurant,** 15100 Highway 238 (541–846–6082). Of massive log construction, the inn offers seven large guest-room suites using decor that depicts the history of the area. Enjoy fine dining in the inn's restaurant, Wednesday through Sunday starting at 5:00 P.M.

Entering Grants Pass via Highway 238, you'll cross the Rogue River on the ca. 1931 **Caveman Bridge,** which is on the National Register of Historic Places. For helpful visitor information write or stop by the well-stocked Grants Pass Visitor Information Center, 1995 NW Vine Street (541–476–7717; www.visit grantspass.org).

The **Rogue River** earns its nickname, "the fishingest river in the West," if you judge from the large number of folks who fish its pools and riffles year-round. The best chinook salmon angling is reported to take place from mid-April through September, whereas trout fishing picks up in August and again in December through March. Local tackle shops sell bait, supplies, the required licenses, and salmon/trout tags. Ask about catch regulations.

You can fish from the shore at parks along the river or hire a drift-boat guide for half days or full days—a tradition since the early 1930s, long before an 84-mile stretch of the river between Grants Pass and Gold Beach on the south coast was designated part of the National Wild and Scenic system. More adventurous anglers can check out the three- and four-day guided fishing trips down this section of the Rogue that are offered by licensed outfitters from September 1 to November 15; the visitor information center will have current information.

## Primer on Pears

Once considered fit for only royalty to eat, pears are not only basking in renewed popularity, but even we commoners have access to them. The Rogue River Valley of southern Oregon grows some of these special fruits:

**Bartlett:** One of the first pears of the season, Bartletts turn from green to bright yellow; they have the definitive sweet, mellow, and buttery taste known to pears; and they hold their shape well for baking and poaching.

**Anjou:** The most abundant of winter pears, Anjous are light green or yellow-green and sport a creamy flesh, slightly spicy flavor, and thin edible skin.

**Bosc:** With a russet brown skin, the Bosc has a creamy and tender flesh that offers an aromatic and full-bodied flavor. It's a good baking and cooking pear.

**Comice:** The chubby pear with a short neck and thick, short stem is greenish-yellow, often with a reddish blush. Often called the queen of pears, it is juicy, sweet, and best eaten fresh; it's wonderful as a dessert pear served with cheeses.

The most common summer white-water trips use large, inflatable oar-and-paddle rafts, inflatable kayaks, drift boats, or the popular jet boats. As you drift along with an expert guide handling the oars, the Rogue River ripples, cascades, boils, churns, and spills over rocks and boulders, through narrow canyons and gorges, and along quiet, pondlike, and peaceful stretches—rimmed on both sides by forests of Douglas fir, madrona, and oak and reflecting sunlight, blue sky, and puffy white clouds from its ever-moving surface.

You can also enjoy a one-day guided raft trip on the river or a four-hour, 36-mile jet-boat excursion to **Hellgate Canyon,** stopping at OK Corral for a country-style barbecue dinner served on a large deck overlooking all that marvelous river and wilderness scenery. Local kids love to entertain jet-boat passengers by swinging out over the river on long ropes attached to bankside trees, dropping and splashing—among much clapping and raucous laughter—into the river near lovely **Schroeder County Park and Campground,** just a few miles west of downtown and off US 199, the Redwood Highway. For information and reservations contact **Hellgate Jetboat Excursions** in Grants Pass (541–479–7204).

If you'd like to remain a little closer to civilization, consider spending the night at **Ponderosa Pine Inn Bed & Breakfast,** 907 Stringer Gap Road in nearby Grants Pass (541–474–4933).

For good eats in Merlin try **Backroad Grill** (541–476–4019), open for dinner Wednesday through Sunday.

If you're in the area on a Saturday, check out the fabulous **Grants Pass Grower's Market**—the fresh-baked cinnamon rolls, breads, and pastries are to die for, not to mention the farm-fresh fruits, vegetables, and herbs. The market is set up at Fourth and F Streets, 9:00 A.M. to 1:00 P.M.

Check out the live theater offerings at **Stardust Repertory Theatre,** 424 SW Sixth Street (541–472–9614), and at **Barnstormers Little Theatre,** between Sixth and Seventh Streets at 112 NE Evelyn Avenue in Grants Pass (541–479–3557). Barnstormers is one of the oldest community theaters in the state. Also, check out the season's plays and musicals offered by **Rogue Music Theatre** at Rogue Community College, a few miles east of Grants Pass (541–479–2559).

Before heading north via I–5 toward Roseburg, or going west via the Redwood Highway (US 199) toward Cave Junction and the south coast, plan a natural history stop at **Wildlife Images Rehabilitation and Education Center.** Originally started to nurse injured birds of prey back to health, the center now aids and nurtures all types of injured or orphaned wild animals, from bears and fawns to raccoons and beavers. To arrange a guided tour, call ahead, (541) 476–0222; www.wildlifeimages.org.

# Spiced Pear Fans from
# Pine Meadow Inn Bed and Breakfast

"We especially enjoy serving this dish in the fall, with pears from our garden," says innkeeper Nancy Murdock.

3 ripe pears, red Anjou preferred

½ cup apple, apricot, or peach juice

½ cup sherry

1 teaspoon cinnamon

¼ teaspoon cloves

1 tablespoon brown sugar

¼ cup berry preserves

6 sprigs of thyme or other herb, about 2 inches long

Serves 6

Cut each pear in half and cut out core center section. Turn each half over on cutting board and cut partially into thin vertical slices, leaving half intact. Spray a baking dish with nonstick spray and carefully place each pear half face down in the dish (use a spatula). Mix together the juice, sherry, spices, and brown sugar and pour over the pears; reserve 1 tablespoon of the mixture. Bake in 350-degree oven 20–30 minutes.

Mix the reserved juice with the preserves and spread a tablespoon or so of this mixture on six small serving plates.

When pears are cooked, remove each half carefully with a spatula, place each face-down on serving plate, and fan the vertical slices. Place a sprig of thyme or other herb in the center crevice as a garnish.

For another scenic side trip, take the 20-mile, paved, twisting road east of Cave Junction, located 30 miles southwest of Grants Pass via US 199, up to the **Oregon Caves National Monument** (541–592–2100). Located in the heart of the Siskiyou Mountains at an elevation of 4,000 feet, the prehistoric marble and limestone underground caverns were discovered by Elijah H. Davidson in 1874, although native peoples, of course, knew about the caves for centuries before white people arrived.

Although guided walks through the caves can be taken year-round, avoid midsummer crowds and long lines by planning a trip in either early spring or late fall, after Labor Day. Better yet, try a midwinter visit in the snowy wonderland, bringing along your snowshoes or cross-country skis.

The cave tour, somewhat strenuous, lasts about seventy-five minutes and is not recommended for those with heart, breathing, or walking difficulties;

canes and other walking aids are not permitted inside the caverns. And though children under six are prohibited from entering caves, a babysitting service is available for a nominal fee. *NOTE:* The caverns are a chilly forty-one degrees Fahrenheit inside; dress warmly and wear sturdy shoes.

Then, too, you could arrange to stay the night at the rustic ***Oregon Caves Chateau*** (541–592–3400), built in 1934 and now on the National Register of Historic Places. It's a handsome cedar structure with twenty-two guest rooms (sans telephones or TV), some overlooking a waterfall and a pond, others the Douglas fir–clothed canyon or the entrance to the caverns. The chateau's restaurant serves dinner, offering steak, seafood, chicken, and a selection of Northwest wines, with Cave Creek close by—it bubbles right through the dining room. The old-fashioned coffee shop is open for breakfast and lunch. The Oregon Caves Chateau operates from mid-June to September.

Or, you can bed down in a log-lodge–style guest room or in a comfy tree house suite located near the banks of the scenic Illinois River by calling the friendly folks at ***Erin Lodge Bed & Breakfast,*** 29025 Redwood Highway, Cave Junction (541–592–4253; www.erinlodge.com). If you'd like to experience a summer camp for families that also features tree houses, call ***Out 'N' About Treesort*** located near Cave Junction (541–592–2208; www.treehouses.com).

For the current status of ***Kalmiopsis Wilderness*** hiking trails and for maps and additional information, contact the Illinois Valley Visitor Center, 201 Caves Highway, Cave Junction (541–592–2631). Locals say the nearby ***Wild***

## Wine Tasting in Southern Oregon

**Ashland Vineyard & Winery**
2775 East Main Street, Ashland
(541) 488–0088
Open 11:00 A.M. to 5:00 P.M. Tuesday
through Sunday

**Bridgeview Vineyard & Winery**
4210 Holland Loop Road, Cave Junction
(877) 273–4843
Open 11:00 A.M. to 5:00 P.M. daily

**Foris Vineyards Winery**
654 Kendall Road, Cave Junction
(800) 843–6747
Open 11:00 A.M. to 5:00 P.M. daily

**Valley View Winery**
125 West California Street
Jacksonville
(800) 781–9463
Open 11:00 A.M. to 5:00 P.M. daily
except holidays

**Weisinger's of Ashland**
3150 Siskiyou Boulevard, Ashland
(800) 551–9463
Open 10:00 A.M. to 6:00 P.M. daily
June through September, 11:00 A.M.
to 5:00 P.M. October through May

***River Brewing & Pizza Company*** (541–592–3556), open daily, is a companionable spot to eat and to sample ales brewed on the premises.

***McGrew's Restaurant*** (541–596–2202) in nearby O'Brien is well known for steaks and seafood. Call for reservations.

From here continue west on the scenic Redwood Highway (US 199) toward Crescent City, California, and to the heart of the Redwood National and State Parks. For helpful maps and information, stop at the Hiouchi Visitor Center on US 199, just 8 miles east of Crescent City. Redwood National Park Headquarters and Visitor Center is located at 1112 Second Street in Crescent City (call 800–343–8300 for maps and information). Ask about Myrtle Creek Botanical Area, Jedediah Smith Redwoods State Park, Stout Grove, Lake Earl Wildlife Area, Point St. George Lighthouse, North Fork Smith River Botanical Area, Rowdy Creek Fish Hatchery, and the lily fields, all located near Crescent City in Del Norte County of northern California. From Crescent City it's an easy drive north on U.S. Highway 101 to Brookings and Gold Beach on the southern Oregon coast.

# The Umpqua Valley

Early travelers in the mid-1800s came through southern Oregon by stagecoach over those rough, dusty, and sometimes muddy roads from central California on their way north to the Oregon country. The trip from San Francisco to Portland took about sixteen days, the fare being about 10 cents a mile. Stage stations were situated every 10 or so miles, and the big crimson-colored stages, built to carry the mail and as many as sixteen passengers, were an important link in the early development of the Northwest.

Completion of the railroad in 1887 through the Willamette and Umpqua Valleys south to California brought a sudden halt to the overland mail stage. Although this marked the end of a colorful chapter in Northwest history, nevertheless today's traveler can recapture a bit of that history. For a look at one of the oldest stage stops in the state, detour from I-5 at Wolf Creek, about 20 miles north of Grants Pass. Here you will find ca. 1883 ***Wolf Creek Inn*** (541–866–2474), a large, two-story, classical revival–style inn that is still open to travelers.

Purchased by the state and completely restored in 1979, the inn is now administered by the State Parks and Recreation Department. Hearty meals are served in the dining room, and guest rooms are available on the second floor. When you walk into the parlor, which is furnished with period antiques, you might notice the sunlight filtering through lace-curtained windows and imagine a long-skirted matron or young lady sipping a cup of tea while waiting for the next stage to depart. The inn's pleasant dining room is open to the public for breakfast, lunch, and dinner year-round (except New Year's).

If time allows, take the Sunny Valley exit from I–5, exit 71, and visit the **Applegate Trail Interpretive Center.** In this impressive log structure, you and the kids can sample more intriguing history of the region, particularly that of the Applegate brothers, Jesse and Lindsay, who in 1846 blazed a new trail to Oregon from Fort Hall, Idaho, entering the Willamette Valley from the south. The center, located at 500 Sunny Valley Loop (888–411–1846), is open daily from 10:00 A.M. to 5:00 P.M. (closed during winter months).

Hamlets and small communities like Remote, Camas Valley, Days Creek, Tiller, Lookingglass, Riddle, and Glide contain many descendants of both early miners and pioneers. These folks live in the remote areas of the Umpqua River east and west of Roseburg. There are a few native peoples left, too—a small community of Cow Creek Indians.

Also hidden away on the county roads—look for the bright blue Douglas County road signs with yellow numbers—and in the small valleys near Roseburg are some of the region's first vineyards and wineries. More than thirty years ago the first varietal grapes were planted by Richard Sommer at **Hillcrest Vineyard,** and from these first roots eventually emerged a thriving colony of vintners just west of Roseburg—Davidson Winery, Giradet Wine Cellars, Lookingglass Winery, Callahan Ridge Winery, Hillcrest Vineyard, Umpqua River Vineyards, and Henry Winery.

To reach the wineries, drive through the oak-dotted, rolling hills west of Roseburg. Call ahead to make certain the tasting rooms are open; some of the vineyards are open only by appointment. The Roseburg Visitor Center, at 410 SE Spruce Street (541–672–9731; www.visitroseburg.com), will have helpful maps and may be willing to call ahead for you. If you want to explore the side roads a while longer, ask for *A Guide to Historic Barns* and *A Driver's Guide to Historic Places.*

Wind southwest a few miles from Roseburg to Winston to visit **Wildlife Safari** (541–679–6761; www.wildlifesafari.org), a 600-acre, drive-through wild-animal reserve of more than a hundred different species of animals and birds representing Africa, Asia, and more exotic areas of the world. Among the wildlife living here are the Tibetan yak, wildebeest, eland, lion, elephant, ostrich, hippopotamus, rhinoceros, and cheetah. Ask the staff if Sneeze, the female African elephant, is still available for rides.

Since 1980 Wildlife Safari has been operated by the Safari Game Search Foundation, a nonprofit organization dedicated to preserving endangered species, conducting animal-related research, providing educational programs for elementary schools throughout the Northwest, and rehabilitating injured wildlife. A world leader in the research on and breeding of cheetahs, the organization has successfully raised more than one hundred cheetah cubs here in the past twenty years and is one of the largest providers of cheetahs to zoos throughout the world.

The reserve is open daily year-round from 9:00 A.M. to dusk. It offers the **White Rhino Restaurant** and Casbah Gift Shop along with a small RV park, picnic areas, and free kennels for Fido. Wildlife Safari reserve is about 4 miles west of I–5 from the Winston exit via Highway 42. There is an admission fee.

For exhibits of some of the region's natural history, as well as logging and mining equipment dating from the 1800s, detour from I–5 just south of Roseburg—at the Fairgrounds exit—to visit the **Douglas County Museum of History and Natural History** (541–957–7007; www.co.douglas.or/museum), located in the large contemporary structure next to the fairgrounds. After poking around the vintage logging and mining equipment in the courtyard, be sure to look inside for the fine exhibit of old photographs. Though the photographs are yellowed with age, the weathered faces in them mirror hope and determination as well as hardship and even heartbreak; the exhibit offers a poignant look into Oregon's pioneer past. The museum is open daily from 9:00 A.M. to 5:00 P.M. A shady park next door offers picnic tables and parking for recreational vehicles.

If you pass through the community of Glide—it's about 17 miles east of Roseburg—the last weekend in April and notice lots of cars parked near the Community Building, be sure to stop to see whether the annual **Glide Wildflower Show** (541–677–3797; www.glidewildflowershow.org) is in progress. At this show some 300 native plants and flowers from the southern Oregon region are displayed in colorful arrangements by local naturalists and wildflower lovers. Don't miss it; it's great fun and also offers a chance to meet the locals and chat about botanical favorites over a cup of coffee.

Another pleasant side trip from Roseburg weaves farther east on Highway 138 into the southern **Cascade Mountains.** The two-lane asphalt ribbon plays hide-and-seek with the **North Umpqua River** and with many frothy waterfalls carrying names like Toketee, Lemolo, White Horse, Clearwater, and Watson. **Watson Falls** is noted as the second highest in Oregon, a 272-foot drop down a rugged cliff; access is from a well-marked ½-mile trail. The falls and nearby parking areas, beginning about 20 miles east of Glide, are well marked. A section of the scenic river, also well marked, is open just to those who love fly fishing; the fly fishing section between Glide and Steamboat is especially scenic.

*Steamboat Inn* (800–840–8825; www.thesteamboatinn.com) offers rustic but comfortable rooms and cabins that overlook the chortling Umpqua River— you'll likely want to sit on the wide deck for hours and soak in the wilderness. Guests enjoy gourmet fisherman dinners in the knotty-pine dining room. You could also check on the cozy accommodations at nearby *Steelhead Run Bed & Breakfast* (800–348–0563; www.steelheadrun.com) on the Umpqua River. From here you can continue east on Highway 138 to connect with *Poole Creek Campground* at Lemolo Lake (541–498–2531) and with newly reno-vated *Lemolo Lake Lodge* (541–643–0750; www.lemololakeresort.com); with *Diamond Lake* and its wide range of fishing, camping, and resort facilities; and with *Crater Lake National Park* (see beginning of this chapter for details). Along the route take a break and pull in at *North Umpqua Store* (541–498–2215) at Dry Creek, off Highway 138, for cold beverages, food sup-plies, and local gossip.

To see another section of the Umpqua River, detour west from I–5 onto Highway 138 at Sutherlin, just north of Roseburg. This meandering rural route carries travelers to *The Big K Guest Ranch,* located at 20029 Highway 138 W (800–390–2445; www.big-k.com) near Elkton on 2,500 acres of rolling Douglas fir forest in the Umpqua River Valley. The guest ranch complex overlooks "the loop," the biggest bend and a scenic stretch of the Umpqua River that is known for good fishing—smallmouth bass, steelhead, shad, and chinook salmon, depending on the season. The river bubbles and meanders past the ranch, through the Coast Range, and empties into the Pacific Ocean at Reedsport. The Kesterson family offers guests a number of outdoor options. You can swim in the resident pool, go horseback riding, bicycle, hike, try your hand at horse-shoes or the sporting-clay range, arrange for a river float trip, or even go on a wild turkey hunt. Home-style fare is offered in the river-rock fireplace dining room in the main lodge; accommodations are in cozy log cabins.

Plan one last detour before entering the lush Willamette Valley region: a stop in the small community of Oakland, nestled in the oak-dotted hills just north of Sutherlin. About twenty-five years ago, when the area's lumber mill closed, Oakland felt an economic decline common to many timber towns throughout the Northwest. The townsfolk's response, though, was decidedly uncommon—they worked to have their ca. 1852 community designated the *Oakland Historic District* and placed on the National Register of Historic Places, the first such district in Oregon to be so recognized, in 1967.

Begin with a stroll on Locust Street, poking into a few of its antiques shops and boutiques. Then stop at *Tolley's Restaurant and Antiques* (541–459–3796) for lunch or dinner, during which you'll be surrounded by more antiques, an old-fashioned soda fountain, and a lovely curved staircase of gleaming wood. The restaurant and ice-cream parlor are open daily for lunch; the intimate balcony dining room is open Wednesday through Sunday from 5:00 to 9:00 P.M. You can also eat outdoors on the patio with a view of the koi pond and lush plantings.

Next browse through another gaggle of antiques shops, snoop into the historic **Lamplighter Pub,** and inspect memorabilia and old photographs at the **Oakland Museum,** open daily from 1:00 to 4:30 P.M. except holidays (541–459–3087). Conclude your visit by walking farther up both sides of Locust Street to see vintage commercial structures, art galleries, and Victorian-style houses. Ask at Tolley's if the Oakland Gaslight Players are doing summertime melodramas in the renovated high school building at the upper end of Locust Street.

## Places to Stay in Southern Oregon

### ASHLAND

**A-Dome Studio Bed & Breakfast**
8550 Dead Indian Memorial Road
(541) 482–1755

**Country Willows Bed & Breakfast**
1313 Clay Street
(541) 488–1590

**Cowslip's Belle Bed & Breakfast**
149 North Main Street
(541) 488–2901

**The Iris Inn Bed & Breakfast**
59 Manzanita Street
(541) 488–2286

**Lithia Springs Inn**
2165 West Jackson Road
(800) 482–7128

**Oak Hill Bed & Breakfast**
2190 Siskiyou Boulevard
(541) 482–1554

**Palm Cottages Motel**
1065 Siskiyou Boulevard
(877) 482–2635

### BLY

**Aspen Ridge Resort**
Highway 140
(541) 884–8685

### GRANTS PASS

**Ponderosa Pine Inn B&B**
907 Stringer Gap Road
(541) 474–4933

**Weasku Inn Historic Fishing Resort**
5560 Rogue River Highway
(800) 493–2758

### KLAMATH FALLS

**Best Western Olympic Inn**
2627 South Sixth Street
(541) 882–9665

**Lake of the Woods Lodge, Cabins & RV Resort**
950 Harriman Route
(541) 949–8300

**Rocky Point Resort, Restaurant, and RV Park**
28121 Rocky Point Road
(541) 356–2242

**Thompson's Bed & Breakfast**
1420 Wild Plum Court
(541) 882–7938

### MEDFORD

**Cobblestone Cottages Bed & Breakfast**
2281 Ross Lane
(541) 772–0898

**Windmill Inn of Medford**
1950 Biddle Road
(800) 547–4747

### MERLIN

**Morrison's Rogue River Fishing Lodge**
8500 Galice Road
(800) 826–1963

### PROSPECT

**Prospect Historic Hotel B&B and Dinnerhouse**
391 Mill Creek Drive
(near Crater Lake)
(800) 944–6490

# Places to Eat in Southern Oregon

## ASHLAND

**Apple Cellar Bakery Restaurant**
2255 Highway 66
(541) 488–8131

**Cucina Biazzi**
568 East Main Street
(541) 488–3739

**Morning Glory Cafe**
1149 Siskiyou Boulevard
(541) 488–8636

**Omar's Restaurant**
1380 Siskiyou Boulevard
(541) 482–1281

**Señor Sam's Mexican Grill**
1634 Ashland Street
(541) 488–1262

## EAGLE POINT

**Barbwire Cafe**
Highway 62
(541) 830–0560

## GRANTS PASS

**Laughing Clam Restaurant**
121 South West G Street
(541) 479–1110

## JACKSONVILLE

**Bella Union Cafe**
170 West California Street
(541) 899–1770

## KLAMATH FALLS

**Mr. B's Steakhouse**
3927 South Sixth Street
(541) 883–8719

## MEDFORD

**Casa Ramos Mexican Restaurant & Cantina**
1253 North Riverside
(541) 776–2808

**Donut Country Coffee Shop**
1119 East Jackson Street
(541) 779–7699

## MERLIN

**Galice Resort on the Scenic Rogue River**
11744 Galice Road
(541) 476–3818

## SHADY COVE

**Two Pines Smokehouse**
21377 Crater Lake Highway 62
(541) 878–7463

# HELPFUL TELEPHONE NUMBERS AND WEB SITES FOR SOUTHERN OREGON

**Ashland Visitor Center**
(541) 482–3486
www.ashlandchamber.com

**Bicycle Adventures**
www.bicycleadventures.com

**Britt Festivals**
(800) 882–7488
www.brittfest.org

**Grants Pass Visitor Center**
(800) 547–5927
www.visitgrantspass.org

**Great Basin Visitor Center**
Klamath Falls
(800) 445–6728
www.greatbasinvisitor.info

**Illinois Valley Visitor Center**
Cave Junction
(541) 592–2361

**Illinois Valley Forest
Service Ranger District**
Cave Junction
www.fs.fed.us/r6/siskiyou

**Jacksonville Visitor Center**
(541) 899–8118
www.jacksonvilleoregon.org

**Klamath National Wildlife Refuge**
Klamath Basin, and Bear Valley Refuge
(541) 883–5732

**Medford Visitor Center**
(541) 776–4021
www.visitmedford.org

**Oregon Cabaret Theatre**
Ashland
(541) 488–2902

**Oregon Shakespeare Festival**
www.osfashland.org
Tudor Guild Gift Shop,
(541) 482–0940
ticket sales, (541) 482–4331
*NOTE:* No performances on Monday

**Oregon State Parks and
Campgrounds**
(800) 551–6949 (general information)
(800) 452–5687 (reservations)

**Roseburg Visitor Center**
(800) 444–9584
www.visitroseburg.com

**Shasta Sunset Dinner Train**
(530) 964–2142
www.ShastaSunset.com

**Southern Oregon University
Theatre Arts**
Ashland
(541) 552–6348

# Southeastern Oregon

## The Old West

Southeastern Oregon is the state's "big sky" country, made up of its three largest and least-populated counties: Harney, Malheur, and Lake. The whole of many states on the East Coast could fit into this wide-open country in the Beaver State's far southeastern corner. In the 28,450-square-mile area containing just Malheur and Lake Counties, there are fewer than ten people per square mile—now, that's elbow room with room to spare.

The stark, panoramic landscapes here evoke images of western movies; one can easily imagine cowboys riding "Old Red" and "Big Blue," herding cattle through sagebrush-blanketed valleys and across rushing streams, sending scouts up narrow canyons to flat-topped buttes or along alkali lakes far ahead. The horizon stretches wide in all four directions in this massive high desert country, broken now and then by shaggy pinnacles, ridged rimrock canyons, and fault-block mountains.

Hudson's Bay Company explorer-trapper Peter Skene Ogden, along with other fur traders who came in the mid-1820s, had a fairly easy trek into the region because resident Native Americans had already carved numerous trails, often following deer and antelope trails. The ancient Paiute Indians

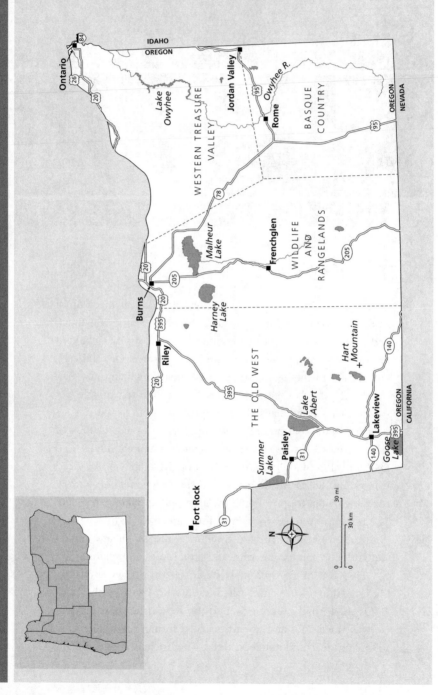

Ontario

IDAHO
OREGON

26

20

Lake
Owyhee

Jordan Valley

WESTERN TREASURE VALLEY

84

95

Owyhee R.

Rome

BASQUE COUNTRY

OREGON
NEVADA

95

78

20

Malheur
Lake

Frenchglen

WILDLIFE AND RANGELANDS

205

205

Burns

20

395

Harney
Lake

Riley

20

395

THE OLD WEST

Hart
+ Mountain

140

Lake
Abert

Lakeview

OREGON
CALIFORNIA

Paisley

31

Summer
Lake

140

Goose
Lake

395

Fort Rock

31

N

30 mi

30 km

0

0

hunted, traveled the animal trails, gathered seeds, and dug camas bulbs for centuries before Ogden's party arrived in 1826.

Other white people passed through in the 1850s, during the California gold rush. Early cattle barons then grabbed millions of acres of the southeastern desert country for rangeland in the 1870s and 1880s. The region still contains a number of the old ranches, and raising beef cattle remains one of the primary occupations—along with raising sheep, which was introduced by the immigrant Basques in the 1890s. There is a wonderful **Basque Museum** that history buffs may want to visit; it's located at 611 Grove Street in nearby Boise, Idaho (208–343–2671; www.basquemuseum.com), and is open Tuesday through Friday from 10:00 A.M. to 4:00 P.M. and on Saturday from 11:00 A.M. to 3:00 P.M. The annual Basque festival, the St. Ignatius Festival, is held the last weekend in July; call the museum for further information.

In 1843 Capt. John C. Frémont, a topographic engineer, was sent to the territory by the U.S. government to explore the region. He is responsible for naming many of the bold features of Lake County encountered during this winter expedition. You can follow his north-south route on Highway 31, the **Fremont Highway**, which skirts the Fremont National Forest and Gearhart Mountain Wilderness and is accessed from Lakeview, near the Oregon-California border, or from U.S. Highway 97 south of Bend and just south of La Pine.

## TOP HITS IN SOUTHEASTERN OREGON

**Diamond Loop and Blitzen Valley Auto Tour Route**
south of Burns

**Fort Rock State Park and Fort Rock Homestead Village Museum**
Fort Rock

**Four Rivers Cultural Center**
Ontario

**Harney County Historical Society Museum**
Burns

**Keeney Pass Oregon Trail Site & Oregon Trail Museum**
Nyssa

**Lake Owyhee and Owyhee River**
north of Jordan Valley

**Malheur National Wildlife Refuge**
south of Burns

**Rome Columns**
toward Jordan Valley

**Schminck Memorial Museum**
Lakeview

**Vale Murals**
Vale

## High Desert Field Trip

Take two seventh-grade homeroom teachers, one physical education teacher, two parents, and forty-seven seventh-graders from a K–8 elementary school in northeast Portland. Then, after spending the school year raising funds and planning, climb aboard a yellow school bus with tents, food, gear, and a friendly bus driver and head across the Cascade Mountains to Oregon's high desert for three days of school under the sky. My teaching partner, Dale Brown, and I led the trip in May 1970. The learning curve for the kids was astronomical, and I learned as much as they did. Our studies took us as far south as Fort Rock and Hole-in-the-Ground and as far north as Pilot Butte, Newberry Crater, Lava Butte, Lava Cast Forest, Lava River Cave, Arnold Ice Cave, and Skeleton Cave.

We set up camp at Tumalo State Park near Redmond in the group camp area alongside the Deschutes River, in the company of tall ponderosa pine and shorter juniper trees. Can you imagine making forty-seven sack lunches every morning? Thank goodness for those two wonderful parents, who did most of the cooking! One of the highlights was the day we visited Fort Rock, and several students spied an eagle's nest with a baby eaglet in it. Each afternoon we returned to camp by 3:30 or 4:00 P.M. so the kids could splash in the river before dinner. After dark, sitting around the crackling campfire, Dale would read spine-tingling tales from author Robert Service like his narrative poem "The Cremation of Sam McGee." Then we'd all fall into our sleeping bags and sleep like logs. I wonder if those kids, now grown, ever think about our three-day outdoor school under the high desert sky.

If time allows, detour from US 97 at La Pine onto Highway 31 and follow the signs to **Fort Rock State Park** (about 30 miles). You get the most dramatic perspective by walking up and inside the volcanic remnant, rising 325 feet from the high desert floor and surrounded by miles and miles of pungent sagebrush. It's more than ½ mile across inside. If you're lucky, you might spot a baby eagle in its nest. Notice the large wave-cut formations on the east flank, carved by eons-old inland seas that once covered this vast region.

Although the tiny community of **Fort Rock** offers one gasoline station, a cafe, and a grocery store, it's best to also bring your own supplies such as sunscreen, wide-brimmed hats, and drinking water. The high desert gets *very* hot and dry during summer months, with temperatures in the high eighties and nineties. Stay long enough, however, to visit **Fort Rock Homestead Village Museum** (541–576–2251). Walk into several vintage structures filled with pioneer memorabilia and furnishings that date from those original homestead days. Open Memorial Day weekend through September, Friday through Sunday from 10:00 A.M. to 4:00 P.M.

If you'd like to experience a bit more high desert outback country, deep into the sagebrush, continue south and east to the small community of *Christmas Valley*. If you arrive after sundown, you won't need to throw your bedroll under the sage and stars, however, because all the comforts of civilization are found here. The *Christmas Valley Desert Inn Motel* (541–576–2262) offers kitchenette units, telephones, trail biking, a nine-hole golf course, and a small airstrip.

As you continue south on Highway 31, you could pause in Silver Lake for dinner at *Cowboy Dinner Tree Restaurant* (541–576–2426; www.cowboy dinnertree.homestead.com/main.html) on South Hager Mountain Road. Don't let the looks of the ramshackle, shacklike structure turn you away. Made of rough-sawn lumber, it once housed cowboys; parts of it are more than fifty years old. A lone tall juniper guards the rear of the building. Rusted bridles and bits and old cast-iron skillets adorn the walls. Located about 4 miles south of Silver Lake, it's a honkin' drive from anywhere: about 87 miles from Lakeview, 25 from Christmas Valley, 150 from Klamath Falls, and 70 from Bend. There is no espresso machine here, and no alcohol is served. There is no menu—you eat what the chef cooks, which is beef or chicken. Once seated inside, you dive into bowls of fresh salad greens and hearty soup while the staff grills your twenty-two- to twenty-four-ounce marinated sirloin steak or your whole chicken on a grill out in the lean-to area behind the kitchen. These monster entrees are served with baked potatoes loaded with butter and sour cream and a pan of luscious rolls. Save room for dessert, too. Cowboy Dinner Tree Restaurant is open for dinner at 5:00 P.M. Thursday through Sunday during summer months and Friday through Sunday during winter months. Don't even think of stopping by without calling first—reservations are a must because of limited seating. Call the hosts at (541) 576-2426.

## cowboycritique

As you enter or leave Lakeview, notice the new cowboy welcome signs that adorn the entry points. Actually, these tall, painted, cutout wood figures have caused the locals some concern, because many feel the old cowboy figures were more authentic. "I don't like the new cowboy," said one shop owner. "He looks too much like a city guy."

Continuing south about 40 miles on Highway 31 from Silver Lake, travelers find *The Lodge at Summer Lake* at 53460 Highway 31 (866–943–3993; www.thelodgeatsummerlake.com). It's located directly across the highway from the Fish & Wildlife ranger station. At the ca. 1940s hostelry you can choose from seven motel rooms or three cedar cabins at the edge of a large bass pond, and a bunkhouse. In the main lodge where the restaurant is located you'll find a comfy great room and cozy fireplaces. The lodge is owned by two couples who decided to forgo big-city life and head to this scenic high desert valley that sits at an elevation of about 4,300 feet.

Ten miles farther south, **Summer Lake Inn,** located at 47531 Highway 31 (800–261–2778; www.summerlakeinn.com), offers upscale lodgings in several cabins paneled in warm cedar, in elegant self-contained cottages with fireplaces and kitchens, and in comfy rooms in the main lodge.

Outdoor activities in the region include fly fishing the Chewaucan River along with bird and wildlife viewing along the ridges rimmed with fragrant pine, sagebrush, and juniper. Also try backcountry bicycling, rockhounding, stargazing, or fishing for bass and trout at Ana Reservoir and in the nearby Sycan, Sprague, and Ana Rivers. *NOTE:* The lakes in this area along Highway 31 are shallow wetlands often visited by snow geese and sandhill cranes on their spring and fall migrations along the Pacific Flyway.

If you trek through the area in September around Labor Day weekend, check out the **Lake County Fair,** featuring the largest and oldest amateur rodeo in the Northwest, the **Paisley Rodeo.** You'll notice cowboys and cowgirls riding their horses through the streets of nearby Paisley, a frontier town on the Chewaucan River along the Fremont Highway, and you'll also spot the old watering trough and hitching post downtown.

Just 2 miles north of Lakeview is **Old Perpetual,** a geyser that spouts about 60 feet above the ground. The underground water heats to a temperature of some 200 degrees, erupting in a frothy, billowy column. The geyser spouts once every sixty to ninety seconds in the winter and every four to ten minutes in the summer.

## Country-Western Ballads That Go with Southeastern Oregon

"Easy on the Eyes, Hard on the Heart," Terri Clark

"Let's Take It One Step at a Time," George Strait

"My Heart Has a History of Lettin' Go," Paul Brandt

"We Really Shouldn't Be Doin' This," George Strait

"I'm Old Enough to Know Better But Still Too Young to Care," Wade Hayes

"All My Exes Live in Texas," George Strait

"Love Gets Me Every Time," Shania Twain

## TOP ANNUAL EVENTS IN SOUTHEASTERN OREGON

**John Scharff Migratory Bird Festival**
Burns; early April
(541) 573–2636

**Jordan Valley Rodeo**
Jordan Valley; mid-May
(541) 856–2460

**Thunderegg Days**
Nyssa; July
(541) 372–3091

**Hang Gliding Festival**
Lakeview; Fourth of July weekend
(541) 947–6040

**Japan Nite Obon Festival**
Ontario; third Saturday in July
(541) 889–8012

**Lake County Fair and Roundup**
Lakeview; Labor Day weekend
(541) 947–6040

For a pleasant overnight stay near Lakeview, try the newly renovated rooms at *Hunter Hot Springs Resort,* on U.S. Highway 395 (541–947–4242; www.huntersresort.com) and next to Old Perpetual geyser. You and the kids can enjoy the hot mineral springs swimming pool in the enclosed courtyard as well as watch gaggles of geese and ducks sail in and land for the night on other hot-springs pools nearby. If you visit around the Fourth of July, you'll often see groups of colorful hang gliders, with their pilots strapped aboard, soaring in from nearby Blackcap Mountain aiming for the landing zone on the resort's grounds.

There's also a little gem of a museum in Lakeview, *Schminck Memorial Museum* (541–947–3134), located in a small bungalow ½ block south of the courthouse at 128 South E Street. Administered by the Oregon State Society, Daughters of the American Revolution, the collection numbers more than 7,000 pieces that were collected over a lifetime by Lula and Dalpheus Schminck. The couple developed the collecting habit and spent many hours recording, labeling, and displaying their finds. You'll see fashions of the 1880s such as bustles, bows, high-button shoes, fancy fans, combs, hats, hatpins, parasols, beads, and bags. One of the splendid collections is composed of 74 vintage quilts dating from 1806 to 1820. Browsers can also see pipes, canes, spectacles, gold watches, personalized shaving mugs, and tools and tack of the period, as well as Indian artifacts and baskets from Lake County. Visit this little gem Tuesday through Saturday, 10:00 A.M. to 4:00 P.M. except December and January.

For eateries in Lakeview try *The Burger Queen* at 109 South F Street (541–947–3677); *Green Mountain Bakery,* 512 Center Street (541–947–4497); *Jerry's Restaurant,* 508 North Second Street (541–947–2600); *Happy Horse*

*Deli* at 728 North Fourth Street (Highway 140), (541–947– 4996); and *Honker's Coffeehouse* at 25 North E Street (541–947–4422) for tasty coffee and espresso drinks. Further information for lodging and dining in the Lakeview area can be obtained from the Lake County Visitor Center (877–947–6040; www.lakecounty chamber.org).

Or, if hunting's your passion, just south of Lakeview and near Goose Lake at the base of the Warner Mountains, just across the California border, contact the folks at *Honker Inn Lodge* (530–946–4179) to ask about special packages for hunting antelope, duck and goose, deer, blue and ruffed grouse, and spring ground squirrels (the county's number-one rancher's pest). Guide service is also available to hunt on private ranches.

If time allows, head east via Highway 140 to see whether the pelican colony is nesting at *Pelican Lake,* about 28 miles east of Lakeview. Turn north at the hamlet of Adel—a restaurant and a gas station are situated here— and proceed on a paved side road for a mile or so. This road continues another 15 miles to the small ranching community of Plush; along the way you might see deer, Canada geese, and sandhill cranes, particularly during the migrations in late fall.

For an alternate and closer route to Plush, head east from Lakeview on Highway 140 for about 15 miles, passing the small *Warner Canyon Ski Area.* The ski area offers fourteen runs, a 730-foot drop in elevation, and both down-hill and cross-country skiing. There are marked trails for snowmobiling enthusiasts as well. You'll reach the top of Warner Pass at 5,846 feet, then turn north and drop steeply into picturesque Warner Valley some 19 miles to *Plush.* You'll find one store with groceries and gas here. This small ranching community on the edge of Hart Lake serves as the gateway to *Hart Mountain National Antelope Refuge.* The 275,000-acre federal wildlife refuge was established in 1930, and the mountain was named for the heart-shaped brand of a former cattle ranch located nearby; the word was apparently misspelled. Along its mountain slopes and canyons clothed with groves of aspen, yellow pine, mountain mahogany, and sagebrush flourishes one of the largest herds of pronghorn antelope in the United States. The larger mule deer, with prominent ears, are seen in the area as well.

*NOTE:* The numerous all-weather gravel roads found in this region are often bumpy, steep, and one lane wide; always have a full tank of gas, extra water, and food supplies before heading into the hinterlands. Be prepared to change flat tires as well. Diesel fuel is usually available only in the larger cities, and gas stations along remote stretches close at dusk. The high desert is unforgiving regardless of the season; days can be hot and dry, nights chilly or freezing.

## OTHER ATTRACTIONS WORTH SEEING IN SOUTHEASTERN OREGON

**Ghost town, Ruby Ranch, and
Charbonneau's grave**
Danner

**Ghost town with post office**
Westfall

**P Ranch**
Frenchglen

**Peter French Round Barn**
Diamond

Thus well equipped, you can try out your natural-history–exploring persona and enjoy a more relaxed pace while carefully negotiating the narrow all-weather road north of Plush, which climbs *very* steeply for 27 miles to **Hot Springs Campground** (541–947–2731; www.fws.gov/refuges) atop 7,710-foot Hart Mountain. You'll pass the refuge headquarters at the top and then continue about 5 miles south to the campground, where you can immerse your road-weary body in a natural hot-water spring right next to the sky. The pool is rimmed with a low lava rock wall—and the night sky is jammed with glittering stars. Pitch your tent, walk the short trail to the summit overlook, and watch for eagles, badgers, and bighorn sheep, as well as the antelope and deer that are protected here (they feed in the early morning and at dusk).

The Hart Mountain National Antelope Refuge area is also well known to rock hounds for its agate nodules, fire opal, crystals, and sun stones. For gem-hunting locations open to the public, check with the ranger at the refuge headquarters; or pick up maps and obtain directions from the U.S. Fish & Wildlife refuge visitor information center in Lakeview at 18 South G Street (541–947–3315), particularly if you want to go to the sun-stone area.

Backtracking to Plush, you can connect with US 395 by heading northwest along the hogback for about 31 miles of good all-weather dirt road. In the distance you'll see Coyote Hills and **Abert Rim** rising 2,000 feet above the plateau, filling the western horizon along the edge of Abert Lake. Its 800-foot lava cap ends in a sheer precipice.

This 30-mile-long scarp is a nearly perfect fault, one of the largest exposed faults in the world. On huge boulders at the base are pictographs drawn by early Indians who lived in the region; arrowheads, rock foundations of primitive huts, and bleached bones have also been discovered in the area.

This southeastern region is dotted with beds of lakes formed thousands of years ago. Some lakes evaporated; others found outlets or were clogged by showers of volcanic ash. Some contain water during the brief rainy season; others are always dry; and still others retain only enough moisture to become meadows. You'll see chalky white alkali around many of the lakes' shores, as the lakes shrink during the summer months.

Head north on paved US 395, entering Harney County and passing Wagontire and stopping at *Riley,* a distance of about 60 miles. Here mule deer share the browse with shaggy range bulls that look the size of locomotives. Gas up at Riley or continue east some 25 miles on U.S. Highway 20, stopping in the larger community of *Burns* to replenish gas and food supplies.

Just east of Riley you can detour at the state rest area and walk the ½-mile *Sagehen Hill Nature Trail* to become acquainted with the native shrubs, plants, and bird species of the high desert region. At eleven self-guided stations, visitors identify big sagebrush (take a small leaf, rub it between your palms, and sniff the wonderful fragrance); bitterbrush, with its dark green leaves and yellow springtime flowers; western juniper, one of the dominant trees, its blue-green berries loved by many bird species; low sagebrush; and Idaho fescue, an important native bunchgrass that grows on the high desert.

Along the trail you may also see dwarf monkey flower, western yarrow, blue-eyed Mary, owl clover, lupine, and wild parsley. Keep an eye out for red-tailed hawks, golden eagles, turkey vultures, and prairie falcons, as well as sage grouse, mourning doves, mountain bluebirds, and Oregon's state bird, the melodious western meadowlark.

Look toward the west to spot Wagontire Mountain, Squaw Butte, and Glass Buttes. On a clear day you can see Steens Mountain to the south and east; it's composed of hundreds of layers of basalt lava that were thrust more than 1 mile above the plateau about fifteen million years ago. Directly south is *Palomino Buttes,* part of a Bureau of Land Management area for wild horses

## Harney County

Harney County boasts the distinction of being the largest county in the United States, at 10,228 square miles. It also has the smallest population of any county in the state, just more than 7,000.

"This figure doesn't include cattle, sheep, horses, or wildlife," says one longtime resident with a grin.

"The concepts of remote, lonely, and off the beaten path take on new meaning here," says a native Oregonian who lives south of Burns.

# Cowboy/Cowgirl Primer 101

**Attributes of an authentic cowboy/ cowgirl in southeastern and eastern Oregon:**

Well-worn jeans

Long-sleeved shirt with slightly frayed collar

Well-worn boots

Well-seasoned, wide-brimmed hat

Well-seasoned face: wrinkles around the eyes, skin slightly leathery and often sunburned

Laughs easily, often squints, often smiles and waves and says "howdy"

Hair slightly unkempt, sometimes balding on top (sorry, cowboys)

Drives well-aged pickup truck often with bales of hay on board, no canopy, radio tuned to local country-western station

Usually owns more than one horse, saddle, and set of tack

Prefers well-aged whiskey or beer; never orders a skinny latte with hazelnut syrup

Uses words and phrases like *doin', no how, ain't, goin' to the rodeo,* and *yes ma'am*

Prototypes: Robert Redford at age sixty or friends Marc and Rachel K. of eastern Oregon

**Attributes of a faux cowboy/cowgirl, any location other than southeastern or eastern Oregon:**

Designer jeans and designer shirt with designer logo

Designer sunglasses

Uses sunblock

New lizard-skin boots

New wide-brimmed hat

Does not laugh easily, never squints, rarely waves, waits for others to say hello

Hair blown dry, never unkempt

Drives new pickup with clean canopy on back, state-of-the-art CD system on board

Most likely has never ridden a horse, wouldn't think of owning one

Prefers designer ales and microbrews to whiskey, orders skinny lattes with foam

Uses words and phrases like *cool, awesome, foxy, later,* and *meet you on the slopes*

Prototypes: Tom Cruise, Martha Stewart

that covers about 96,000 acres. Often bands of wild horses, each numbering from thirty to sixty, are seen along the roads in the area.

One such area, ***Palomino Buttes Horse Management Area,*** can be accessed about ½ mile east of the Sagehen rest area by turning south on the gravel road labeled "Double-O." The wild horses are wary of humans, however, so binoculars and lack of noise may help you to spot them.

By now even the most confirmed city dweller should have relaxed into the quiet strength of the high desert, and the notion of becoming an amateur geologist or naturalist, even for a brief time, will seem appealing. These wide-open spaces also had an appeal for an eclectic mix of early settlers—first trappers and miners, then cowboys, cattle barons, and sheepherders, each, of course, displacing the native peoples, many of whom were ultimately sent to reservations.

The cattle barons and sheepherders were, needless to say, on less than friendly terms in those early days, and many bloody skirmishes occurred between the two groups until the federal government intervened. Today nearly 75 percent of the land in southeastern Oregon is managed by the U.S. Bureau of Land Management.

## Wildlife and Rangelands

If your visit to the region coincides with the early spring migration, consider taking in the *John Scharff Migratory Bird Festival* in Burns (www.migratory birdfestival.com). Meet bird lovers from all over the Northwest, participate in guided bird-watching walks, see films and slide shows, and hear interesting lectures given by noted waterfowl experts. You can also take in an auction and a western art show. For dates—the festival usually takes place the first or second weekend of April—contact the Burns–Harney County Visitor Center, 76 East Washington Street, Burns (541–573–2636; www.harneycounty.com).

*Burns,* in its earliest years, was the capital of the old cattle empire—the surrounding areas were ruled by cattle barons like Peter French and Henry Miller—but by 1889 the town amounted to a straggling frontier village of one dusty main street bordered by frame shacks. During the next thirty-five years, the settlers waited for the expanding railroad system to reach their town. A colorful throng gathered to see the first train arrive in September 1924—the cattle ranchers wearing Stetsons, the cowboys sporting jingling spurs on their high-heeled boots, and the Paiute Indians attired in their brightly hued native dress.

Another colorful throng, this one composed of bird species and wildlife, gathers just south of Burns near Harney and Malheur Lakes on the *Malheur National Wildlife Refuge.* On your way into the refuge, stop at the National Refuge headquarters for information on current road conditions and which bird species are in residence. The headquarters is located on the south shore of Malheur Lake, 30 miles south of Burns via Highways 78 and 205. The headquarters and its visitor center (541–493–2612) are open weekdays from 8:00 A.M. to 4:30 P.M. *NOTE:* Check water and weather conditions on the refuge when planning a visit.

While at the refuge headquarters, stop at the *George M. Benson Memorial Museum,* just next door, where you can see nearly 200 beautifully mounted specimens of migratory birds. The museum is open daily.

For seminars on local history, geology, and birds and wildlife and for guided trips, folks can contact the *Malheur Field Station* (www.malheur fieldstation.com), also located just next to the National Refuge headquarters and the museum. This nonprofit "Desert Wilderness Program" is supported by twenty-two schools and by such prestigious organizations as the Audubon Society, The Nature Conservancy, and the Oregon High Desert Museum in Bend. Outdoor classes for students of all ages, from all over the region, and including Elderhostel programs for seniors sixty and older, are held here year-round.

Travelers can also bunk in one of the trailers or dorm rooms (bring your own sleeping bag) at the Malheur Field Station and can arrange for meals here as well. For information and reservations—the latter are a must, especially during spring and autumn bird migration seasons—contact the staff at Malheur Field Station (541–493–2629).

Use the helpful maps provided by the U.S. Fish & Wildlife Service and the U.S. Department of the Interior obtained at refuge headquarters as you explore this magnificent wildlife refuge, which received official approval from President Theodore Roosevelt in 1908. The lakes, ponds, marshes, mudflats, and grain crops of the refuge are now managed for the benefit of both resident and migratory wildlife. Prior to this intervention early settlers had engaged in unrestricted hunting of the birds, and plume hunters had nearly wiped out the

## Tips for Successful Bird-Watching at the Malheur Wildlife Refuge

Stay in your vehicle; it makes an excellent observation and photographic blind.

Drive slowly and remain on posted roadways; the wildlife and waterfowl will be less frightened and more inclined to remain where they can be observed.

Use binoculars and telephoto lenses; take black-and-white as well as color photos.

Go on your own or join a naturalist-guided tour; get current information from refuge headquarters (541–493–2612). Bring water and beverages, sandwiches for the kids; pack out your own litter.

Enjoy and identify the types of bird talk: gabbles, honks, whistles, twitters, low quacking, rattle-honks. Encourage the kids to take their own photos and keep a journal or natural-history diary.

swans, egrets, herons, and grebes to obtain and sell their elegant feathers to milliners in San Francisco, Chicago, and New York.

Continue south on Highway 205 toward *Frenchglen,* journeying on a two-lane road that will take you through the heart of the Malheur Wildlife Refuge, with its 185,000 acres of open water, marshes, irrigated meadows and grainfields, riparian grassy areas, and uplands. You'll first notice antelope bitterbrush, sage-brush, and western juniper, followed by quaking aspen and mountain mahogany at elevations above 4,000 feet.

Although the largest concentration of migratory birds usually occurs in March and April, many varieties can be seen throughout the year here—includ-ing the mallards, Canada geese, and greater sandhill cranes that gather noisily to feed in the *Blitzen Valley* grainfields just south of refuge headquarters, Rat-tlesnake Butte, and Buena Vista Ponds. Great blue herons, white pelicans, trumpeter swans, long-billed curlews, great egrets, snowy egrets, and many kinds of ducks, geese, and hawks also rest and often nest on the refuge; many of these species can also be seen on the large marshes and ponds near Burns. "This is archetypal wilderness at its best," says one refuge naturalist.

Just south of Malheur and Harney Lakes, in the shadow of a commanding, 9,670-foot fault block known as Steens Mountain, tiny *Frenchglen Hotel* sits like a miniature sentinel reminding visitors of the pioneer past. Built in the late 1870s by the early cattle baron Peter French, the hotel is now owned by the state and managed by the State Parks and Recreation Department. Along with other bird-watchers and photography buffs, you can reserve one of the eight postage stamp–size guest rooms. The evening meal is served family style, accompanied by lively exchanges between guests, who compare fishing

Frenchglen Hotel

exploits, bird-watching areas, wildflower finds, and ghost towns discovered in the area. Next morning the aroma of freshly brewed coffee will lure you downstairs to an enormous breakfast of such delights as giant blueberry pancakes, eggs, sausage, and fresh seasonal fruit. For information—reservations are a must, especially for meals—call the innkeepers at (541) 493–2825. The hotel is open from March through October.

Naturally, you'll work off this hearty morning meal by poking into the nearby Frenchglen Mercantile; the village has a population of about ten, depending on the time of year. If you have a hardy vehicle, preferably with four-wheel drive, and want to take in spectacular vistas way off the beaten path, drive the 69-mile **Steens Mountain Loop Drive,** which begins just 3 miles south of Frenchglen. *NOTE:* Allow two to three hours for this panoramic drive. There are two campgrounds on the north section of the loop drive. **Steens Mountain Resort** (800–542–3765), also on North Loop Road, offers RV hookups, cabins, a bunkhouse, and tent space.

Check with the Bureau of Land Management visitor information trailer in Frenchglen for current road conditions—don't attempt this route in rainy or icy weather. On the one-way gravel road, the steep climb through sagebrush to juniper, through groves of quaking aspen, and into alpine wildflower-strewn meadows is deceivingly gradual.

Then you are suddenly next to the sky, at nearly 10,000 feet above the desert floor, and are pulling off at **East Rim Viewpoint** to gaze at ancient glaciated valleys and down at the Alvord Desert, more than a mile below. Keep an eye out for kestrels, golden eagles, bald eagles, prairie falcons, bighorn sheep, and deer during summer months—and black rosy finches at the summit.

If the Steens Mountain Loop Drive seems a bit strenuous for your automobile, consider the easier, 26-mile **Diamond Loop.** This loop trek is reached from an 18-mile side road, a section of the **Blitzen Valley Auto Tour Route,** as you head east from the Malheur National Refuge headquarters—where you can pick up a brochure for this self-guided auto tour.

On this western section of Diamond Loop, stop at **Diamond Craters Natural Area** for a self-guided hike through lava cones, ropy lava flows, cinder cones, spatter cones, and other unusual volcanic remnants scattered over several square miles. *NOTE:* Stay on the firmly packed roadway to avoid getting stuck; more than one vehicle has sunk to the hubs in the tephra—decomposing volcanic ash that is found in several areas near the roadway. For current regional maps, auto guides, and hiking information, contact the Burns District Bureau of Land Management office, 12533 Highway 20 West, Hines (541–573–4400; www.blm.gov/or).

At the northeast corner of Diamond Loop, you can see one of the state's oldest, most unusual structures: a round barn built a hundred or so years ago by cattle baron Peter French. It was used for breaking horses during winter months. You can also see the historic P Ranch location near Frenchglen.

From 1872, when he arrived with a herd of cattle and six Mexican vaqueros, until 1897, Peter French expanded his holdings and cattle operation to the point where he controlled nearly 200,000 acres, ran some 45,000 head of cattle and more than 3,000 horses, and built a dozen ranches encircling his domain on the west side of Steens Mountain. (Rulers of the enormous areas to the north and east were cattle barons John Devine and Henry Miller.) Peter French and his partner were fatally shot by disgruntled neighboring ranchers on the day after Christmas in 1897.

If you're into interesting old **ghost towns,** the kind that offer weathered structures like schools, stores, dance halls, saloons, and houses, you can snoop about and have fun photographing such places of the past as The Narrows (1889), Blitzen (late 1800s), Stallard Stage Stop (from 1906 to 1913), Ragtown Townsite, and Alberson Townsite (1907). Andrews (from 1898 to 1918), once known as Wildhorse, sits at the eastern base of Steens Mountain, and all that's left of this once-popular haven for ranchers and sheepherders is a weathered structure that served as a dance hall; the old saloon stood nearby but was destroyed by fire during the summer of 1996. Ask for maps and directions to these sites at the Harney County Visitor Center, 76 East Washington Street in Burns.

For a comfortable overnight stay about as far into the hinterlands as you can drive, located off Highway 205 at the south end of the Diamond Loop Drive, the **Hotel Diamond** (541–493–1898; www.central-oregon.com/hoteldiamond/) offers five small bedrooms on the second floor with baths down the hall, like the "olden days." The hostelry does extra duty as general store, deli, and post office for Diamond's six or so enthusiastic residents. Hearty dinners are served to hotel guests and to travelers in the hotel's small restaurant. The hotel is open March 15 to November 15 and is located about 50 miles south of Burns.

You might also be interested in the **Kiger Mustang Viewing Area,** located just a few miles east and south of Highway 205. A number of wild horses, from among the twenty different management areas in which they roam, are rounded up by Bureau of Land Management personnel every three to four years to thin the herds. These animals are offered for adoption as part of the national **Adopt-a-Horse program.** Horse adoption events take place at the **Oregon Wild Horse Corral** facility in Hines, where folks who have qualified take part in the lottery drawing for the wild horses. Those whose numbers are drawn get to choose the mustang they wish to adopt. For further information contact the BLM office in Burns (541–573–4400, www.blm.gov/or and www.wildhorseandburro.blm.gov).

The *Harney County Historical Society Museum* in Burns contains many informational displays and vintage photographs that allow a peek into this fascinating Old West section of Oregon. The museum, located at 18 West D Street (541–573–5618), is open May through September, Tuesday through Saturday from 9:00 A.M. to 5:00 P.M.

If your travel schedule or the weather prevents a trip from Burns into the Malheur National Wildlife Refuge and Peter French's historic Blitzen Valley, try the shorter *Lower Silvies River Valley Drive,* via Highway 78, just southeast of Burns in the scenic Harney Valley. Here you can see ducks, geese, and sandhill cranes in March and April and avocets, ibis, terns, curlews, and egrets through July.

A scenic overnight option is *Lone Pine Guest Ranch,* located on Lone Pine Road just 3 miles east and north of Burns via US 20. Here the Davis family shares their spectacular view from two suites situated on the edge of a wide rim that overlooks Steens Mountain, the Silvies River and Five Mile Dam area, and the Harney Valley—the high desert at your feet. Each suite is fully self-contained with private bath, kitchenette, cozy sitting area, and wide deck. For reservations contact Fran Davis at (541) 573–2103 or (541) 573–7020; www.lone pineguestranch.com. Children are welcome.

If you'd like to stay closer to town, you could call the innkeepers at *Sage Country Inn Bed & Breakfast,* 351½ West Monroe Street in Burns (541–573–7243; www.sagecountryinn.com). In the large Victorian farmhouse, guests can choose from three comfortable guest rooms with private baths. Your delicious breakfast might include French toast with whipped banana cream and sugar-cured ham along with fresh fruit, juices, and Vienna coffee blend.

Before heading out of the Burns area, you could also try out the following eateries: the *Meat Hook Steak House,* 673 West Monroe Street (541–573–7698), for a great selection of steaks from Harney County beef, open Monday through Saturday, 11:00 A.M. to 10:00 P.M.; *Figaro's Italian Kitchen,* 63 North Buena Vista Avenue (541–573–5500), open daily 11:00 A.M. to 9:00 P.M.; *Broadway Deli,* 530 North Broadway (541–573– 7020), for sandwiches, soups, pastries, and espresso; and *Treat Yourself Espresso,* 604 West US 20.

From Burns you can head east on US 20 toward Ontario and the Oregon-Idaho border, west on US 20 toward Bend and central Oregon's high desert country, southeast via Highway 78 toward the town of Jordan Valley, or continue south via Highway 78 and U.S. Highway 95 to the Oregon-Nevada border. *NOTE:* Remember that distances in this remote section of the Beaver State are deceiving and that food and gasoline services are also remote and many hours apart. Always have current state maps, keep track of distances and the time of day, refill your gas tank before heading into the sagebrush and alkali desert country, and arrange ahead for overnight accommodations (unless you are camping).

# Basque Country

At Burns Junction, about 92 miles southeast of Burns, turn east on US 95. After roughly 15 miles, turn north on a gravel-surfaced road just beyond the hamlet of Rome (gas, groceries, and RV campsites here) and opposite the OWYHEE CANYON ROAD sign. The intriguing **Rome Columns** can be seen about 3½ miles down the dusty road. The columns are huge formations of sandstone and fossil-bearing clay from Oregon's prehistoric past that jut some 1,000 feet into the intense blue sky. Surrounded by yellow-blooming sagebrush, the creamy-colored battlements, stained with rich browns and deep reds, overlook the peaceful ranch and farm valley of the nearby **Owyhee River.**

Eons ago this high desert area was actually a lush tropical paradise, as evidenced by many species of shell and animal fossils found throughout the layers of ancient riverbeds and lake beds. Those emigrant pioneers who detoured south through this region in the early 1840s carved their names in the soft sandstone; later the area also served as a stage stop.

Just north of the bridge, across the Owyhee River, you could turn right to the Bureau of Land Management guard station, which has a small grassy area, picnic tables, potable water, a restroom, and public boat ramp. The homey **Rome Station Cafe,** 3605 US 95 (541–586–2295), offers eats and conversation with local folks. At Burns Junction you can find **Three Js Cafe,** 4740 US 95 West (541–586–3051), also open daily.

Just 33 miles east of Rome, the community of **Jordan Valley** sits at an elevation of 4,389 feet, virtually on the Oregon-Idaho border. This small town became the unlikely home of a band of Basque immigrants who, in the 1890s, left their homelands in the French and Spanish Pyrenees. The Basques, being sheepherders, also brought lambs and ewes to the Jordan Valley. By the turn of the twentieth century—and after countless bloody skirmishes—sheepherding replaced cattle ranching in this far southeastern corner of the state.

Originally an important way station on a supply line between the mining camps of California and Idaho, Jordan Valley soon became a major sheep-trading center and the home of the Basque settlers and their families. Near the old Jordan Valley Hotel in the center of town, you can see remnants of a hand-hewn stone court where early Basque townspeople played *pelota,* an energetic game similar to handball.

Stop at the **Old Basque Inn Restaurant** for tasty local food; the eatery is located in Jordan Valley on North US 95 (541–586–2800) and is open most days for dinner starting at 5:00 P.M. For an overnight stay try the Sahara Motel (541–586–2500) or the Basque Station Motel (541–586–9244). Other than primitive camping, these two motels are the only overnight options in the Jordan Valley area.

For current information about the region, about the annual **Jordan Valley Big Loops Rodeo,** held each May, and about other colorful Basque festivals held during summer and fall, contact the Nyssa Visitor Center, 14 South Third Street, Nyssa (541–372–3091).

# Western Treasure Valley

From Jordan Valley head north on US 95 about 18 miles, turning onto an all-weather gravel road that angles northwest toward **Leslie Gulch–Succor Creek.** The rugged road—accessible to all but low-slung automobiles, which won't do so well—drops into a canyon where sandstone cliffs seem to loom higher, as well as to hover closer together. Their deep pinks, flamboyant purples, vibrant oranges, and flaming reds splash across the brilliant blue sky, the stark landscape littered here and there with pungent sage and bitterbrush. This scenery is guaranteed to buckle the knees of the toughest cowpoke or the most cynical urban dweller.

Miles of dirt roads and trails are available to hikers, backpackers, and off-road vehicles in the Leslie Gulch area, managed by the Bureau of Land Management. If you move quietly and carefully, you may see wild horses and bighorn sheep roaming through the canyons, as well as chukars (small partridges) dashing across dusty roadbeds and up steep talus slopes. Look for thunder eggs—oblong rocks, rough on the outside but usually containing beautiful crystal formations on the inside—at nearby **Succor Creek Canyon,** and look for agates along the banks of the Owyhee River. The best time to visit is April through June, although snow is possible in early May. Summers are hot and dry, with temperatures of ninety degrees and above; by late September the nights are frosty. *NOTE:* There are primitive restrooms and drinking water at the **Succor Creek Recreation Area Campground,** restrooms and primitive camping but no water at Leslie Gulch campground. Check for ticks after hiking—they can carry Lyme disease. For maps and current information, check with the Vale District Office of the Bureau of Land Management, 100 Oregon Street, Vale (541–473–3144).

A better alternative is the campground just south of Owyhee Dam at Lake Owyhee State Park, on the shores of **Lake Owyhee**—about 23 miles from

Adrian, off Highway 201 (Adrian is about 20 miles north of Succor Creek State Recreation Area). There are thirty-one electrical hookups at Lake Owyhee State Park, as well as a public boat ramp and a dock. For campground reservations call the Oregon State Parks reservation center at (800) 452–5687.

If you plan a trip into this remote area, be sure to have a full tank of gas, plenty of food and beverages, extra containers of water, sturdy shoes, and camping gear.

Be sure to stop and see the imposing *Owyhee Dam,* located north of the campground. Begun in 1926 and completed in 1932, the dam rises 405 feet from bedrock, is 255 feet thick at its base in the sandstone and basalt canyon, and is 30 feet thick at the top. The structure represents one of the largest and most important irrigation developments in the state, for the Owyhee River waters stored in the large lake behind the dam are used not only for year-round recreation but also to irrigate an extensive area of high desert that would otherwise remain an arid wasteland.

## Viewing Wildlife in the Owyhee Wild River Area

By visiting where animals hunt, feed, rest, nest, and hide you can almost always find them, but you'll have the best chance if you move very slowly, whether walking or driving. When walking, avoid wearing bright solid colors; rather, wear clothing that blends with the surrounding habitat colors. Sunrise and sundown are the best times to watch for wildlife, which is when they most actively look for food and water. The federal lands of the Owyhee Canyon from the dam to the mouth of the canyon have been designated as a Watchable Wildlife Area, part of a national program to foster appreciation of America's wildlife heritage. Bring binoculars and a good field guide.

### ANIMAL SPECIES IN THE AREA (YEAR-ROUND)

Wild horses, bighorn sheep, deer, coyote

River otters, long-tailed and short-tailed weasel, mink, beaver

Bobcat, jackrabbit, porcupine, marmot, striped skunk

### BIRD SPECIES IN THE AREA (MOST YEAR-ROUND)

Black-crowned night heron, great blue heron, American kestrel (sparrow hawk)

Long-eared owl, great horned owl, common nighthawk, golden eagle

Killdeer, spotted sandpiper, nighthawks, chukar, northern bald eagle (winter visitor)

For wildlife and bird lists, maps, camping, and other information, contact the BLM Vale District office, 100 Oregon Street (541–473–3144).

Near the communities of Nyssa, Vale, and Ontario—located on the Oregon-Idaho border about 25 miles north of Owyhee Dam and Lake Owyhee—you can see evidence of the Owyhee River waters bringing life to lush fields of sugar beets, potatoes, onions, and alfalfa. Notice the tall green poplars and shaggy locust trees around homesteads, then rows of fruit trees gradually giving way to wheat and grazing lands.

In *Nyssa,* a thriving community for the dairy and poultry industries, a large beet-sugar refining plant also produces and ships many tons of sugar each day. Between the three communities of Nyssa, Vale, and Ontario, you can see broad fields of blooming zinnias, bachelor buttons, and other flowers grown for the garden seed market; vegetables are grown here, too. Midsummer is a good time to see the fields of flowers in gorgeous bloom—and you might also smell the pungent, dark-green peppermint plants that cover large fields as well.

In the sagebrush-covered rimrock hills above these fields, a number of Basque sheepherders still sing and echo their distinctive native melodies while they and their sheepdogs tend large flocks. Many Mexican-American families also live in the area, as do a large number of Japanese-Americans.

The *Four Rivers Cultural Center,* located at 676 SW Fifth Avenue in Ontario (541–889–8191; www.4rcc.com), celebrates the heritage of four rivers important to the vitality and growth of this region: the Malheur, Payette, Owyhee, and Snake. The 10,000-square-foot museum also features a comprehensive look at the variety of cultures that live in the Treasure Valley area. A walk through the museum introduces visitors first to the Paiute Indians, who lived off the land for thousands of years until they were displaced by miners, ranchers, and settlers. Next you'll learn about the Basques, who came from Spain and started out as sheepherders; many Basque families still live in the area. Then there are the Mexican vaqueros, who brought the western buckaroo tradition to the area; other Hispanic families followed in the 1930s and 1940s.

## rivers

Oregon is blessed with nearly 90,000 river miles through the state. "Rivers are pathways of life . . . rivers create landscape . . . rivers refresh the spirit . . . rivers feed the soul . . . rivers carry culture and are replete with history."—The *Oregonian,* December 1991

Perhaps the most poignant story depicted at the museum, however, is that of the Japanese-American families who found new homes on Oregon's far eastern border. Many of these families were released in the early 1940s from World War II internment camps on the West Coast because they were willing to relocate and work on farms in Ontario, Vale, and Nyssa. Their former homes, land, and possessions had been confiscated by the U.S. government. After the war many of these families chose to remain here. An annual event on the third Saturday of July, *Japan Obon Nite Festival,* celebrates the Japanese-American culture, costumes, food, and traditions. The museum complex also contains a 640-seat performing-arts theater, meeting spaces, cafe, and gift shop. Visit the Japanese Garden containing plantings, rocks, a gazebo, and reflecting pool just adjacent to the center. The center is open daily except major holidays from 9:00 A.M. to 5:00 P.M. For information and current dates for the annual ethnic festivals held in the area, contact the Ontario Visitor Center, 676 SW Fifth Avenue, Ontario (541–889–8012).

There is also a well-stocked State Welcome Center at the Ontario rest area on Interstate 84 (I–80 North) about ½ mile from the Oregon-Idaho border.

For eateries in Ontario try *Casa Jaramillo,* 157 SE Second Street (541–889–9258); *Brewsky's Broiler,* 49 NW First Street (541–889–9550); *Romio's Pizza & Pasta,* 375 South Oregon Street (541–889–4888); *Jolts & Juice,* 17 SE Third Avenue (541–889–4166); and *Sorbenots Coffee House,* 213 West Idaho Avenue (541–889–3587).

From nearby Nyssa travel west and north on Enterprise Avenue, which is actually a section of the Oregon Trail. Stop at the *Keeney Pass Oregon Trail Site* and look up and down the draw at the deep wagon ruts cut into the soft clay. Here you can also read about some of the hardships experienced. From Amelia Knight's diary entry dated August 5–8, 1853, for example, you'll read this: "Just reached Malheur River and campt, the roads have been very dusty, no water, nothing but dust and dead cattle all day."

For the pioneers, the hot mineral springs near *Vale* were a welcome stop for bathing and washing clothes. At the *Malheur Crossing* marker, located between the bridges on the east edge of Vale, notice the deep ruts left by the heavy wagons pulling up the grade after crossing the river. Also, while in town, notice the *Vale Murals.* Painted on buildings throughout the community, the large and colorful murals depict poignant scenes from the Oregon Trail journey. At *Red Garter Ice Cream Saloon,* 293 Washington Street West in Vale (541–473–2294), you could pause for cool libations.

The pioneers actually entered what is now Oregon at old Fort Boise—in Idaho, just a few miles east of Nyssa—a fur-trading post established in 1834 by the British Hudson's Bay Company. Here the wagons forded the Snake River, the settlers often having to remove the wheels before the wagons could float across. From Malheur Crossing, where the pioneers enjoyed a welcome soak in the hot springs, the wagon trains continued northwest, met the Snake River again at Farewell Bend, and then made their way northwest toward The Dalles and the most difficult river passage from there downriver to Fort Vancouver—the mighty Columbia River.

History buffs can also walk a 1-mile trail to view wagon ruts at the *Oregon Trail Historic Reserve* in southeast Boise, Idaho, or, better yet, head east about 65 miles farther to visit the splendid new *Oregon Trail History and Education Center* at Three Island Crossing State Park in Glenns Ferry, Idaho (208–366–2394; www.idahoparksandrecreation.idaho.gov). The state of Idaho boasts a large section of clearly visible ruts carved by thousands of those horse- and oxen-drawn wagons during the 1840s migration from Independence, Missouri, to the Oregon Country.

An alternate route, the old *Central Oregon Emigrant Trail,* is followed rather closely by US 20 west from Vale, just north of Keeney Pass. In 1845 a wagon train of some 200 pioneers, led by Stephen Meek, first attempted this route. Unfortunately about seventy members of the group died from hardship and exposure when the wagon train wandered for weeks on the high desert, bewildered by the maze of similar ridges, canyons, and washes. Meek was attempting to find a shortcut to the Willamette Valley. The survivors finally reached the Deschutes River, near Bend, and followed it to The Dalles.

Take US 20 toward *Burns* for a nostalgic look at more of the wagon ruts, as well as a view of the vast sagebrush desert those first pioneers struggled to cross. Later, between 1864 and 1868, the *Cascade Mountain Military Road* was laid out following the Central Oregon Emigrant Trail. This new road connected with the old *Willamette Valley Road,* which brought travelers across the central Cascade Mountains to Albany, in the lush central and northern Willamette Valley.

In those days wagon trains, some ½ mile long, carried wool and livestock from the eastern Oregon range country to the Willamette Valley, returning with fruit, vegetables, and other food supplies. Stagecoaches, conveying both mail and passengers, added their own dramatic chapter to the history of the Cascade Mountain Military Road. Every settlement on the route drew all or part of its livelihood from this transportation link. From historians, by the way, we learn that the first automobile to cross the United States was driven over this route, in June 1905.

As travelers now speed along modern US 20 between Vale and Burns, a drive of about two hours, note that this same trip took two full days and one night for the stagecoaches to complete. The trip was hot and dusty, with a change of horses taking place every 15 miles. Images of a Roy Rogers or a John Wayne western movie come to mind, with a stagecoach pulled by a team of horses bumping across the sagebrush desert.

About midway between Vale and Burns, you'll pass through *Juntura,* a poplar-shaded village nestled in a small valley where the North Fork of the Malheur River joins the South Fork. Stop to see the lambing sheds near the railroad tracks. This was long a major shipping point for both sheep and cattle; the entire valley and surrounding range country were once dominated by the legendary Henry Miller, one of the powerful cattle barons of the late 1800s.

You can see a shearing and dipping plant by turning south from Juntura on an all-weather gravel road and then proceeding for about 4 miles, toward the tiny community of Riverside. For camping or a late-afternoon picnic, head north from Juntura to **Beulah Reservoir.** The Bureau of Land Management's **Chukar Park Campground,** situated on the North Fork of the Malheur River, has nineteen sites; the county has a primitive campground on the lake as well. *NOTE:* Drinking water needs to be packed in here.

About 4 miles north of the campground is a good area for day hikes at **Castle Rock,** an extinct volcano cone that rises to an elevation of 6,837 feet. For maps and further information about Chukar Park Campground, day hiking, and fall hunting in the area, contact the BLM's Vale District Office, (541) 473–3144.

Tired of camping? Well, you could call the folks at **Blue Bucket Inn at 3E Ranch** and linger one more day or so in cowboy country. Here you can hole up in a cozy cottage with a kitchen; stop in Burns to load up on groceries. You can, if you're so inclined, help out on a 2,600-acre working cattle ranch, located on a scenic stretch of meadow and rangeland that borders the central fork of the Malheur River—25 miles west of Juntura and some 50 miles from Burns. The grub is good—snacks are served on arrival, and dinner can be arranged at an additional charge. A full country breakfast is included. For current information and to make reservations, call the innkeepers at (541) 493–2375.

## Places to Stay in Southeastern Oregon

### BURNS

**Crystal Crane Hot Springs**
59315 Highway 78
(541) 493–2312

**Lone Pine Guest Ranch**
HC 71-51 Lone Pine Road
(541) 573–2103

**Sage Country Bed & Breakfast Inn**
351½ West Monroe Street
(541) 573–7243

### CHRISTMAS VALLEY

**Christmas Valley Desert Inn Motel**
(541) 576–2262

### DIAMOND

**Hotel Diamond**
10 Main Street
(541) 493–1898

### FRENCHGLEN

**Steens Mountain Cabins & RV Park**
North Loop Road
(541) 493–2415

### HINES

**Best Western Rory & Ryan Inns**
534 US 20 North
(541) 573–5050

### LAKEVIEW

**Best Western Skyline Motor Lodge**
(541) 947–2194

Hunter Hot Springs Resort
Highway 395
(541) 947–4242

**ONTARIO**

Best Western Inn
251 Goodfellow Street
(541) 889–2600

Historic Creek House
Bed & Breakfast
717 SW Second Street
(541) 823–0717

Super 8 Motel
266 Goodfellow Street
(541) 889–8282

**SUMMER LAKE**

The Lodge at
Summer Lake
53460 Highway 31
(541) 943–3993

Summer Lake Inn
47531 Highway 31
(800) 261–2778

**VALE**

Sears & Roebuck Home
Bed and Breakfast
484 North Tenth Street
(541) 473–9636

# Places to Eat in Southeastern Oregon

**BURNS**

Apple Peddler Restaurant
540 US 20
(541) 573–2820

## HELPFUL TELEPHONE NUMBERS AND WEB SITES FOR SOUTHEASTERN OREGON

Harney County Visitor Center
Burns
(541) 573–2636
www.harneycounty.com

*Lake County Examiner*
(since 1880), published every Thursday
(541) 947–3378

Lake County Visitor Center and
Oregon Welcome Center
(877) 947–6040
www.lakecountychamber.org

Malheur National Wildlife Refuge
(541) 493–2612

National Cowgirl Museum
www.cowgirl.net

Ontario Visitor Center
(888) 889–8012
www.ontariochamber.com

Oregon Natural Desert Association
www.onda.org

U.S. Fish & Wildlife Service
www.fws.gov

**CABINS AND FIRE LOOKOUTS FREMONT NATIONAL FOREST**

Lakeview Ranger District
(541) 947–3334

Paisley Ranger District
(541) 943–3114

Silver Lake Ranger District
(541) 576–2107

**CAMPGROUNDS INFORMATION**

U.S. Bureau of Land
Management (BLM)
(541) 573–4400

**The Book Parlor Espresso**
181 North Broadway
(541) 573–2665

**Broadway Deli & Espresso**
530 North Broadway
(541) 573–7020

**Meat Hook Steak House**
673 West Monroe Street
(541) 573–7698

**JORDAN VALLEY**

**Old Basque Inn Restaurant**
North US 95
(541) 586–2298

**Three J's Cafe**
Burns Junction
4740 US 95 West
(541) 586–3051

**LAKEVIEW**

**The Burger Queen**
109 South F Street
(541) 947–3677

**Green Mountain Bakery**
512 Center Street
(541) 947–4492

**Honker's Coffeehouse**
25 North E Street
(541) 947–4422

**Jerry's Restaurant**
508 North Second
(541) 947–2600

**NYSSA**

**Twilight Restaurant**
212 Main Street
(541) 372–3388

**ONTARIO**

**Brewsky's Broiler**
49 NW First Street
(541) 889–9550

**Jolts & Juice**
17 SE Third Avenue
(541) 889–4166

**Romio's Pizza & Pasta**
375 South Oregon Street
(541) 889–4888

**Rusty's Pancake & Steak House**
14 NW First Street
(541) 889–2700

**SILVER LAKE**

**Silver Lake Cafe**
Highway 31
(541) 576–2221

**VALE**

**Red Garter Ice Cream Saloon**
293 Washington Street West
(541) 473–2294

# Central Oregon

## Lava Lands

Carpeted with pungent sagebrush, juniper, and ponderosa pine, Oregon's central high-desert country offers generous amounts of sunshine and miles of wide-open spaces at elevations of 3,000 feet and higher. Where ancient Indian fires once blazed on the shores of volcanic lakes and long-ago hunters left tracks and trails through pine and juniper forests, both Oregonians and out-of-staters now come to fish, hunt, camp, hike, and golf. Climbing high rocks and mountains, spelunking in lava-tube caves, and going alpine as well as cross-country skiing offer even more adventure.

The first white people to venture into central Oregon were hunters who trapped beaver for their lush pelts. Capt. John C. Frémont, a topographic engineer, was sent from the East Coast to map the region in the 1840s, although both Peter Skene Ogden and Nathaniel Wyeth traveled through the area before Frémont's trek.

Tempted by luxuriant meadows and grasses, the first emigrants to settle in the region raised cattle and sheep, and many ranches still operate in the area. Although Indian chief Paulina

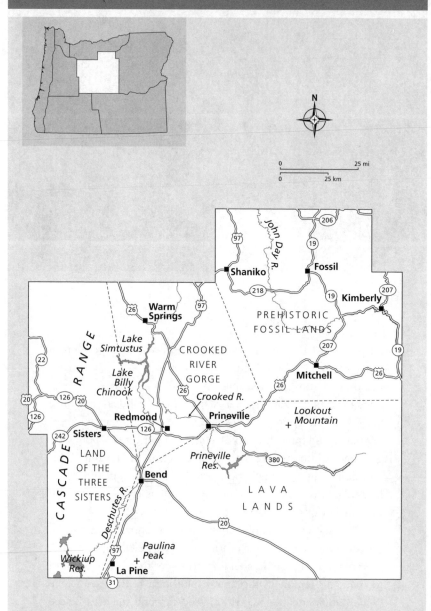

0    25 mi

0    25 km

206
97
19
Fossil
Shaniko
218
19
Kimberly
207
26
Warm
Springs
97
PREHISTORIC
FOSSIL LANDS
207
19
Lake
Simtustus
CROOKED
RIVER
GORGE
RANGE
22
Lake
Billy
Chinook
Mitchell
26
26
20
126
20
126
Crooked R.
126
Redmond
Prineville
Lookout
+ Mountain
126
Sisters
242
126
LAND
OF THE
THREE
SISTERS
Prineville
Res.
380
Bend
CASCADE
Deschutes R.
L A V A
L A N D S
20
Wickiup
Res.
Paulina
Peak
+
97
La Pine
31

John Day R.

and his Paiute tribe fought against white settlement, peace eventually won out. Named for the old chief, the ***Paulina Mountains,*** rising south of Bend, offer a reminder of an important chapter in the area's colorful history.

To get your bearings when arriving in Bend—the largest city and hub of the central region—start from the downtown area and drive to the top of nearby ***Pilot Butte,*** at an elevation of more than 4,000 feet. Here you'll have a panoramic view of not only this sprawling mountain resort community, but no fewer than a dozen gorgeous snowcapped volcanic peaks to the west, in the Cascade Range. Incidentally, this is a great place to see fireworks on the Fourth of July.

The mountain peaks rise along the far horizon like vanilla ice-cream cones. Notice first the largest "double scoopers"—Mount Jefferson, Mount Washington, Broken Top, Three Sisters, Mount Bachelor, and Ollalie Butte. Dusty and tired members of the pioneer wagon trains, as they lumbered across the harsh, unforgiving high desert, used to sight on Pilot Butte so as to maintain their bearings after having crossed the Snake River near the present communities of Ontario, Nyssa, and Vale in the eastern section of the state. Today the road to the top of Pilot Butte is paved, and the viewpoint area is wheelchair accessible.

For one of the best introductions to the natural history of this vast, unique region, visit the ***Oregon High Desert Museum,*** just 5 miles south of Bend via U.S. Highway 97 toward Lava Butte. On the 150-acre site you can investigate a rimrock canyon, a marsh area, meadows, a flowing stream, a prehistoric cave, and other natural habitats for plants, birds, and wildlife native to the high desert. Self-guided interpretive paths shoelace in and around each life zone. You'll be able to tell a chipmunk from a ground squirrel—both have stripes along their backs, but the chipmunks have stripes on their cheeks, too—before

## TOP HITS IN CENTRAL OREGON

**Cascade Lakes and Century Drive**
(mid-June through October or until first snows), Bend

**Historic Shaniko**
Shaniko

**John Day Fossil Beds National Monument**
John Day

**Kinzua Hills Golf Course**
Fossil

**Lava Cast Forest**
Bend

**Newberry National Volcanic Monument**
La Pine

**Pine Tavern Restaurant**
Bend

**The Museum at Warm Springs**
Warm Springs

arriving at the main entrance of the orientation center. "It's the relationship between people, the animals, and the desert habitat that we hope visitors come to understand and appreciate," said Donald Kerr, the museum's founder and former director.

Watch mischievous river otters frolic in their indoor-outdoor pool; say hello to friendly porcupines like Cuddles, Thistlebritches, Barbs, and Cactus; and peer into the trunk of a ponderosa pine to learn about its growth. You and the kids can also hear museum staff and volunteers tell about gopher snakes, birds of prey, or desert weather patterns.

In the museum's *Earle A. Chiles Center,* visitors enjoy a nostalgic dawn-to-dusk walk through eight historic scenes portraying sights, sounds, and authentic memorabilia of the settling of the West. You'll hear desert bird songs, wind and rain, and water rushing through an old mine sluice; you'll see the glow of a blacksmith's fire; and you'll smell the wood and leather in the saddlery.

For a schedule of workshops, lectures, traveling exhibits, and special events offered year-round, contact the Oregon High Desert Museum, 59800 South US 97, Bend (541-382-4754; www.highdesertmuseum.org). The museum is open daily, except on major holidays, from 9:00 A.M. to 5:00 P.M. Enjoy, too, browsing in the Silver Sage Trading Store and having a snack in the Rimrock Cafe.

For another panoramic view of the region, continue south from Bend along US 97 for about 10 miles to *Lava Butte,* stopping first at the *Lava Lands Visitor Center* (541–593–2421) at its base for an intriguing look at the region's volcanic past. Colorful, animated displays simulate natural phenomena such as a volcanic eruption and an earthquake. Outdoors you can also walk the *Trail of the Molten Land* or the *Trail of the Whispering Pines,* both short self-guided tours near the visitor center. Managed by the Deschutes National For-

## TOP ANNUAL EVENTS IN CENTRAL OREGON

**Sisters Rodeo**
Sisters; June
(541) 549–0251

**Sisters Outdoor Quilt Show**
Sisters; mid-July
(541) 549–0251

**Draft Horse Show**
Redmond; late July
(541) 923–5191

**Central Oregon Pee Wee Rodeo**
Deschutes County Fairgrounds
Redmond; late August
(866) 800–3976, www
.redmondcofc.com

est, the well-stocked center is open mid-April to mid-October from 9:00 A.M. to 5:00 P.M.

The road leading up to 500-foot Lava Butte, the extinct, reddish brown volcanic cone looming above the visitor center, is steep but well paved with red cinder rock, and there's a large parking area at the top. With camera or binoculars in hand, walk the easy self-guided trail around the top of the butte for spectacular views of ancient lava fields to the north and south and of those ever-present ice-cream-cone mountain peaks.

You're now gazing at a vast area in which folks have lived for more than 9,000 years. The earliest visitors probably came from the Great Basin area of Idaho and Utah to hunt and gather food. About 7,000 years ago the eruptions of Mount Mazama—now Crater Lake, to the south—and nearby Mount Newberry produced about 200 times the amount of ash, pumice, and debris created by the eruption of Mount Saint Helens in Washington State in 1980. As you continue walking around the rim of Lava Butte, you can also see the Paulina Mountains, Newberry Crater, and the latter's two alpine lakes, Paulina and East Lakes, directly to the south and east.

If time allows, continue a few miles south on US 97 and take the 10-mile side trip into **Lava Cast Forest,** winding east through ponderosa pine, bitterbrush, and manzanita on a red cinder gravel road into the high desert hinterlands. Access it from US 97, turning east on Forest Service Road 9720, just opposite the Sunriver Resort turnoff. Pick up an illustrated guide at the beginning of the paved trail and enjoy twelve descriptive stops along the easy 1-mile route. As you walk the path, notice the characteristic cinnamon-colored bark of the tall ponderosa pine; then, as you reach the sunny, open lava plain, notice the smaller version of the pine, nature's own bonsai, or dwarf, trees.

Though short and stunted—struggling to grow in the volcanic lava, with its rough, jagged, and clinkerlike surfaces—the trees may actually be very old, their root systems enlarged to help fight the extreme environment. You'll also see dead trees bleached white by the desert weather, stark skeletons hunched in the black lava. During spring, flowering wild currant and bitterbrush ornament the volcanic landscape with pale pinks and yellows. Look, too, for red Indian paintbrush and rock penstemons blooming in crevices and crannies.

Peer into vertical and horizontal tree casts that about 6,000 years ago were enormous pines engulfed by slow-moving molten lava from **Mount Newberry.** At station 9 along the trail you can actually see the source of the lava flow, toward what remains of the mountain, to the southeast. The rounded cylindrical casts are the only remnants of the lush forest that once clothed Mount

Newberry's slopes. Station 11 offers another grand view of the other snow-capped peaks in the Cascade Mountain Range, to the west.

Although there is no potable water at Lava Cast Forest, there are a couple of picnic tables, as well as an outdoor restroom, in the shade of tall ponderosa pines. You'll also find a few benches along the trail, affording sunny spots for a picnic lunch. Be sure to pack drinking water or canned beverages, especially on warm summer days, when temperatures can climb to the eighties or nineties.

Further information about this geologic phenomenon can be obtained from the Deschutes National Forest headquarters in Bend, at 1645 U.S. Highway 20 East (541–383–5300). The office is open year-round, Monday through Friday, from 8:00 A.M. to 4:30 P.M.

For a closer look at the remains of Mount Newberry, drive to the start of **Newberry Crater Auto Tour,** just 8 miles south of the Lava Cast Forest and Sunriver Resort turnoffs, and wind about 13 miles up to Paulina and East Lakes. Another way to get wide-angle views of all this spectacular geology is to arrange an airborne sightseeing tour in a Cessna 172 (seats three) or a Cessna 206 (seats five). For current schedules, rates, and reservations, check the Web site at www.flightshopinc.com, or call the friendly folks at the Flight Shop Inc., located at Bend Municipal Airport, 63132 Powell Butte Road (541–388–0019).

When 9,000-foot Mount Newberry collapsed in a fiery roar thousands of years ago, a large caldera, 4 to 5 miles across, was formed; it was blocked by further eruptions over the next million or so years, creating two lakes, Paulina and East, rather than the single lake exemplified by, say, Crater Lake to the south.

**East Lake** is known for producing some of the largest trout ever caught in the United States; both German brown and eastern brook trout weighing in at more than twenty-five pounds have been reeled in here by dedicated anglers. Both lakes have campgrounds and boat docks, and both offer fishing boats and motors for rent. **East Lake Resort** offers rustic accommodations (541–536–2230; www.eastlakeresort.com), and the lakeside campground here

## OTHER ATTRACTIONS WORTH SEEING IN CENTRAL OREGON

**City of Fossil Museum**
Fossil

**Headwaters**
Metolius River

**Forest Fire Hot Shots Memorial**
Ochoco Creek Park, Prineville

**Old Mill District**
Bend

## Arnold Ice Cave: Bend's Early Refrigeration

The early settlers of Bend quarried huge chunks of ice from nearby Arnold Ice Cave and hauled these to town on horse-drawn wagons. For about ten years this ice was used as the primary method of refrigeration for the families and shopkeepers of Bend. Since that time thick layers of ice have re-formed within the cave, completely covering the lower stairway. You can peer into the icy darkness safely from the upper stairway, near the cave's wide entrance. The ice cave is located out China Hat Road; for information and directions contact the staff at Lava Lands Visitor Center, 58201 South US 97, Bend; (541) 593-2421.

offers great views. At *Paulina Lake* there is also a rustic lodge and tiny cabins, as well as rowboats and fishing equipment for rent. Because legal seasons, bag limits, and types of tackle are highly variable, anglers who want to get licenses to fish the many lakes and rivers in central Oregon are advised to obtain current copies of the official regulations from the Oregon Department of Fish and Wildlife, 61374 Parrell Road, Bend (541–388–6363).

Although the first white person to see the two lakes was explorer Peter Skene Ogden, in 1826, he didn't find those wily trout. Fish were introduced into both lakes years later by the State Fish and Game Department; the fish hatchery is on the Metolius River near Sisters and Black Butte. The mountain was named for John Strong Newberry, a physician and noted geologist who, in 1855, accompanied the Williamson expedition to explore possible railroad routes through the central section of the state.

As you bask in the warm sun on the boat dock at Paulina Lake at a level of 6,331 feet, inside Newberry's crater, notice the large peak looming some 2,000 feet higher into the deep blue sky—that's *Paulina Peak,* also named for the Paiute Indian chief. During the summer, drive up to Paulina Peak on the hard-surface gravel road for stupendous views. If you're itching to bring your horse to the high desert, you'll find riding trails here, too, and you can bunk at the nearby *Chief Paulina Horse Camp* (541–383–4000). For a bit more comfortable lodging, you can stay at *Paulina Lake Resort* (541–536–2240; www.paulinalake.com), in one of a dozen rustic knotty-pine, housekeeping cabins. The lodge restaurant serves lunches and dinners and a Saturday-night barbecue. The resort is open in the summer for fishing and December through March for snowmobiling and cross-country skiing.

Before retracing your route back to US 97, detour on the marked Forest Service side road located between the two lakes to see the large lava flow of

## The Old West Is Due East

Not too many years ago, Bend was a relatively quiet central Oregon mill town rather off the beaten path. Freight trains clattered through loaded with wood and wood products. Loggers, hunters, and backcountry hikers in wool shirts and boots drank regular beer. There were no espresso shops. When I first visited Bend in 1970, accompanied by forty-seven seventh-graders, you could motor along US 97 from either end of town in less than fifteen minutes. My teaching colleagues and I, along with two parents, brought the kids to the high desert for three days of school in the out-of-doors. There were no crowds of tourists, no hoards of snowboarders, no lines of bicyclists. We had elbow room with room to spare.

Be prepared, however, for a distinct change when visiting the Bend of the 2000s. "You used to see more pickup trucks than BMWs or sport-utility vehicles," says one resident. "Quail used to walk through my backyard, but now there's a new subdivision." Bend has metamorphosed into a high-altitude mecca of ski runs and groomed cross-country ski trails, classy resorts and upscale subdivisions, trendy boutiques and factory-outlet stores, espresso shops and gourmet eateries. Those folks who cling to the independent spirit that is so ingrained in the Northwest are moving farther and farther east toward Burns, Baker City, Joseph, even Halfway, a small town near the Idaho border. But even among the many changes in Bend, it's possible to find great places to breathe crisp mountain air and smell pungent ponderosa pine, aromatic juniper, and savory sagebrush. It just takes a bit longer to find them now.

glassy black obsidian used by Native peoples to fashion arrowheads and other implements; lovely **Paulina Creek Falls** is close by as well. During winter the main paved road into the lakes is plowed for the first 10 miles to the Sno-Park parking area, allowing for backcountry snowmobiling and cross-country skiing; Sno-Park permits can be purchased in Bend or La Pine. This entire 56,000-acre geologic area has been designated the **Newberry National Volcanic Monument.**

Summer campers, those without horses, can try the campground along East Lake, but if these sites are full, try larger **La Pine State Park** along the **Deschutes River** just a few miles south and west of US 97, in the La Pine Recreation Area. For campground reservations call the state toll-free number, (800) 452–5687, or see the Web site www.oregonstateparks.org. Incidentally, on the last Saturday in July, in the park's log amphitheater, you can hear melodious four-part harmony from singers who gather here each year for the Barbershop Quartet Concert.

Are golfing and sleeping indoors rather to your liking? For a western-style bed-and-breakfast experience located on a golf course, check with innkeepers

Doug and Gloria Watt at **DiamondStone Guest Lodge,** 16693 Sprague Loop, La Pine (541–536–6263; www.diamondstone.com). The Watts offer comfortable log lodge-style rooms, a suite on the second floor, and another on the main floor; both offer great views of Mount Bachelor, the Three Sisters, and Broken Top. Guest rooms come with queen or king beds, cozy down comforters, TVs, and private baths. Morning brings welcome smells of freshly brewed coffee, homemade breads, and hot-from-the-oven muffins. The inn is about halfway between Sunriver and La Pine and about 25 miles south of Bend. The nine-hole **Quail Run Golf Course,** with its wide fairways edged by tall ponderosa pines, is just putting distance from the inn and is open to the public; for tee times call (541) 536–1303; www.oregongolf.com/quail_run.

While exploring Oregon's high desert country, you must go spelunking in at least one lava cave. The most accessible is **Lava River Cave,** in **Lava River Caves State Park,** just off US 97 north of Sunriver Resort and Lava Cast Forest. With lantern in hand—lanterns are available for a nominal fee at the park entrance station—and sturdy shoes on your feet, proceed toward the cave's yawning entrance. The trail drops over volcanic rocks, bridged by stairs, leading to the floor of the first large, cool chamber. There you might see stalactites and stalagmites of ice, which often don't melt completely until late June or early July.

Negotiate another stairway up to the main tunnel and walk the winding passageway, your lantern reflecting ghostly shadows all along the way. The enormous cave is nearly 60 feet high and 50 feet wide in places, larger than the tunnels beneath New York's Hudson River. Conversations echo from the cave's farthest recesses, returning as eerie voices from the darkness.

Geologists explain that the great cavernous tunnel, which runs for about 5,000 feet through solid lava, was once the course of a molten lava river. Along the walls are remnants of the lava current—slaggy crusts in some places, rounded and overhanging cornicelike shelves in other places—marking the

## Ask a Geologist!

The U.S. Geological Survey offers a program on the Internet, Ask a Geologist—log onto www.usgs.gov/ and pose your question about roadside geology. You'll be directed to a helpful source on the Internet, or a specialist in the field may answer your inquiry. Help the kids and grandkids pose good questions about the fascinating geology of central Oregon; encourage them to set up an informal three-ring-binder field notebook, which can be taken along in the car. You'll spawn a crowd of roadside geology buffs in no time at all.

various levels of old volcanic streams. Notice where the walls are coated with a glaze of varying smoothness, while from the ceiling hang "lavacicles," volcanic stalactites formed by dripping lava.

Lava River Cave, located about 12 miles south of Bend, is open May through September, from 9:00 A.M. to 4:00 P.M. daily. Picnic facilities are available in the park, but no drinking water is provided. *NOTE:* Temperatures inside the lava caves range from thirty to forty-five degrees, so be sure to dress warmly. Avid spelunkers can obtain information about Skeleton Cave and Wind Cave, both near Bend, from the Bend–Fort Rock Ranger District in Bend (541–383–4000) or from the staff at Lava Lands Visitor Center (541–593–2421), just a mile north of Lava River Cave.

Novice spelunkers should note the following safety tips: Explore caves in a group, never alone; bring an ample supply of light sources—a lantern and/or a powerful flashlight for each member of the party, and also candles and matches; dress warmly—lava caves are rarely warmer than forty-five degrees, even on hot summer days.

For another spectacle, this one next to the nighttime sky at a brisk altitude of 6,300 feet, head east from Bend via US 20 about 35 miles to **Pine Mountain Observatory,** where you can snoop at the moon, the planets, star clusters, nebulas, and galaxies through a 15-inch research telescope managed by students and instructors from the University of Oregon. In addition to the 15-inch telescope are two other Cassegrain telescopes, with mirrors of 24 and 32 inches, that are used by the staff to collect data on the planets and stars.

To reach the site, just beyond the Millican gas station, turn south on the all-weather gravel road, take the right fork near the base of the mountain, and wind 9 miles up to the parking area next to the sky. Though the Pine Mountain Observatory is usually open Friday and Saturday, May through September, with viewing at dusk, visitors are asked always to call ahead—(541) 382–8331, after 3:00 P.M.—to make arrangements before driving out to the observatory. Stargazers are advised to wear warm clothing, bring flashlights with red bulbs or red coverings (so as not to interfere with the visibility of the stars), and dim their cars' headlights as they approach the parking area.

While exploring Bend, have lunch or dinner at one of the city's oldest eateries, the **Pine Tavern Restaurant** (541–382–5581; www.pinetavern.com), overlooking **Mirror Pond** on the Deschutes River near **Drake Park.** One 125-foot ponderosa pine grows right in the middle of the pond-side dining room. A mere 250 years old, the cinnamon-barked tree blends nicely with the room's rustic decor and has been growing right through the roof for about 70 years, since the establishment began welcoming diners in 1936. Especially tasty are the warm sourdough scones, similar to Indian fry bread, delicious

# Stargazing: from Castor and Pollux to Regulus and Orion

In the wide, unpolluted skies of central Oregon, one's view of the heavens— with or without a telescope—is amazing. With the magnification of a telescope lens, the likes of star clusters, nebulae, and galaxies come into view, and the past, present, and future seem to merge in time. But even without the aid of a telescope you can easily see the high-desert sky jam-packed with glittery stars—from low on the horizon to far overhead—and the sight is truly awesome. Having lived in the city most of my life, I didn't realize how star-deprived I was; the lights of the city prevent one from seeing this marvelous nighttime show. So, your assignment is to get yourself off to the hinterlands of the high desert and to lie down after dark on a pile of sleeping bags, blankets, and pillows and enjoy the glittery spectacle. Take the kids, take the grandkids, take the grandparents—everyone deserves to see this!

Learn about the mysteries of the night sky through these helpful sources:

Rose City Astronomers
www.rca-omsi.org

Mount Hood Community College
Planetarium Sky Theater
Gresham, www.starstuff.com/
theater.htm; (503) 491–7297

Oregon Star Party
Offers a mid-August weekend
held under the stars in central Oregon for
amateur astronomers
www.oregonstarparty.org

Do-it-yourself star-viewing spots:
Haystack Reservoir State Park; the
Cove Palisades State Park; Prineville
Reservoir State Park; Ochoco State
Park. All are located in the Redmond
and Prineville areas north and east of
Bend, and all offer tent and RV sites.

with honey butter. Located downtown, at 967 NW Brooks Street, the restaurant is open for lunch Monday through Saturday from 11:30 A.M. to 2:30 P.M., for dinner daily from 5:30 to 9:30 P.M.

While in the downtown area, stop by the ***Deschutes Historical Center,*** at 129 NW Idaho Street (541–389–1813) in the 1914 Reid School building, which was placed on the National Register of Historic Places in 1979. Among the fine displays are old farm tools; well-used pioneer crockery; native arrowheads; thunder eggs, Oregon's state rock; and a 530-page chronicle of the region's early history, which was compiled by sifting through old family records and census data. The center is open Tuesday through Saturday from 10:00 A.M. to 4:30 P.M.

If you have a canoe, save time for a leisurely paddle with a gaggle of swans, mallards, and Canada geese on Mirror Pond at lovely Drake Park. You could also call the staff at Bend Metro Parks and Recreation (541–389–7275) for information about canoeing classes, held during spring, summer, and fall.

For delicious baked goodies, and for breakfast or lunch, stop at **Westside Bakery,** located just west and south of Drake Park at 1005 NW Galveston Street (541–382–3426). House specialties include chocolate almond mound torte, chocolate raspberry mousse torte, Black Forest cake, and lemon poppy-seed torte. The pies are to die for: apple, marionberry, coconut cream, and special-order pies such as key lime, cherry, and banana cream. Or have breakfast or lunch at one of the downtown eateries such as **Alpenglow,** 1040 NW Bond Street (541–383–7676); the locals rave about the breakfast fare here. Other eateries in Bend that serve great espresso, fresh pastries, gourmet sandwiches, fresh salads, soups, and lox and bagels include **Dilusso Coffee Shop** at 1135 NW Galveston Avenue (541–383–8155); **Big-O-Bagels,** 1032 NW Galveston (541–383–2446); and the legendary **Pilot Butte Drive-In,** 917 NE Greenwood Avenue (541–382–2972).

Located near Drake Park and Mirror Pond, two hospitable bed-and-breakfast inns welcome travelers to the Bend area. **The Sather House Bed & Breakfast,** at 7 Northwest Tumalo Avenue (541–388–1065; www.satherhouse.com), was built in 1911 by a Norwegian immigrant family of ten and was restored in 1994 by innkeeper Robbie Giamboi. Four comfortable guest rooms are located on the second floor and come with such agreeable amenities as a Battenburg lace coverlet, a Victorian draped headboard, cozy terry robes, and a claw-foot soaking tub. The second inn, equally inviting, is **Lara House Bed & Breakfast,** located at 640 NW Congress Street (541–388–4064). This handsome Craftsman-style home, built in 1910, has six guest rooms that come with private baths. Breakfast is often served in the solarium, which overlooks the landscaped grounds and Drake Park.

For helpful information about the Bend area, contact the Bend Visitors Association, 63085 North Highway 97 (800–800–8334; www.visitbend.com). Ask, too, about shops and eateries in the newly renovated Old Mill District.

## Land of the Three Sisters

Heading west from Bend on US 20, you'll find that the Three Sisters—**South Sister, Middle Sister,** and **North Sister**—form a stunning mountain backdrop against the deep blue sky of central Oregon as you make your way to Sisters, Black Butte, and the headwaters of the Metolius River. The snowy peaks form an elegant trio; you could even imagine them enjoying a sisterly gossip session over cups of hot steaming espresso or lattes!

## The Three Sisters

The three mountains, North Sister, Middle Sister, and South Sister (with elevations of 10,085, 10,047, and 10,358 feet, respectively), are climbed by experienced climbers, with North Sister requiring the most advanced physical preparation and skills, including rock climbing and snow climbing. Climbers carry and know how to use ice axes and crampons. All climbers participate in regulation classes before attempting to climb any mountain in the Cascade Range. The USDA Forest Service Sisters Ranger Station (541–549–7700) administers this area.

If you haven't yet had supper, you could stop by the **Tumalo Feed Company** (541–382–2202), a family steak house and old-fashioned saloon. The eatery is located at 64619 Highway 20 in Tumalo, about 4 miles northwest of Bend.

Or you can check out several good options in Sisters, "Food for your inner cowpoke," says one local cowgirl—**Coyote Creek Cafe** (541–549–9514), which offers mesquite-broiled specialties, in Three Winds Shopping Center at the western edge of town, open daily all summer and on weekends in winter 8:00 A.M. to 9:30 P.M.; and **Depot Deli** (541–549–2572) in the center of town at 250 West Cascade Street, which has great sandwiches, soups, and pastries. For tasty made-daily pies (especially the marionberry pie), doughnuts, breads, and pastries, stop by **Sisters Bakery** at 251 East Cascade Avenue (541–549–0361). For great coffee and espresso, in addition to freshly roasted coffee beans, stop by **Sisters Coffee Company,** 273 West Hood Avenue (541–549–0527). And just for fun take in a current film at the new **Sisters Movie House** (541–549–8800; www.sistersmoviehouse.com), where you can order a juicy burger or homemade panini and eat in the cafe or have your fare delivered to your theater seat.

The community of **Sisters,** transformed into an Old West tourist town with wooden boardwalks and western-style storefronts, is filled with interesting shops, lovely boutiques, and old-fashioned eateries. **Hotel Sisters** is one of the few early structures remaining, now restored as an 1880s-style restaurant, **Bronco Billy's Ranch Grill** (541–549–7427).

In mid-July take in the spectacular **Sisters Outdoor Quilt Show** (www .stitchinpost.com), and in mid-June hang out with cowboys and cowgirls at the **Sisters Rodeo;** call the Sisters Visitor Center (541–549–0251) or the rodeo office (541–549–0121) for current information. Creekside City Park offers tent and RV spaces during summer months; it's close to downtown shops and eateries.

If time allows, detour about 5 miles west of Sisters and head north another 5 miles to Camp Sherman to see the headwaters of the Metolius River, bubbling directly from the lower north slopes of Black Butte. At the **Wizard Falls Fish Hatchery,** a few miles downriver from Camp Sherman, you can see where those wily trout are raised to stock the more than one hundred lakes in the high Cascades. The Metolius is well known to fly fishers for its enormous wild trout, and nearby **Lake Billy Chinook,** behind Round Butte Dam, offers some of the best kokanee—or landlocked salmon—troll fishing in the region.

Walk along the ½-mile **Jack Creek Nature Trail** near Camp Sherman to see native plants and wildflowers thriving in a lush, spring-fed oasis that contrasts with the dry, open forest floor strewn with long pine needles and ponderosa pinecones the size of large baseballs. Peer over the footbridge at Camp Sherman to spot some of the largest trout you've ever laid eyes on, playing hide-and-seek in the clear waters of the Metolius.

If you want to sleep out here under the fragrant ponderosa pines, you can usually find a spot for your tent or RV at the more than a dozen Forest Service campgrounds, but note that these are very busy on summer weekends. Before departing Sisters, stop by or call the Sisters Ranger Station (at the west edge of town) for maps and information, (541) 549–7700. For sleeping indoors close to a crackling fire, try vintage 1920s-style **Metolius River Lodges** (800–595–6290; www.metoliusriverlodges.com) for rustic cottages on the banks of the river; **Metolius River Resort** (800–818–7688 or 541–595–6281; www.metoliusriver resort.com) for new cabins with river-rock fireplaces, no pets allowed; or mid-1930s **Lake Creek Lodge** (800–797–6331; www.lakecreeklodge.com), which has rooms in the main lodge or pine-paneled cabins with fireplaces, heated outdoor pool, tennis court, and stocked fishing pond and creek. But be sure to plan a fine-dining evening at the **Kokanee Cafe** (541–595–6420) in Camp Sherman, just around the corner from Camp Sherman Store & Fly Shop. This out-of-the-way cafe is open for dinner seasonally, May through October, and the nightly fresh fish specials are legendary.

If you're looking for a quiet retreat a bit closer to civilization, consider **Black Butte Ranch** (800–452–7455; www.blackbutteranch.com), located about 8 miles west of Sisters. Nestled on some 1,800 acres of ponderosa pine forest and meadows at the base of 6,436-foot Black Butte—a volcanic cone whose warm innards keep it virtually snow-free all year—the area was, from the late 1800s to about 1969, a working cattle ranch and stopping-off place for sheep and wool coming from eastern Oregon across the Cascade Mountains to the Willamette Valley. Today you can stroll or bicycle along paths that wend around guest quarters, condominiums, and private vacation residences. If you play golf or tennis, you can choose from two eighteen-hole golf courses and nineteen open-air tennis courts. Or you can paddle a canoe on the small lake just beyond the restaurant and dining room; nestle in front of a friendly fire and watch the squirrels dash about the ponderosa pine just outside a wide expanse of windows; or curl up for a snooze amid the utter quiet in this peaceful spot. During winter you can bring Nordic ski gear and enjoy cross-country treks on those flat meadows, which are covered with snow from November through March.

Just west of Sisters on Highway 126, you may see a number of woolly llamas in large grassy meadows belonging to the 350-acre private Patterson Ranch. Gentle creatures with high intelligence and great curiosity, the llamas are raised here, at one of the largest llama-breeding ranches in North America. You can stop by the roadside to see them.

For information about guided llama hikes, contact **Oregon Llamas Adventures** in Bend, (541–389–6855). The Sisters Area Visitor Center, located at 164 North Elm Street (541–549–0251; www.sisterschamber.com), will also have helpful information about the area.

There are several comfortable bed-and-breakfast inns within shouting distance of the Three Sisters mountains, pleasant places to hunker down for the night. For amenable digs within walking distance of shops and cafes in Sisters, there's **Blue Spruce Bed & Breakfast,** 444 South Spruce Street (541–549–9644). Vaunell and Bob Temple welcome their guests to spacious rooms on the second floor with king beds, western memorabilia, gas log fireplaces, and cozy sitting areas. Then, at **Juniper Acres Bed & Breakfast** (541–389–2193), located at 65220 Smokey Ridge Road between Sisters and Bend, you could meet Della and Vern Bjerk and hole up in their log home, situated on ten acres of young- and old-growth juniper and with floor-to-ceiling windows framing views of the snowcapped Three Sisters, Mount Washington, Mount Jefferson, Brokentop, and Mount Bachelor. Guests are offered Della's great breakfast, which might include pineapple-guava-raspberry juliuses, baked pears, an egg-cheese-broccoli soufflé, fresh baked coffee cake, and orange muffins.

The Cascade Mountains form an effective weather barrier, with their forested foothills, sparsely clad higher slopes, and snowy volcanic peaks extending down the midsection of the Beaver State and siphoning those heavy rain clouds from the Pacific Ocean to the west. Most of this moisture falls as snow in the high Cascades from November through April, leaving less moisture for the high-desert regions east of the mountains. Spring snowmelt gurgles into hundreds of lakes, creeks, and streams, tumbling down the mountainsides to larger rivers that find their way nearly 250 miles to the Pacific Ocean, completing the eternal cycle.

As emigrant families made the first wagon-train crossing of the central Cascades south of Bend across Pengra, later renamed **Willamette Pass,** toward

Eugene in late fall 1853, they found that the first snows of late autumn had already whitened most of the mountain peaks. With 300 wagons, the half-starved, weary group was nearly stranded in the high country until guided safely to Eugene by resident pioneers who had earlier begun to open the route over the pass.

Your visit to the high Cascades wouldn't be complete, however, without including the 87-mile *Cascades Lakes National Forest Scenic Drive,* which meanders along the same routes traversed by the Native peoples, botanist David Douglas, and explorers like John Frémont, Nathaniel Wyeth, Peter Skene Ogden, and Kit Carson. Designated a National Forest Scenic Byway in 1989, this nearly 100-mile highway loop from Bend south to the *Wickiup Reservoir* is more commonly called Century Drive by most of the locals. In 1920 the original Indian trails, horse trails, and wagon roads were finally replaced by a main wagon road from Bend to Sparks Lake and the Elk Lake area.

During summer and early fall, before snow season, take the well-paved cinder road to wind your way through ancient lava beds to 6,000-foot *Mount Bachelor* and down through pine forests, skirting more than a dozen alpine lakes—Sparks, Elk, Big Lava, Little Lava, Cultus, Little Cultus, Deer, North Twin, and South Twin—on whose shores are many campgrounds and places from which to fish. Fly-fishing-only lakes include *Davis, Sparks,* and *Fall River.* A more quiet spot, much loved by serious fly fishermen/women is Davis Lake, at the far south end of Century Drive, beyond Wickiup Reservoir. At Cultus and Little Cultus Lakes, an interesting mixture of ponderosa pine, Douglas fir, white fir, white pine, sugar pine, and spruce grows along the road into the lake area; here, too, are some of the few places along the drive that offer shallow sandy beaches. Cultus Lake allows motorboats and offers some of the best waterskiing and Jet Skiing in the area. Family-friendly *Cultus Lake Resort* (800–616–3230; www.cultuslakeresort.com) is open from May through October and offers canoe and rowboat rentals.

There are summer hiking and camping areas at most of the lakes, as well as winter cross-country ski trails along the route; during winter, visitors enjoy skiing to Elk Lake, where rustic *Elk Lake Lodge* (541–480–7228; www.elklake resort.com) remains open year-round. Good sources for maps and information are the Deschutes National Forest Headquarters in Bend (541–383–5300) and the Central Oregon Visitor Center in Bend (800–800–8334; www.visitbend.com).

During summer months visitors can ride one of the Mount Bachelor ski chairlifts for grand top-of-the-mountain views of more than a dozen snowy peaks, of shaggy green forests, and of sparkling mountain lakes. It's a stunning panorama.

# Fast Facts about Mount Bachelor

**Elevation:** 5,700 feet at base, 9,065 feet at summit

**Acres of skiing:** 3,686

**Vertical drop:** 3,365 feet

**Number of alpine ski runs:** seventy-one

**Maximum alpine ski-run length:** 2 miles

**Ski season:** generally November through April

**Alpine terrain ratings:** 15 percent novice, 25 percent intermediate, 35 percent advanced intermediate, 25 percent expert

**Chairlifts:** Eleven, including seven express chairs

**Average annual snowfall:** 250–300 inches; average snowfall at base is 150–200 inches

**Day lodges:** Six, including Sunrise Lodge, mid-mountain Pine Marten Lodge, and the Cross Country Lodge

**Cross-country skiing:** Twelve trails with 35 miles of machine-groomed tracks

**Ski report:** (541) 382-7888

**Information and reservations:** Ski school, equipment rental, winter activities; (800) 829-2442; www.mtbachelor.com

**Number of skiers and snowboarders served every season:** 600,000

**How to beat the crowds:** Plan to stay during the week or on Sunday, ski early or late in the day, avoid holiday weekends and spring break weeks; also, try out other winter activities such as horse-drawn sleigh rides, Alaskan husky dogsled rides (from Sunrise Lodge), tobogganing and inner tubing, snowshoeing (some walks are led by members of the Forest Service), snowmobiling, and ice skating.

Located just west of Elk Lake and directly south of McKenzie Pass, the 247,000-acre ***Three Sisters Wilderness*** offers more than 250 miles of trails that skirt alpine meadows, sparkling streams, glittering patches of obsidian, ancient lava flows, old craters, and dozens of small lakes, as well as glaciers at higher elevations. About 40 miles of the ***Pacific Crest National Scenic Trail*** runs through this vast region, which in the late 1950s was set aside as a wilderness. Check with the Sisters Ranger Station (541–549–7700) for current maps and information about backcountry hiking and camping.

Protected by the National Wilderness Preservation Act of 1964, the Three Sisters Wilderness—along with more than fifteen million acres of other land so designated across the United States—permits visitors to travel only by foot or by horse; no vehicles are allowed. Oregon has set aside thirteen such wilderness areas, seven of them located from south to north in the Cascade Mountains.

Like the early mountain men, explorers, and naturalists, experienced and well-equipped backpackers will often stay out for four or five days at a time in the high country, letting the wilderness saturate every pore. The Three Sisters Wilderness is accessible from mid-July through October for hiking and from November through June for snow camping and cross-country skiing. Snow often reaches depths of 20 feet or more at the higher elevations, and hikers may encounter white patches up to the first week of August.

Most of the high mountain lakes are stocked with eastern brook, rainbow, and cutthroat trout. From Lava, Elk, and Sparks Lakes, you can access trails into the Three Sisters Wilderness, walking just a short distance if time doesn't allow an overnight trek with backpacks and tents.

The wilderness outback is not your thing? Instead check out the cozy cabins and three scenic lakeside campgrounds at **Suttle Lake** (www.thelodgeat suttlelake.com)—Blue Bay, South Shore, and Link Creek—located about 15 miles west of Sisters via US 20 (call 877–444–6777 for campground reservations). **The Boathouse Restaurant** (541–595–2628) at the marina offers Northwest fare and great views of the lake. Enjoy walking the trail around the lake as well as boating, fishing, sunning, and swimming.

During summer and fall you might enjoy seeing the high mountain country on horseback, just as explorers like Lewis and Clark, John Frémont, and Kit Carson did in the early 1800s. The **Metolius-Windigo Trail,** built in the 1970s by horse lovers in cooperation with the Sisters, Bend, and Crescent ranger districts staff, offers a network of riding trails, as well as campsites with corrals. The Metolius-Windigo Trail runs through the spectacular alpine meadow and high backcountry from Sisters toward Elk Lake and then heads south, following Forest Service roads and sections of the **Old Skyline Trail,** toward **Crescent Lake** and **Windigo Pass,** located off Highway 58, about 60 miles south of Bend.

For horse campers the familiar crackling warmth of a morning fire mixes well with hands that hold mugs of hot coffee before breaking camp and saddling up. The creak of saddle leather punctuates the crisp morning air; the clop of the horses' hooves echoes through the pines; the air smells fresh and clean. Most horse campers are lured by both the wilderness and the simple joys of riding, and many assist hikers in the **Adopt-a-Trail** program. The Forest Service provides materials and consultation, whereas various hiking and trail-riding groups maintain or build new trails.

If you're itching to mount a horse and ride into the ponderosa, check with the folks at **Black Butte Stables & Pack Station** (541–595–2061). Half- or full-day rides take visiting cowboys and cowgirls into high pine forests and meadows and offer great views of the snowcapped mountains. Overnight pack trips can also be arranged. For year-round riding visit the **Eagle Crest Equestrian Center** at 1522 Cline Falls Road off Highway 126 toward Redmond (541–923–2072). Rides here follow trails along the Deschutes River and through the juniper and sage canyon, then open to wide mountain views. For folks who can bring their own horses, there are a number of high-country campgrounds available with horse facilities along the Windigo Trail, including Cow Camp Horse Camp and Graham Corral Horse Camp, both at 3,400-foot elevation; Sheep Springs Horse Camp, at 3,200-foot elevation; Whispering Pines Horse Camp, at 4,400-foot elevation; and Three Creeks Meadow Horse Camp, at 6,350-foot elevation. Maps and additional information can be obtained from Hoodoo Recreation Services (541–822–3799; www.hoodoo.com) and the Sisters Ranger Station (541–549–7700).

To try your hand at high-altitude camping without a horse but with suitable camping gear, warm sleeping bags, warm clothing, and plenty of food and beverages, take Forest Service Road 16 south via Elm Street from Sisters for 18 miles to a little-known gem at about 6,000 feet elevation, **Three Creeks Lake Campground.** There is no piped-in water, there are restrictions on boats with motors, and there are only ten campsites in this pretty forest campground. For current information check with the Sisters Ranger Station. At this altitude it will be chilly at night and in the early morning, even during the summer months.

## Crooked River Gorge

About a million years ago, lava spilled into the Crooked River canyon upriver near the community of Terrebonne and flowed nearly to Warm Springs. As you drive though this area, stop at **Peter Skene Ogden Wayside,** just off US 97. Stand at the low stone wall and peer into a 300-foot-deep rocky chasm where the Crooked River, at its base, is still searching for that old canyon. It is more than an awesome sight. *NOTE:* Keep close watch on children here and keep all pets on a leash.

If time allows, drive into the Crooked River Gorge via Highway 27 from Prineville to the large **Prineville Reservoir State Park**—a gorgeous drive into the heart of the gorge and, at its base, the ancient river. There are campgrounds on the lake, which offers fishing throughout the year, including ice fishing in winter. For more information contact the Prineville–Crook County Visitor Center, 390 NE Fairview Street (541–447–6304). And if you're a rock hound, ask about the annual Thunderegg Days held during midsummer. To get to Prineville, head east from Redmond for about 20 miles on U.S. Highway 26.

Of the nation's nine smoke-jumper bases, eight are in the Northwest, and one, **Redmond Smokejumper Base,** is located at the USDA Forest Service Redmond Air Center, just off US 97 south of Redmond, at 1740 SE Ochoco Way, just beyond the Redmond Airport. If you call ahead for tour information (541–504–7200), you may get to watch hotshot trainees jump from the practice tower in their full smoke-jumping regalia as well as see how the parachutes and harnesses are repaired, rebuilt, and repacked. Note, however, that spring and fall are the best times to arrange a visit; the center may be closed to guests if a summer fire emergency occurs.

If you like golf, the **Juniper Golf Club** just south of Redmond welcomes all travelers who enjoy the game. Call ahead for a tee time (541–548–3121) for either nine or eighteen holes of golf under a vibrant blue sky and with lush green fairways lined with ponderosa pine, pungent juniper (one of the aromatic cedars), and yellow flowering sagebrush. For another eighteen holes of golf, head to **Crooked River Golf Course,** located south of Redmond and near Terrebonne (800–833–3197; www.crookedriverranch.com). The high desert scenery along the golf course is awesome. For a complete list of public courses, contact the Redmond Visitor Center, 446 SW Seventh Street, (541–923–5191; www.visitredmond.com).

For a fun adventure taking travelers back to the early 1800s, plus dinner aboard a train, call the **Crooked River Railroad Company** in Redmond (541–548–8630) to ask for a current brochure that details the year's offerings. On this western-theme dinner train, which winds about 20 miles into the Crooked River canyon and valley, you can expect to see not only juniper, sagebrush, and red rimrock, but occasionally also fictional and real characters from the early West. For additional details check out the Web site, www.crookedriverrail road.com; the site also offers good links to regional visitor associations and visitor centers and an interesting link to famous lady outlaws. You'd rather eat closer to civilization? Try **Mustard Seed Cafe** at 614 NW Cedar Avenue in Redmond (541–923–2599), open daily from 7:00 A.M. except Sunday and Monday.

Then, too, you could detour at Terrebonne, a few miles north of Redmond, and drive out to spectacular **Smith Rock State Park** to watch the rock climbers before heading north on US 97 toward Madras and the Warm Springs Indian Reservation. The rock climbing at Smith Rock is considered some of the best and most challenging anywhere in the world. As you crane your neck upward to watch the brightly Lycra-clad men and women scale the steep red-rock inclines, you may hear words of encouragement in more than a dozen languages—from French, Italian, and German to Swedish, English, and Japanese.

Free climbing, the most popular form of rock climbing, allows only the use of the rock's natural features to make upward progress; however, safety ropes are allowed, to stop a fall. You'll notice climbers on the ascent using just their hands and feet to perch on small outcroppings or to clutch narrow crevices as they carefully negotiate a route to the top; the object is to climb a particular section, or route, "free" without using the safety ropes.

You'll find shady places to picnic here, as well as an easy, ten-minute trail you can walk down to the meandering Crooked River. Then cross the footbridge for a close encounter with those enormous, almost intimidating vertical rocks that nature has painted in shades of deep red-orange, vibrant browns, and pale creams. Be sure to stay a safe distance from the climbers, because loose chunks of rock can dislodge and plummet to the ground. The best picture-snapping view of Smith Rock and the Crooked River, by the way, is from the far end of the parking area, near the turnaround—an absolute showstopper at sunrise or sunset. *NOTE:* A forest fire swept through the area during summer 1996; although the view is still awesome, it will take many years for Mother Nature to repair the scorched juniper trees.

Located in the heart of the Warm Springs Indian Reservation, ***Kah-Nee-Ta Resort*** (800–554–4786 or 541–553–1112; www.kahneeta.com) is nestled alongside the Warm Springs River at the base of another bright copper-and-amber canyon just a few miles from the community of Warm Springs. The moment you turn off US 26 at Warm Springs and wind down from stark rimrock ridges and sparsely clad hills into the multicolored canyon, city cares will seem far away. The area easily recalls scenes from a well-worn Zane Grey novel or a colorful Charles Russell painting.

The charm of Kah-Nee-Ta owes as much to its culture as to its unique rimrock setting. A sense of the Native American past permeates the air, while the unobstructed desert landscape encourages a gentle sifting away of those citified cobwebs. Long walks are a must here—meander down a paved path next to the Warm Springs River, which bubbles alongside The Village, and catch whiffs of pungent sage, bitterbrush, and juniper.

The resort, owned and operated by the Confederated Indian Tribes of Warm Springs, began welcoming visitors in 1964 with the opening of The Village, which offers comfortable cottage units, a number of large tepees for rustic outdoor-style camping (you bring your own sleeping bags and such), and hookups for recreational vehicles. Three mammoth swimming pools and a bathhouse are fed by the hot mineral springs. On a sagebrush-carpeted bluff just above The Village is the spacious contemporary lodge that opened in 1972. Wrapped around its own jumbo-size pool, the lodge is a good choice if you like your getaways a bit swankier.

After settling in, one of the best things to do is to lower your travel-weary frame into one of the hot mineral baths located in the bathhouse at The Village. Follow this leisurely private soak with a sweat beneath several layers of sheets and blankets. Yes, sweat. Profusely. You'll emerge cleansed, relaxed, and quite likely a new person—the experience is one of Kah-Nee-Ta's most memorable offerings.

Eateries on site include an informal cafe at The Village; the Pinto Coffee Shop or the outdoor patio overlooking the swimming pool up at the lodge; and the elegant Juniper Room, also at the lodge. An entree prepared with Cornish game hen called Bird-in-Clay, a house specialty, is worth ordering ahead—notify the dining-room staff about three hours in advance. With its stuffing of wild rice and juniper berries, the dish is delicious; you receive your own miniature mallet made of juniper to break open the clay covering.

With a massive stone entry shaped like a tribal drum and brick walls fretted with a traditional native basket pattern, *The Museum at Warm Springs* (541–553–3331; www.warmsprings.com/museum) resonates with the cultural past and present of the three Native American tribes—Wasco, Warm Springs, and Paiute—who live in this spectacular rimrock canyon near the Deschutes River. The museum is one of the premiere tribal-owned museums in the United States, and visitors can see one of the most extensive collections of Native American artifacts on a reservation. From late spring through early fall, enjoy living-history and dance presentations, storytelling, and craft demonstrations of basketry, beadwork, and drum making. Be sure to stand in the song chamber, where you can hear traditional chanting. Many Indian elders hope that the museum will be an important link to the younger members of the Confederated tribes, teaching them, as well as visitors, about their languages, religions, and cultures. Located just off US 97 in Warm Springs, on Shitake Creek, the museum is open daily from 9:00 A.M. to 5:00 P.M.

## Prehistoric Fossil Lands

*Shaniko,* located at the junction of US 97 from the Bend-Redmond-Madras area and Highway 218 from the John Day area, was an important shipping point for wheat, wool, and livestock at the turn of the twentieth century. The bustling town at the end of the railroad tracks was filled with grain warehouses, corrals, loading chutes, cowboys, sheepherders, hotels, and saloons. Known as the Wool Capital, the town was named for August Scherneckau, whom the Indians called Shaniko and whose ranch house was a station on the old stage route from The Dalles to central Oregon.

The last of the battles between the cattle ranchers and the sheep ranchers were fought near Shaniko in the mid-1850s; for some twenty-five years the former resisted what was considered an invasion of their territory by "those ornery sheepherders." The sheep won, however, and still dominate the rangelands on the high desert. In fact, you should be prepared to wait a considerable amount of time for flocks of the woolly critters to cross various highways throughout the region when the herds are moved to and from mountain pastures in both spring and fall.

Although Shaniko is mostly a ghost town today, a few energetic citizens are breathing new life into the old frontier village. The ***Historic Shaniko Hotel*** (541–489–3441 or 800–483–3441; www.shaniko.com), no longer tired and weather-beaten, was renovated in the mid-1980s. A wide plank porch once again wraps around both sides of the redbrick hotel, graceful arched windows sparkle in the morning sun, and oak doors with new glass panels open into a lace-draped, plant-filled lobby that holds one of the original settees and an antique reception desk. The oak banister, refinished and polished, still winds up to the second floor.

Hanging brass plaques also identify sixteen refurbished guest rooms, each named for an early Shaniko pioneer. Shiny brass lamps have replaced bare light bulbs; plush carpeting covers floors that earlier sported tired, cracked linoleum; firm mattresses offer rest in place of creaky old springs; lovely linens and floral spreads grace beds that once offered mismatched and worn blankets; and new private bathrooms keep guests from having to trek to the far end of the hall.

Old farmhouse near Shaniko

What's there to do in Shaniko? Well, mosey over to the gas station and buy a soft drink; capture with a camera or paintbrush the weathered romance of the old school, the jail, and city hall or the water tower and the hotel; peer into old buildings and wonder who lived there; or just sit on the porch swing and reflect about the days when Shaniko bustled with cowboys, ponies, sheepherders, sheep, train whistles, and steam locomotives.

The hotel restaurant, *Shaniko Cafe* (541–489–3415), open daily from 7:00 A.M. to 9:00 P.M., serves moderately priced meals. *Shaniko Ice Cream Parlor* (541–489–3392), around the corner from the hotel, offers sandwiches as well as ice cream from April to October.

Hopefully, you refilled your picnic basket and cooler in Bend, Redmond, or Madras before heading to Shaniko and can now continue east on Highway 218 for about 20 miles, driving into the *John Day Fossil Beds National Monument* area. Stop to see the palisades of the *Clarno Unit*, just east of the John Day River. This unit comprises about 2,000 acres. Not only the leaves but also the limbs, seeds, and nuts of the tropical plants that grew here forty to fifty million years ago are preserved in the oldest of the Cenozoic era's layers, the Clarno formation, named for Andrew Clarno, an early white settler who home-

## Wheeler County Is Fossil Country

You've had your fill of civilization for a bit? You have the urge to be alone with just your own thoughts? Two excellent choices come to mind: the scenic John Day River, which flows through Wheeler County; and the John Day Fossil Beds National Monument, all 14,000 acres of it scattered about the 1,713 square miles of the least-populated county of the state. The concept of population density is practically unknown here, averaging about one person per square mile.

The first time I visited the John Day area, I was unprepared for the Clarno Unit's oddly shaped and deeply weathered spires and palisades; the Sheep Rock Unit's bluish green cliffs; and, particularly, the low, rounded Painted Hills, with their bands of colors that looked like softly running watercolors. I was unprepared for the solitude and peacefulness of the place. The sky went on forever. The parking area was empty. It was early in the day—a soft breeze was blowing through the sagebrush and scattering the dry tumbleweeds about. I heard the distinctive call of the meadowlark (our state bird). Even inserting film into my camera seemed too jarring a noise for this peaceful place, so far off the beaten path. But the long light of early morning is a wonderful time to shoot photos of the Painted Hills. The long, warm light of evening is an equally good time to shoot photos here. Early spring and fall are good times to visit; summers are normally quite hot and very dusty (always bring fresh drinking water with you).

steaded here in 1866. The formation is a mudflow conglomerate that has been battered by eons of weather; you'll notice the unusual leftovers—eroded pillars, craggy turrets, top-heavy pedestals, natural stone bridges, and deep chasms. Walk up the slope from the picnic area to stand amid these intriguing shapes and notice pungent-smelling sagebrush and junipers dotting the otherwise barren hills where a tropical forest once grew. *NOTE:* There is no fresh drinking water here. And although they usually hide in rock crevices, keep an eye out for the western Pacific rattlesnake while you're in this area.

According to analysis of the bone and plant fossils unearthed here, first by a cavalry officer and then by Thomas Condon, a minister and amateur paleontologist who settled in The Dalles in the 1850s, an ancient lush tropical forest once covered this region. This humid life zone of eons past contained palm, fig, cinnamon, hydrangea, sequoia, and ferns, together with alligators, primitive rhinoceroses, and tiny horses. As you walk along the interpretive ***Trail of the Fossils,*** notice the many leaf prints in which every vein and tooth has been preserved in the chalky-colored hardened clays.

When Condon first learned of the area, through specimens brought to The Dalles, he explored it and found other hidden clues to Oregon's past. In 1870 he shipped a collection of fossil teeth to Yale University, and during the next thirty years, many of the world's leading paleontologists came to Oregon to study the John Day fossil beds. The three large units in the region, encompassing more than 14,000 acres, were designated a national monument in 1974 and are now under the direction of the National Park Service. The digging and collecting of fossil materials are coordinated by two Park Service paleontologists, and evidence of new species of prehistoric mammals continues to surface as the ancient layers of mud, ash, and rock are washed and blown away by rain and wind each year. The Oregon Museum of Science and Industry's ***Hancock Field Station,*** located on the Clarno Unit and near the small community of Fossil and the John Day River, offers outdoor workshops and fossil-hunting field trips for kids of all ages during the summer. For information about current programs call (541) 763–4691 or check www.omsi.edu.

If you discover some interesting fossil remains while exploring the area, the park staff encourages reporting their locations so that the findings can be identified and catalogued into the computer.

To visit the ***Painted Hills*** Unit, 3,000 acres in size, continue on Highway 218 to Fossil, head south past ***Shelton Wayside and Campground***—a lovely oasis and a good picnic spot—and turn onto Highway 207 toward Mitchell, a total of about 60 miles. Find the turnoff to the Painted Hills just a few miles west, then continue 6 miles north to the viewpoint.

The vast array of cone-shaped hills you'll see here are actually layer upon layer of volcanic ash from those huge mountains, such as Newberry and Mazama, once looming to the south, that collapsed in fiery roars thousands of years ago. Some of the layers of tuff are stained a rich maroon or pink, others are yellow-gold, and still others are black or bronze. The colors are muted by late afternoon's golden light and at sunset turn a deep burgundy. As you behold this barren, surrealistic landscape, you'll blink and wonder whether you aren't really looking at a marvelous watercolor or oil painting.

For a closer view of the brilliantly colored bands of tuff, walk along the ½-mile trail from the overlook or drive to nearby **Painted Cove Trail.** NOTE: Remember to take plenty of fresh drinking water with you into both the Clarno and the Painted Hills Units.

Later, returning to Mitchell, you might plan a coffee break at **Bridge Creek Cafe** (541–462–3434), located right on US 26. Here friendly conversation is offered along with breakfast, lunch, and dinner. The cafe is open daily from 8:00 A.M. to 7:30 P.M., with shorter hours during winter months.

Continuing east on US 26 about 30 miles, stop at **Picture Gorge** before turning north on Highway 19 for a couple of miles to the **Cant Ranch Historical Museum.** At Picture Gorge you can easily see the oldest to youngest major formations, all marching across the landscape in orderly layers of mud, ash, and rock—the Picture Gorge Basalt, about fifteen million years old; Mascall Formation, about twelve million years old; and the narrow ridge on top, named the Rattlesnake Formation, about three million years old. You can easily see where the two oldest formations were tilted southward together and eroded before the Rattlesnake Formation was laid down across them, horizontally.

Located just across Highway 19 from Cant Ranch Historical Museum is the splendid new **Thomas Condon Paleontology Center,** where fossil replicas and actual specimens from the three units are displayed and identified. You can also watch park staff prepare the fossils for exhibiting, and you can ask questions about the specimens you find and report. In the orchard nearby a collection of farm implements from the Cant Ranch is being restored, and in the main ranch house one of the rooms has been set aside to look just as it did some sixty years ago, complete with original furnishings and an arrangement of Cant family photos. The new paleontology center is open daily from 8:30 A.M. to 4:30 P.M. Drinking water is available at Cant Ranch and also at the Foree Deposit area in the nearby **Sheep Rock Unit;** both facilities are also wheelchair accessible. This unit is 9,000 acres in size. You can walk along self-guided nature trails along the base of blue- and green-tinged cliffs. Additional information and maps are available from the John Day Fossil Beds National Monument located at 32651 Highway 19 (541–987–2333; www.nps.gov/joda).

Campgrounds in the area include those at **Shelton Wayside State Park;** the **Clyde Holiday Wayside** on US 26 near Mount Vernon, about 30 miles east of the Paleontology Center; and the primitive camping areas in the **Strawberry Mountain Wilderness,** south of John Day and Canyon City. Current camping information is also posted in each unit of the park.

The **Fish House Inn Bed & Breakfast** (541–987–2124 or 888–286–3474; www.fishhouseinn.com) in nearby Dayville offers three comfortable guest rooms in the main house, a charming 1908 bungalow, and a small cottage that sleeps four. During warm weather, innkeepers Mike and Denise Smith serve a hearty breakfast outdoors under the trees. "We serve our own blend of freshly roasted gourmet coffee, too," adds Denise. The Smiths also offer facilities for several RVs and a few tent sites. Within walking distance is the John Day River, a city park with a tennis court, a small cafe, and several country stores.

There are a limited number of motels and restaurants in Mount Vernon and Mitchell; more can be found in Prineville or in John Day, the latter about 5 miles east of Mount Vernon. For current information contact the Grant County Visitor Information Center, 281 West Main Street, John Day (541–575–0547 or 800–769–5664).

Since you're also smack in the middle of Oregon's high-desert fossil country, you could head west on Highway 19 for about 45 miles to the community of Fossil and plan an expedition to the public fossil beds. For accommodations check with **Fossil Lodge,** located at 808 Main Street, and just next door **Bridge Creek Flora Inn Bed & Breakfast** at 828 Main Street (541–763–2355; www.fossilinn.com). "Bridge Creek Flora refers to the geological layer where many of the plant fossils are found," explains owner Lyn Craig. She and husband Mike welcome guests to their two cozy inns and offer guests the use of rock hammers and buckets for fossil digging. On the exposed bank directly

## Lonerock's Outdoor Post Office

Tucked at the bottom of a deep canyon at the edge of the Blue Mountains, Lonerock, population hardly seventy, is framed by tall ponderosa pine and western juniper. Perched on a wood fence some nineteen mailboxes await circulars, junk mail, and first-class mail. It's said there's room for two more mailboxes should you want to move there—it's 25 miles from Fossil, 34 miles from Heppner, and 22 miles from Condon. If you'd prefer to just stay overnight, there are swell digs at historic **Hotel Condon** (800–201–6706; www.hotelcondon.com). Enjoy good eats at the hotel restaurant or at the **Condon Country Cafe** (541–384–7000), or do lunch and espresso at **Country Flowers Coffee Shop & Deli** (541–384–4120). They're all located on Main Street; you can't get lost.

## Field Trip to Fossil Country

On one visit to Wheeler County, with those forty-seven seventh-graders we hauled from Portland all over Oregon during the school year of 1970, we stopped in the small town of Fossil at the junction of Highway 218 and Highway 19 (about three hours from the Portland area). Now promise you won't tell the whole world, but you can park at the high school and find behind it one of the richest fossil beds in the state, which is not only easily accessible but also is open for public collection. I still have my shoebox of fossil treasures from that trip—one of my favorites is a thin piece of shale with the perfect imprint of a dawn redwood branchlet and its distinctive flat needles. You and the kids can hunker down there behind the high school and poke about the fossil beds to find numerous species of fossilized plants, including alder, maple, beech, dawn redwood, and pine. A small shoebox and soft tissues make good collection equipment. The fossil beds were exposed in 1949 during the construction of the high school and have been used ever since by amateurs and professionals. Bring a picnic, bring the kids, and enjoy.

beyond the high school football field, you'll find many species of fossilized plants and trees imprinted in small and large pieces of shale, such as dawn redwood, pine, alder, and maple. It's a wonderful geology lesson for the youngsters as well as for oldsters.

By now, however, you may be hankerin' for a horse-and-cattle ranch experience. There's one to be had at 16555 Butte Creek Road, not far from Fossil. Here at **Wilson Ranches Retreat Bed & Breakfast** (866–763–2227; www .wilsonranchesretreat.com), Phil and Nancy Wilson offer seven comfortable rooms in the large renovated bunkhouse. Mornings bring hearty breakfasts served around a large knotty-pine table. Phil Wilson might cook up a gaggle of sausages or bacon, scrambled eggs, and biscuits for guests, family, and the wranglers. Around lunchtime the cowboys join guests and family for another gargantuan feast of, for example, elk-meat chili, roast beef, corn bread, and potato salad. You can go hiking, tour in a 4-wheel-drive truck, or even saddle up and rent a gentle steed for riding on the ranch trails. Or you could just lean on the fence and watch the process of branding the calves, which happens three times a year.

If you head west from Mitchell toward Prineville and Redmond, completing the western loop into high-desert fossil country, plan to picnic or camp at **Ochoco Lake State Park,** just on the western edge of the **Ochoco National Forest.** Notice the stands of western larch, often called tamarack, a tall graceful conifer with lacy needles that turn bright lime green in the fall. An interesting side trek is the 10-mile drive on a mostly gravel-surfaced Forest Service road to see **Stein's Pillar.** The basalt pillar rises some 250 feet from the forest floor, ancient layers of clay jutting into the deep blue sky. For information about hiking and camping in the area, contact the Ochoco National Forest Ranger District in Prineville (541–416–6500; www.fs.fed.us/r6/centraloregon). Access the road to Stein's Pillar just across the highway from the Ochoco Lake State Park turnoff.

For information about motel accommodations, contact the Prineville–Crook County Visitor Information Center, 390 NE Fairview Street, Prineville (541–447–6304).

---

# Where in Oregon Can You Find a Six-Hole Golf Course?

Although this may seem like a rather odd question, Oregon's only approved, USGA-rated six-hole golf course is located 10 miles east of Fossil via Highway 218. The *Kinzua Hills Golf Course* is nestled in the tall pines of the Blue Mountains near the old lumber company–owned town site of Kinzua (it closed in 1978). The golf course is open from May until early fall, and you can play six holes for $5.00, twelve holes for $10.00, and eighteen holes for $15.00, or golf all day for $20.00. What a deal. For current information call Ione Marler (541–763–3287) or Vada Shurtz (541–763–3351). Fossil is approximately 40 miles from Shaniko via Highway 218. From Portland it's about three hours via the Columbia Gorge route, I–84 to Biggs Junction, then Highway 206 south through Wasco to Condon and 20 miles farther to Fossil. Overnight accommodations include Bridge Creek Flora Inn Bed & Breakfast and the Fossil Lodge (541–763–2355).

---

## Places to Stay in Central Oregon

**BEND**

**Bend La Quinta Inn**
61200 US 97
(541) 388–2227

**Juniper Acres**
**Bed & Breakfast**
65220 Smokey Ridge Road
(541) 389–2193

**The Riverhouse Inn**
3075 North US 97
(541) 389–3111
www.riverhouse.com

**Sather House**
**Bed & Breakfast**
7 NW Tumalo Avenue
(888) 388–1065

**Sunriver Resort and**
**Sunriver Lodge**
south of Bend
(800) 547–3922
www.sunriver-resort.com

**DAYVILLE**

**Fish House Inn**
**Bed & Breakfast**
US 26
(888) 286–3474

**FOSSIL**

**Bridge Creek Flora Inn**
**Bed & Breakfast**
828 Main Street
(541) 763–2355

**JOHN DAY**

**Best Western**
**John Day Inn**
315 West Main Street
(541) 575–1700

**LA PINE**

East Lake Resort, Cabins,
& Campground
South of Bend via US 97
(541) 536–2230

**MADRAS**

Log cabins at the Cove
Palisades State Park on
Lake Billy Chinook
near Madras
(800) 452–5687 (state park
reservation number)

**SISTERS**

Blue Spruce
Bed & Breakfast
444 South Spruce Street
(541) 549–9644

Suttle Lake Resort,
Cabins, Campgrounds
14 miles west of Sisters
via US 20
(541) 595–2628
(541) 549–7700

# Places to Eat in Central Oregon

**BEND**

Cafe Bellisimo
Old Mill District
(541) 330–4322

Goody's Ice Cream
957 NW Wall Street
(541) 389–5185

**CONDON**

Country Flowers
Coffee Shop & Deli
Main Street
(541) 384–4120

Hotel Condon Restaurant
Main Street
(541) 384–4624

**FOSSIL**

The Fossil Cafe
(541) 763–4328

**PRINEVILLE**

The Robin's Nest Cafe
395 North Main Street
(541) 447–8665

**REDMOND**

Local Grounds
Coffeehouse
447 SW Sixth Street
(541) 923–3977

Mustard Seed Cafe
614 NW Cedar Avenue
(541) 923–2599

**SHANIKO**

Shaniko Hotel Cafe
US 97
(541) 489–3415

**SISTERS**

Angeline's Bakery & Cafe
121 West Main Street
(541) 549–9122

Depot Deli
250 West Cascade Avenue
(541) 549–2572

Sisters Coffee Company
243 West Hood Avenue
(541) 549–0527

Sno Cap Drive-In
417 West Cascade Avenue
(541) 549–6151

# HELPFUL TELEPHONE NUMBERS AND WEB SITES FOR CENTRAL OREGON

**Bend Visitor & Convention Bureau**
(800) 949–6086
www.visitbend.com

**Cascade Festival of Classical Music**
Bend, late August
(541) 382–8381
www.cascademusic.org

**Community Theatre of the Cascades**
148 NW Greenwood Street
Bend
(541) 389–0803

**Department of Fish & Wildlife**
Bend Ranger District
(541) 388–6363

**John Day Fossil Beds National Monument**
(541) 987–2333
www.nps.gov/joda

**Madras/Jefferson County Information**
(541) 475–2350
www.madras.net

**Mount Bachelor Ski Report**
(541) 382–7888

**Newberry Volcanic National Monument and Lava Lands Visitors' Center**
(541) 593–2421

**The *Nugget Newspaper***
Sisters
(541) 549–9941
www.nuggetnews.com/

**Oregon Fish and Wildlife**
John Day Ranger District
(541) 575–1167

**Oregon road and mountain pass reports**
(800) 977–6368
www.tripcheck.com

**Oregon State Parks**
campgrounds, yurts, houseboats, cabins, tepees, and camper wagons
(800) 551–6949
(800) 452–5687 (reservations)
www.oregonstateparks.org

**Oregon State Snowmobile Association**
www.oregonsnow.org

**Prineville/Crook County Visitor Information**
(541) 447–6304

**Redmond Area Visitor Information**
(541) 923–5191
www.visitredmond.com

**Sisters Area Visitor Information**
(541) 549–0251
www.sisterschamber.com

**USDA Forest Service Bend–Fort Rock Ranger Station**
Bend
(541) 383–4000
www.fs.fed.us/r6/centraloregon

**USDA Forest Service Sisters Ranger Station**
Sisters
(541) 549–7700

**Wanderlust Tours**
143 SW Cleveland Avenue, Bend
(541) 389–8359
www.wanderlusttours.com
day and moonlight canoeing, caving and volcano tours, April to mid-October; day and moonlight snowshoe treks, snow camping, mid-November to May

# Northeastern Oregon

## Cowboys, Cowgirls, and Ranch Country

Traveling into the far northeastern section of the Beaver State, you'll encounter sizable wheat farms, numerous cattle ranches, and wide-open skies as well as high mountain vistas in the farthest corner. Long before reaching Hermiston, Stanfield, and Echo via Interstate 84 from the Columbia Gorge, you'll begin to see cowboy hats on the heads of guys and gals in cars and pickups that pass. You most likely won't see new lizard-skin cowboy boots on their feet, however, because well-worn leather ones are the norm here. Extremely well-worn. As in southeastern Oregon, travelers find themselves usually above 3,000 feet in elevation, even above 4,000 and 5,000 feet, and, at one viewpoint, a whopping 6,982 feet above sea level.

For a close-up encounter with the not-too-distant past, pause in Pendleton to trek back in time to one of the city's unusual historical places, the *Pendleton Underground.* You'll walk through a section of the underground where scores of Chinese laborers lived during the early days of this Wild West town. Because of the negative feelings against those of Asian backgrounds, the men rarely came above these dimly lit caverns

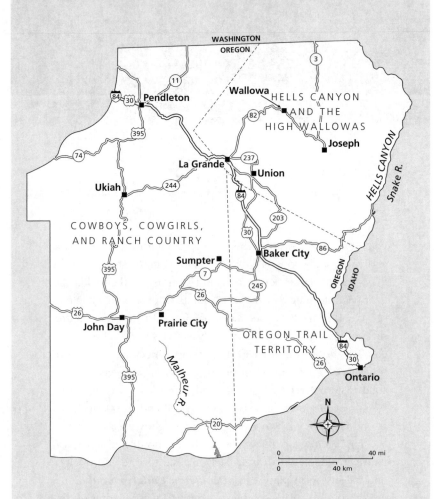

except to work on the construction of the railroad; even their own businesses and services were located in the tunnels. The guided tour starts from the renovated Shamrock Cardroom, 37 SW Emigrant Street, formerly one of the wild-and-woolly honky-tonks that flourished in the early 1900s. Reservations are required and tours run at intervals between 9:30 A.M. and 4:00 P.M.; call (541) 276–0730.

Once each year the ***Pendleton Underground Comes to Life*** is held in early spring, with local folks dressing the part and reenacting colorful scenes of a hundred years ago in the underground—the Shamrock Cardroom, Hop Sing's Laundry, Empire Ice Cream Parlor, the Empire Meat Market, the Prohibition Card Room, and, upstairs in the nearby old hotel, the Cozy Rooms Bordello. For the current schedule call (541) 276–0730 or check with the Pendleton Visitor Center, 501 South Main Street (541–276–7411; www.pendletonoregon.org). You can also ask for information about current tours of the area, which may include vintage barns, ghost towns, and colorful tales about Pendleton's rambunctious early days.

Folks have wrapped up in Pendleton blankets for more than eighty years, and you can watch them being woven during tours offered at the ca. 1909 ***Pendleton Woolen Mill,*** 1307 SE Court Place (541–276–6911; www.pendleton-usa.com). You can also visit the mill store, where robes, shawls, and blankets

## TOP HITS IN NORTHEASTERN OREGON

| | |
|---|---|
| **DeWitt Depot Museum**<br>Prairie City | **Oregon Trail Regional Museum**<br>Baker City |
| **Frazier Farmstead Museum and Gardens**<br>Milton-Freewater | **Pendleton Underground**<br>Pendleton |
| **Geiser Grand Hotel**<br>Baker City | **Sumpter Valley Narrow Gauge Railroad**<br>Sumpter |
| **Haines Steak House**<br>Haines | **Union County Museum and Cowboy Heritage Collection**<br>Union |
| **Hells Canyon National Recreation Area** | **Valley Bronze Foundry**<br>Joseph |
| **National Historic Oregon Trail Interpretive Center**<br>Flagstaff Summit near Baker City | **Wallowa Lake Tramway**<br>Wallowa Lake |

are for sale. Tours are offered on a first-come basis Monday through Friday, 9:00 and 11:00 A.M. and 1:30 and 3:00 P.M. Then you can visit a well-known saddle factory, **Hamley & Co.,** at 30 SE Court Street (541–278–1100; www.hamley .com), to watch the saddle makers at work and also browse the well-stocked cowboy emporium.

Although there are plenty of motels and motor inns in which to bed down in Pendleton, you could also call on the innkeepers at **A Place Apart Bed and Breakfast,** 711 SE Byers Avenue (541–276–0573; www.aplace-apart.com). The Ellis Hampton house was, in its early era, the most expensive and extravagant home on the city's fashionable southeast side. You'll see the handsome staircase, the parlor pocket doors, the shining oak hardwood floors, and the original brass hardware on the doors and windows. In the early 1900s owner Judge Ellis designed the large two-story home for entertaining and social gatherings. Guest rooms come with queen beds, soft down comforters, cozy flannel robes, scented soaps, thick towels, and shared bath. A full breakfast is served in the formal dining room or, on sunny mornings, in the backyard under the huge old linden tree.

Travelers can find another comfortable bed-and-breakfast inn in Pendleton at classical-style **Parker House Bed and Breakfast,** 311 North Main Street (541–276–8581). Breakfast is served in the grand dining room, on the front porch, at the fireplace, or in your guest room, and may include such tasty fare as cheese and shallot quiche, Dutch baby (a type of pancake) with rhubarb banana sauce, or Winter Berry French toast. The innkeeper also provides helpful services for business travelers.

For eateries try the 1950s-style **Main Street Diner** at 349 Main Street (541–278–1952) for great steaks and juicy hamburgers and the **Great Pacific Wine & Coffeehouse,** 403 South Main Street (541–276–1350), which offers a wine shop, espresso bar, and microbrews on tap. Locals also recommend **Stetson's House of Prime** at SE First Street and Court Avenue (541–966–1132). Further information can be obtained from the Pendleton Visitor Center (800–547–8911). For live theater call ahead and see what's playing at **Blue Mountain Community College Theatre** (541–278–5953).

To experience a taste of real ranch life, head east a few miles from Pendleton, take exit 216, and proceed to the small community of Mission. From here head east along the Umatilla River for wide-angle views of pastures, rangelands, and of the Blue Mountains in the distance. You could arrange a stay just past the community of Gibbon, at the **Bar M Ranch** (541–566–3381; www .barmranch.com), where folks have visited since 1938, when the Baker family first opened the old stagecoach stop to city slickers. You can pitch in with ranch chores if you wish, or you can watch and learn from the ranch hands who tend this 2,500-acre spread. By midweek most tenderfoots are ready to ride horseback to an overnight campout in a high mountain meadow. Weekly rates include lodging, meals, hot-springs pool, and horseback riding.

Although the four seasons come and go in the nearby Walla Walla Valley, the *Frazier Farmstead Museum and Gardens* (541–938–4636), at 1403 Chestnut Street in Milton-Freewater, seems preserved in time, resembling a slice of small-town America at the turn of the twentieth century. The six-acre farmstead, with its large, white, ca. 1892 house, gardens, and outbuildings, is located near downtown Walla Walla, Washington. William Samuel Frazier and his wife, Rachel Paulina, first bought a 320-acre land claim here, near the Walla Walla River, and built a cabin in 1868.

The family, including seven children, left Texas in the early spring of 1867 in three wagons and arrived in the valley at the base of the Blue Mountains in late autumn of that year. A plain pine secretary desk transported in one of the wagons is one of the prized pieces you can see in the house. When the farmstead was willed to the Milton-Freewater Area Foundation in 1978, to be maintained as a museum, volunteers from the local historical society cataloged more

## TOP ANNUAL EVENTS IN NORTHEASTERN OREGON

**Pendleton Underground Comes to Life**
early April or May
(541) 276–0730

**Wagons Ho!**
Baker City; late May
(800) 523–1235

**Wallowa Valley Festival of the Arts**
Joseph; mid-June
(800) 585–4121

**Catherine Creek Junior Rodeo**
Union; mid-July
(541) 963–8588

**Friendship Feast and Pow Wow**
(gathering of Native Americans, town residents, and visitors)
Wallowa; mid-July
(541) 886–3101

**Grant County Kruzers Auto Festival**
Prairie City; first Saturday in August
(541) 575–2533

**Bronze, Blues & Brews**
Joseph; early August
(541) 432–2215

**Alpenfest**
Wallowa Lake; late September
(541) 426–4622

**Pendleton Round-Up/ Happy Canyon Pageant**
Pendleton; mid-September
(541) 276–7411

**Hells Canyon Mule Days**
Enterprise; mid-September
(800) 585–4121

than 700 items and memorabilia, including vintage farm equipment, old photographs, heirloom linens, and family letters from the Civil War. The museum is open April through December; visitors are welcome Thursday through Saturday from 11:00 A.M. to 4:00 P.M. Don't miss the wonderful perennial garden behind the farmhouse.

If you hanker after a good cup of java or a tasty meal before leaving Milton-Freewater, stop at **Ron's Place** at 1014 South Main Street (541–938–5229) for great salads, pizza, and steaks; **Old Town Restaurant** at 513 North Main Street (541–938–2025); or **JP's on the Green** at the Milton-Freewater Golf Course, 299 Catherine Street (541–938–0911), for a scenic setting as well as good vittles.

It's time to head into the heart of northeast Oregon's ranch country, driving south via U.S. Highway 395 past **McKay Creek National Wildlife Refuge,** past **Battle Mountain State Park** (where you can camp at a brisk 4,300-foot elevation), and toward Ukiah, Lehman Springs, and the Umatilla National Forest. Speaking of hot water, **Lehman Hot Springs** (541–427–3015; www .lehmanhotsprings.com) has warmed travelers, including Native American families, for hundreds of years. If you'd like to swim or float a spell, detour at Ukiah and access the historic resort via Highway 244 (about an hour south of Pendleton). Bubbling from the ground at temperatures of 140–157 degrees Fahrenheit, the waters are cooled to around 88–92 degrees in the large pool and to 100–106 degrees in the adjacent small pools. Facilities include cabins, RV spaces, and primitive campsites. Closed during winter months.

US 395 connects with U.S. Highway 26 at Mount Vernon, and turning east you'll reach another historic cattle town, John Day. *NOTE:* Stay alert—you may need to halt for a short spell anywhere along this route when cattle herds are being moved from one grazing area to another.

US 26 meanders into the **John Day Valley,** where vast cattle ranches spread to the east and where yellow pine is logged in the Malheur National Forest to the south and north. Native peoples roamed for thousands of years in this region, hunting in the same mountains and fishing the rivers and streams. Many features in the area were named for John Day, the Virginia pioneer, explorer, and trapper who in 1812 traveled through the area with the Overland Expedition of the Pacific Fur Company, on his way to the mouth of the Columbia River and the new fur-trading settlement of Astoria. Throughout this region also live mule deer, Rocky Mountain elk, antelope, mountain sheep, and many species of upland game.

At the **Grant County Museum** (541–575–0362) and also at **Oxbow Trade Company** (541–575–2911), both on South Canyon Boulevard, US 395, in nearby Canyon City (you're at an elevation of 3,197 feet here), you'll see more

## OTHER ATTRACTIONS WORTH SEEING IN NORTHEASTERN OREGON

**Eastern Oregon Livestock Show**
Union (early June)

**Eastern Oregon Fire Truck Museum**
La Grande
(800) 848–9969

**Circa 1912 Elgin Opera House**
Elgin

**Pendleton Round-Up Hall of Fame**
Pendleton
(541) 278–0815

**Tamastslikt Cultural Institute**
Pendleton; (800) 654–9453

**Umatilla County Courthouse and its one-hundred-year-old Seth Thomas clock and clock tower**
Pendleton; www.pendleton-oregon.org

than one hundred vintage horse-drawn vehicles, an old jail from a nearby ghost town—Greenhorn, located just northeast of John Day—and a cabin that reportedly once belonged to poet Joaquin Miller. In its heyday Canyon City bulged with more than 10,000 miners and gold prospectors; gold was discovered here in 1862 by several miners who were on their way to the goldfields in Idaho. Whiskey Gulch, Canyon Creek, and nearby streams produced several million dollars' worth of the gold stuff before the turn of the twentieth century. The museum is open June through September from 9:30 A.M. to 4:30 P.M. Monday through Saturday, and from 1:00 to 5:00 P.M. Sunday.

Each year on a Saturday in mid-May, to usher in and welcome the arrival of spring at this bracing altitude of 4,700 feet, the Seneca townsfolk dive into a load of barbecued fresh oysters at an annual *Oyster Feed.* Community members drive over to the coast the day before to get fresh oysters, and these are barbecued in their shells at the city park and served up with melted butter, garlic bread, salads, and other goodies prepared by the Seneca folks. Other festivities during the day include a men's and a women's canoe race on the nearby Silvies River. Seneca is located on US 395 about 20 miles south of US 26.

Proceeds from the Oyster Feed help to maintain the nine-hole *Seneca Golf Course.* The golf course is usually open by April or May depending on spring snow conditions; pay for your nine holes at the Bear Valley Mini-Mart. The scenic little golf course, built by volunteers, wraps around the Silvies River several times, and golfers go back and forth over a log bridge, a handsome truss style constructed by local builder Storm Carpenter and his volunteer crew.

Year-round activities in the Strawberry Mountain area include hunting, hiking, backcountry camping, fishing on the Malheur River, snowmobiling and cross-country skiing, and spying wildlife such as deer, elk, and antelope. Mountain goats can often be seen up at Strawberry Lake in the Strawberry Mountain Wilderness. For current information on hiking trails, contact Blue Mountain Ranger District, 431 Patterson Bridge Road, John Day (541–575–3000). One of the easiest trails, for example, is the McClellan Mountain Trail #216, a 10-mile hike from 5,600 feet to 7,400 feet elevation. For those in excellent shape, a more difficult hike is the Little Strawberry Lake Trail, a 6-mile hike that ends at Little Strawberry Lake at 7,200 feet elevation. Snow lovers can find a good sledding hill and a rope tow at Dixie Mountain Ski Area, located about 12 miles east of Prairie City via US 26 toward Sumpter. Stop by the Grant County Visitor Center, 281 West Main Street, John Day (541–575–0547) to pick up current maps and brochures about the area. Ask about the **Strawberry Mountain Scenic Route** and about the **Kam Wah Chung Museum.** The former home of a Chinese herbal doctor who served Chinese immigrants who worked in the gold mines at the turn of the twentieth century, this unusual small museum is located on Northwest Canton Street in the John Day City Park.

## Tree Species for Building a Log House—Notes from Builders Storm and Babe Carpenter

**Douglas fir:** Similar to larch in strength but not as uniform if from drier eastern Oregon, limiting lengths to about 55 feet. Fir logs from the moist Cascade Mountains, however, are straight and long.

**Larch:** Often a favorite because of its uniformity, straightness, and structural strength. The Carpenters have used larch logs to span 80 feet, with log lengths up to 95 feet.

**Lodgepole pine:** This slender pine has been used for log homes more than any other species west of the Rocky Mountains. The logs are straight and uniform, moderate in strength, and decay resistant. Log size is limited to 10–15 inches average diameter with lengths up to 55 feet.

**Ponderosa pine:** These logs exhibit a warm, golden color accented with streaks of blue stain. Although not as strong as larch and fir, ponderosa pine logs are available in long lengths and with diameters up to 36 inches.

**Spruce:** These logs are fairly uniform, with a pleasing appearance. Lightweight yet strong.

**Western juniper:** This species of aromatic juniper offers extreme character and shade variation; the logs are also very decay resistant. Great irregularity and taper with butt-to-tip ratios as much as three to one make this species labor-intensive; by using this prolific tree the pressure on species in higher demand can be lessened.

## Saddle Up!

Do you find yourself hankerin' for an out west experience complete with cowboy or cowgirl boots, well-worn jeans, and a western style hat? If so, give these friendly folks a call and head in several directions to find western-style digs in the Beaver State that come with horses, cattle, and wide-angle mountain, river, or high desert vistas along with comfortable guest rooms and great vittles:

**Aspen Ridge Resort**
Bly; (541) 884–8685
www.aspenrr.com

**Bar M Ranch**
Adams; (888) 824–3381
www.barmranch.com

**Big K Guest Ranch**
Elkton; (800) 390–2445
www.big-k.com

**Cow Trails Ranch**
Wamic; (541) 544–3010
www.cowtrails.com

**Flying M Ranch**
Yamhill; (503) 662–3222
www.flying-m-ranch.com

**Lake Creek Base Camp**
Frenchglen; (800) 977–3995
www.steensmountain.com

**Long Hollow Ranch**
Sisters; (877) 923–1901
www.lhranch.com

**Minam River Lodge**
Joseph; (541) 432–6545
www.minamlodgeoutfitters.com

**Rock Springs Guest Ranch**
Bend; (800) 225–3833
www.rocksprings.com

**Willow Springs Guest Ranch**
Lakeview; (541) 947–5499
www.willowspringsguestranch.com

**Wilson Ranches Retreat**
Fossil; (866) 763–2227
www.wilsonranchesretreat.com

For good coffee, espresso, and lunch eats in the John Day area, try *Java Jungle,* 142 East Main Street, John Day (541–575–2224), and *Uptown Girls Coffee, Bakery, & Gifts,* 225 South Front Street in Prairie City (541–820–4292). For good dinner eateries check out *The Grubsteak Mining Company Restaurant* (541–575–2714) on Main Street in John Day and *Shoshoni Winds Restaurant* (541–820–3767) at 128 West Front Street in Prairie City. Locals also rave about eats at *The Snaffle Bit Dinner House* (541–575–2426), with a lively western theme, located on US 395 just south of the traffic light in John Day.

A few miles east, near the small community of Prairie City, the Jacobs family welcomes travelers to *Riverside School House Bed & Breakfast,* 28076 North River Road (541–820–4731; www.riversideschoolhouse.com). Nestled near the headwaters of the John Day River, the old structure dates back to sometime between 1898 and 1905. Guests enjoy a lovely suite in the renovated schoolhouse that comes with cozy sitting areas and a private bathroom.

Airplane buffs might enjoy stopping at Prairie City in early September to take in the *Fly-in Fun Day* at the Grant County Regional Airport (541–575–1151). The event features a mouthwatering barbecue, parachute demonstrations, remote-controlled airplanes, small-aircraft aerobatic demonstrations, and scenic flight rides.

While you're in the area, be sure to plan a visit to the *DeWitt Depot Museum* (800–769–5664). This historic railroad depot in Depot Park in Prairie City contains memorabilia from Grant County's pioneer days. The depot was the end of the line when the Sumpter Valley Railway was extended from Baker City to Prairie City in 1910. It served as the economic lifeline for logging companies, mining outfits, and families for some fifty years before this section of the rail line was finally closed. Rail buffs and volunteers are in the process of reclaiming a section of the rail line in the Sumpter area. The museum is open Wednesday through Saturday from mid-May to October.

Highway 26 winds north and east over Dixie Mountain Pass to Austin Junction, continues toward Unity, and then descends some 50 miles to connect with the Vale-Ontario-Nyssa communities on the Oregon-Idaho border. If you take this route, you could consider detouring at Unity and camping out at *Unity Lake State Park* on the Unity Reservoir. From here you could access Baker City via Highway 245 connecting with Highway 7 between Sumpter and Baker City. If time allows, stop at the *Eldorado Ditch Company Cafe & Lounge* in Unity (541–446–3447) for good vittles, starting at 7:00 A.M.

Before continuing to Baker City, detour at Sumpter for a nostalgic train ride on the *Sumpter Valley Narrow Gauge Railroad* (541–894–2268; www .svry.com). Board the train at the *Sumpter Valley Dredge State Heritage Area* (541–894–2486), then ride behind the puffing, wood-burning 1914 Heisler steam locomotive *Stumpdodger* through the forested valley etched with piles of dredge tailings. The old train once transported gold ore and logs from the hard-rock mountain mines and pine-dotted Sumpter Valley. During the hour-long ride, watch for geese, heron, beaver, deer, and coyotes—and an occasional raid by "honest-to-goodness train robbers." The train runs weekends through the summer and into September.

A live ghost town, Sumpter is home to about 140 residents, four restaurants, two stores, and a restored ca. 1900 church and offers visitors three gigantic flea markets, a winter snowmobile festival, and more than 200 miles of cross-country ski trails. While you are eating at *Scoop-N-Steamer Cafe* (541–894–2236), the *Sumpter Nugget Restaurant* (541–894–2366), or the *Elkhorn Saloon and Cafe* (541–894–2244), you'll most likely encounter one of those old prospectors and hear a yarn or two about the 1800s gold-rush days and how the town was destroyed by fire in 1917. Snoop into more Sumpter history at **Gold Post Museum** located at the visitor center (541–894–2362) and at **Cracker Creek Mining Museum** across from the Sumpter Valley Dredge.

Although you won't find overnight accommodations in any of the abandoned ghost towns in the area, you can find a cozy room to bed down for the night at **Scoop-N-Steamer Log Cabins** (541–894–2236), at the **Depot Motor Inn,** 179 South Mill Street (800–390–2522), or at **Sumpter Bed and Breakfast,** at 344 North Columbia Street (541–894–0048; www.sumpterbb.com). Over a hearty mountain breakfast, you may find yourself in the company of hikers, bikers, history buffs, and, during the winter months, snowmobilers and both downhill and cross-country skiers. *NOTE:* For road conditions on the major mountain passes in the state, call (800) 977–6368 or see www.tripcheck.com. Be prepared to carry traction devices into all highway and byway areas of northeastern Oregon during winter months.

To explore the historic Sumpter area on your own, get a copy of the **Elkhorn Drive Scenic Byway** map, which is packed with helpful information and photographs. This self-guided summertime drive will take you along the 100-mile Sumpter Valley loop, where you can see old mines, abandoned mine

## Ghost Towns Galore

Weathered storefronts, sagging porches and partial fences, breezes rattling through rusted hinges and blowing through falling-down rafters and roofs? Ghost locomotives that run on old tracks through the valleys and mountains? Ron Harr, railroad buff and avid historian of the Sumpter Valley Railroad, says that tales of lost locomotives in the thick pine, fir, and larch forests in the Sumpter area west of Baker City have circulated for years. Such characters as Skedaddle Smith, One-eyed Dick, and '49 Jimmie reportedly lived in Granite in the old days. Travelers can visit this and other remnants of once-thriving mountain towns of northeastern Oregon's gold country. Maybe you'll spot one of the ghost locomotives along the way.

Check out these ghost-town sites:

**Whitney:** 14 miles southwest of Sumpter in the scenic Whitney Valley

**Bourne:** 7 miles up Cracker Creek north from Sumpter

**Auburn:** 10 miles south of Baker City

**Flora:** north of Joseph and Enterprise via Highway 3

For current information and maps, call the volunteers at Sumpter Valley Railway at (541) 894–2268 or (866) 894–2268.

shafts, and even a ghost town or two. If you're a ghost-town buff, visit the remains of several mining towns along the route.

You can obtain a copy of the Elkhorn Drive Scenic Byway map from the Whitman Ranger District in Baker City (541–523–4476).

Located about 16 miles northwest of Sumpter via the Elkhorn Drive Scenic Byway, *Granite,* population 250, sits at a crisp elevation of 4,800 feet and offers travelers a jumbo-size log-style inn, *The Lodge at Granite* (541–755–5200). Owners Pat and Mitch Fielding built the handsome 6,200-square-foot structure of 8-inch pine, two-sided cut, and with the traditional white chinking. Folks can choose from nine pleasant guest rooms on the second floor. Pat, who was the primary chinking guru, serves a continental breakfast to guests. She's also the town's mayor. Pick up dinner grub in Sumpter or ask about Granite's *Outback Cafe.*

# Oregon Trail Territory

The settlement of Baker City grew up around a mill built in the 1860s by J. W. Virtue to process ore brought from those first hard-rock gold mines. By 1890 the town had grown to nearly 6,700, larger than any city in the eastern section of the state, and a fledgling timber industry had been started by David Eccles, who also was founder of the Sumpter Valley Railroad. When mining declined after World War I, loggers, cattle herders, and ranchers replaced those colorful miners and gold prospectors.

The *Baker City Historic District* includes about sixty-four early buildings, some constructed from volcanic tuff and stone. Also worth a visit is the *Historical Cemetery,* located near the high school. For both attractions pick up the self-guided walking-tour map at the visitor center on Campbell Street. And plan a visit, too, to the U.S. National Bank, at 2000 Main Street, where you'll see a whopping, 80.4-ounce gold nugget that was found in the area during the early gold rush days.

To sleep in sumptuous splendor in Baker City, consider the renovated and refurbished 1889 *Geiser Grand Hotel* located at 1996 Main Street (541–523–1889; www.geisergrand.com). Guests choose from thirty suites and guest rooms and enjoy the hotel's historic restaurant and lounge, meeting and private dining rooms, and, perhaps the loveliest, the splendid oval mahogany Palm Tea Court with skylight, all polished and new again. In the hotel eatery, Geiser Grill, you could order such tasty entrees as Buffalo Prime Rib.

Located just a few blocks north of the visitor center, at the corner of Campbell and Grove Streets, is the *Oregon Trail Regional Museum* (541–523–9308), featuring a collection of pioneer artifacts gathered from the Old Oregon

Trail. Often such prized possessions as trunks, furniture, china, silver, and glassware were left along the trail in order to lighten the wagons. The kids will enjoy the historic gold mining exhibits, an impressive gem and mineral collection, and regional Native American baskets, arrowheads, tools, and clothing. Be sure to look for the vintage freight wagon, the old school bus, the large sleigh, and a number of vintage autos and trucks, all stored in a cavernous space to the rear of the building. Each one has a story to tell. The museum is open daily from 10:00 A.M. to 4:00 P.M. but is closed during winter months.

For cozy lodgings in Baker City check with *Off the Beaten Path Bed & Breakfast,* 2510 Court Avenue (541–523–9230) and with *The Baer House Bed & Breakfast,* 2333 Main Street (800–709–7637; www.baerhouse.com). For pleasant eateries in the Baker City area, stop at *Mad Matilda's Coffeehouse* at 1917 Main Street (541–523–4588) for tasty sandwiches, pastries, java, and lively gossip; at *Baker City Cafe,* a local favorite in new digs at 1840 Main Street (541–523–6099); and at *Arceo's* for great Mexican fare served in a cozy caboose located at 781 Campbell Street (541–523–9000). Two other favorites in

## Cycle Oregon

Jonathan Nicholas, sage columnist for the *Oregonian,* our state's largest newspaper, which is based in Portland, says, "Oregon looks its best from the seat of a bicycle." Here's an individual who walks his talk, or in this case, pedals his talk. Some years ago, in 1988, Jonathan hosted the first Cycle Oregon tour, and it's been going strong ever since. My very own sister participated in the second tour in 1989. "My personal best," she said as she recalled pedaling up to the rim of Crater Lake at an altitude of some 6,000 feet. Do many biking enthusiasts join this intrepid bicycling newspaper columnist? Yes, 1,500 of them, to be exact. Cycle Oregon is open to the first 1,500 riders who register (800–CYCLEOR); I think the trip, which takes off in early September each year, has always been filled.

Jonathan says about the Wallowas, "This is the land of [the Nez Percé tribe's] Chief Joseph, a man who understood a great deal about life, liberty, and the pursuit of happiness. He surely would have enjoyed undertaking some of that pursuit on a bicycle." (Source: the *Oregonian,* February 17, 1999.)

I tend to disagree, however, with Jonathan's assertion; I don't think Chief Joseph would have chosen to undertake any journey aboard a bicycle. But Cycle Oregon folks definitely enjoy climbing aboard, and I have no doubt that as long as Jonathan is willing to hunker his buns onto a bicycle seat and host this fabulous event, 1,500 youngsters and oldsters will continue to cycle along with him. Actually, I think I'll volunteer for the support crew. If you're interested in the event, log onto www.cycle oregon.com for all the current details and the route.

Baker City include **Sorbenots Coffee Shop,** 1270 Campbell Street (541–523–1678) and **Barley Brown's Brewpub,** 2190 Main Street (541–523–4266).

From Baker City detour about 5 miles east on Highway 86 to Flagstaff Summit to visit the impressive **National Historic Oregon Trail Interpretive Center** (541–523–1843). This panoramic site overlooks miles of the original wagon trail ruts that have, over the last century and a half since the 1840s and 1850s, receded into the sagebrush- and bitterbrush-littered landscape. Now the ruts are just dim outlines, reminders of the pioneer past, and eyes squint to follow the old trail across the wide desert toward the Blue Mountains, a low, snow-dusted range that hovers on the far northwestern horizon.

In the main gallery of the 23,000-square-foot center, more than 300 photographs, drawings, paintings, and maps depict the toil, sweat, and hardships of the 2,000-mile journey from Independence, Missouri, to Fort Vancouver, Oregon City, and the lush Willamette Valley located south of the Portland area.

The interpretive center is open May 1 through September 30 from 9:00 A.M. to 6:00 P.M. daily and October 1 through April 30 to 4:00 P.M. daily. *NOTE:* Bring wide-brimmed hats and water if you want to walk the nature trails here—summers are hot and dry, with temperatures often 90–100 degrees Fahrenheit.

# Hells Canyon and the High Wallowas

While the Oregon Trail left the Snake River at Farewell Bend, southeast of Baker City toward Ontario, and continued northwest into Baker Valley and over the Blue Mountains toward The Dalles, the ancient river headed directly north, chiseling and sculpting **Hells Canyon**—a spectacular, 6,000-foot-deep fissure between high craggy mountains. To experience this awesome chunk of geography that separates Oregon and Idaho and is the deepest river gorge in the world, head east to Halfway via Highway 86 from Flagstaff Summit.

Included in this vast region are the 108,000-acre **Hells Canyon Wilderness,** the 662,000-acre **Hells Canyon National Recreation Area,** and the **Wild and Scenic Snake River Corridor.** Visit the canyon during spring or early autumn, when native shrubs, trees, and flowers are at their best; summers are quite hot and dry. If possible, take one of the float or jet-boat trips on the river or, if you're in good shape, a guided backpack or horseback trip into the wilderness areas. For helpful information contact the U.S. Forest Service Wallowa Mountain Visitor Center in Enterprise (541–742–4222) or Hells Canyon Adventures (541–785–3352; www.hellscanyonadventures.com).

Try lovely Hewitt Park and the 50-mile Brownlee Reservoir for picnicking, fishing, and camping on the waters of the Snake River behind Brownlee Dam, just south of Halfway.

## MUSEUMS, CULTURAL AND HERITAGE CENTERS IN OREGON

**Columbia Gorge Discovery Center & Wasco County Historical Museum**
The Dalles
(541) 296–8600
www.gorgediscovery.org
Interprets the geological story of the Columbia Gorge and tells the history of the peoples who have lived there.

**Four Rivers Cultural Center**
Ontario
(541) 889–8191
www.4rcc.com
Tells the story of the Northern Paiute tribe and three other cultures of the Treasure Valley area: Basque, Spanish, and Japanese.

**The Museum at Warm Springs**
Warm Springs
(541) 553–3331
www.warmsprings.com/museum
Presents geology, history, heirlooms, and traditions of the Warm Springs, Wasco, and Northern Paiute tribes.

**Tamastslikt Cultural Institute**
Pendleton
(800) 654–9453
www.tamastslikt.com
Presents the history and culture of the Cayuse, Walla Walla, and Umatilla tribes and offers interpretation of the Oregon Trail migration.

You might refill your picnic basket and cooler in Baker City or in Halfway and take the narrow road that winds from Oxbow Dam along a 23-mile scenic stretch of the Snake River down to Hells Canyon Dam spillway and one of the jet-boat launch areas. There is a portable restroom here and a visitor information trailer, but no other services. In late spring you'll see masses of yellow lupine, yellow and gold daisies, and pink wild roses blooming among crevices in craggy basalt bluffs and outcroppings that hover over the narrow roadway. It's well worth the 46-mile round-trip to experience this primitive but accessible section of the Hells Canyon National Recreation Area (541–426–5546; www.fs.fed.us/r6/w-w). You could enjoy your picnic at the boat-launch site or return to **Hells Canyon Park,** located about halfway back to Highway 86. The park offers picnic areas, comfortable grassy places to sit, and a boat launch, all next to the river. Overnight campsites are available at Copperfield Park, located on this scenic drive about 17 miles from Halfway. Check out comfortable bed-and-breakfast inns in the Halfway area—**The Inn at Clear Creek Farm,** 48212 Clear Creek Road (541–742–2238), an especially good choice for families and for nature lovers. **Pine Valley Lodge** offers funky and fun bed-and-breakfast accommodations in downtown Halfway, 163 North Main Street (541–742–2027). For casual eats in Halfway, try **Mimi's Cafe** (541–742–4646), and for juicy prime rib and steaks try **Stockman's** (541–742–2301), both on Main Street.

Heading north from Baker City toward La Grande, take old U.S. Highway 30 instead of I–84 and detour at Haines to eat at one of the best and most well-known restaurants in the northeastern section of the state, *Haines Steak House* (541–856–3639). After the salad bar you'll work your way through a bowl of hearty soup, western-style baked beans, and a delicious charcoal-grilled steak fresh off the rangelands. The restaurant, open for dinner Wednesday through Monday, is on old US 30 in Haines, about 10 miles north of Baker City.

If you pass through this region of the Beaver State in mid-spring, say, late May, continue from Haines on Highway 237, bypassing I–84 for a while longer, and drive slowly through the small community of Union. Pause here to feast your eyes on a number of enormous lilac trees in full, glorious bloom. Many of the original cuttings were brought across the Oregon Trail in the 1840s. Also look for patches of wild iris that bloom profusely in pastures and fields between North Powder and Union.

During winter months folks can enjoy a horse-drawn wagon ride to see some 200 head of Rocky Mountain elk; check with *Elk Viewing Excursions* in North Powder (541–856–3356). Or take the North Powder exit 285 off I–84 and go west to the *Elkhorn Wildlife Area* (541–898–2826). Rocky Mountain elk and mule deer gather at this feeding site December to March.

And, located in the rustic *Union County Museum* (541–562–6003), 333 South Main Street, Union, in a structure built in 1881, you can visit the new home of the extensive *Cowboy Heritage Collection.* Besides showing the evolution of the cowboy myth, from nineteenth-century dime novels to 1940s B movies, you'll see boots, spurs, saddles, and hand-braided ropes galore. The exhibit also spotlights early Texas trail drives, railhead towns such as Abilene and Dodge City, and flinty-eyed frontier marshals. The exhibit is open Monday through Saturday 10:00 A.M. to 5:00 P.M.

Travelers will find pleasant overnight lodgings at the renovated, ca. 1921 *Union Hotel,* 326 North Main Street (541–562–6135; www.theunionhotel.com). Guest rooms come with names like Annie Oakley Suite, Clark Gable Room, and Mount Emily Room. Former owners Twyla and Allen Cornelius bought the seventy-six-room hostelry in 1996 and spent countless hours stripping old paint, repainting, carpeting, and decorating the lobby, ladies parlor, restaurant, and guest rooms. Some forty Main Street properties including the hotel were recently named to the city's new historic district.

In *La Grande,* just a few miles northwest of Union via Highway 203, you could call innkeepers Marjorie and Pat McClure at *Stange Manor Bed & Breakfast Inn,* located at 1612 Walnut Street (541–963–2400). In this spacious Georgian colonial mansion, built in the 1920s by an early lumber baron, you can rest in elegant comfort surrounded by lovely grounds, with several large lilac trees and a collection of old roses.

Eateries in the La Grande area include **Mammacita's,** for great homemade Mexican food (110 Depot Street; 541–963-6223); **Foley Station,** for fine dining (1011 Adams Avenue; 541–963–7473); **Ten Depot Street,** for casual fine dining in a historic brick building with an early 1900s bar (541–963–8766); and **Highway 30 Coffee Company,** 1302 Adams Avenue (541–963–6821), a favorite with many local folks. While out and about La Grande stop by 102 Elm Street to see the vintage fire engines at **Eastern Oregon Fire Museum** (541–963–8588; www.visitlagrande.com), located in the historic former fire station.

Next, drive from La Grande about 65 miles via Highway 82 into Enterprise and Joseph to treat yourself to a ride on the **Wallowa Lake Tramway** (541–432-5331). Snug with three other mountain lovers in a small, open-air gondola, you'll ascend safely in fifteen minutes to the top of 8,200-foot Mount Howard for some of the most breathtaking views in the entire region. More than a mile below, Wallowa Lake shimmers in the afternoon sun, reaching into the **Eagle Cap Wilderness** and mirroring eight other snowcapped peaks. To the east lie the rugged canyons of the Imnaha and Snake Rivers. As one soaks in the alpine vastness of it all, it's easy to understand why Chief Joseph and his Nez Percé tribe fought to remain in this beautiful area in the mid-1800s when the first white settlers began to encroach on their historic territory. At the top of the tramway are short trails for hiking and a snack shop, **Summit Deli & Alpine Patio,** for cold drinks or hot coffee before you head back down the mountain. Call ahead for the current schedule, although the tram is generally open daily from June through August and part time in May and September.

Rather than hanging in the clouds in a gondola you'd prefer being closer to terra firma? Not to worry, call the new **Eagle Cap Excursion Train** and ask about current schedules for scenic train rides through the pines from

Wallowa Lake Tramway

# Go on a Field Trip with Lewis and Clark

The Corps of Discovery, thirty-three folks including Clark's Newfoundland dog, Seaman, paused and camped in the eastern section of the Columbia Gorge and Snake River areas during 1805, on their way to the Pacific Ocean, and in spring 1806, returning home. To learn more about the expedition, and to see some sites where Lewis and Clark were, visit:

**Lewis and Clark Timeline,** etched in pavement in Clarkston, Washington

**Snake River,** from the Clarkston-Lewiston area to Pasco, Washington

**Columbia River,** from Pasco 300 miles to the Pacific Ocean

**Sacajawea State Park,** campground and interpretive center, near Kennewick, Washington

**Maryhill Museum,** with native crafts and carvings, near The Dalles, Oregon, and Goldendale, Washington (www.maryhillmuseum.org)

**Hat Rock State Park,** near Umatilla, Oregon

**Horsethief Lake State Park,** east of Bingen, Washington

**U.S. Highway 12** east through Dayton and Pomeroy and to Lewiston, Washington, roughly parallels the party's return journey in spring 1806

Joseph to Wallowa and from Wallowa west along the Minam River and Elgin (800–323–7330; www.eaglecaptrain.com).

The Wallowa Lake area, 6 miles from Joseph, opens for the summer season on Memorial Day weekend; winter visits offer miles of cross-country ski trails through a snowy wonderland.

If the notion of packing your tent and camping beneath tall alpine fir at the edge of a mountain lake sounds inviting, consider making a reservation at the Wallowa State Park campground; call the state reservation number (800–452–5687). Be sure to call at least six months ahead, because everyone else likes to go off the beaten path here as well. Or you can make reservations at *Wallowa Lake Lodge* (800–585–4121; www.wallowalake.net/eo), perched at the south end of the lake since 1923 and recently renovated. In addition to twenty-two rooms in the lodge, eight cozy cabins with kitchens and fireplaces are also available. In the lodge dining room you can sit at a table overlooking the lake and enjoy delicious entrees from Northwest farms, fields, and streams. The lodge and restaurant are open from May 1 until mid-October, then on weekends during the rest of the year.

For a pleasant overnight bed-and-breakfast experience, about as far off the beaten path as you can get, call innkeepers Sandy and Nick Vidan at *Imnaha River Inn Bed & Breakfast* (541–577–6002 or 866–601–9214) to see about rooms in their 7,000-square-foot log home near the Imnaha River and the hamlet of Imnaha—about 30 miles north of Joseph. Guest rooms come with names like Elk, Fish, Bear, Cowboy, and Indian; baths are shared, but each room has its own sink. Check with the Wallowa County Visitor Center in Enterprise (800–585–4121; www.wallowacountychamber.com) for information about wilderness cabins, RV parks, and other campgrounds.

One fun excursion is a visit to the *Valley Bronze Foundry* (541–432–7551), which offers tours year-round, although schedules may vary, so call ahead. On the one-hour tour, you'll get to see the labor-intensive bronze-casting process, including the "lost wax process," a production method the business has used since it began operation with a handful of workers in 1982. Many elegant bronze sculptures are on display, some of which have been sent as far away as Berlin, Germany.

For maps and information about camping and hiking in the Wallowa Mountains and Eagle Cap Wilderness, contact the U.S. Forest Service Wallowa Mountains Visitor Center (541–426–5546; www.fs.fed.us/r6/w-w). If you'd like to see this spectacular mountain wilderness area, there are experienced guides and outfitters to contact: *Hurricane Creek Llama Treks* (866–386–8735; www.hcltrek.com) or *Eagle Cap Wilderness Pack Station & High Country Outfitters,* 59761 Wallowa Lake Highway, Joseph (800–681–6222). Ask about short or long rides, including overnight pack trips, and ask about Minam Lodge, located in the heart of the Eagle Cap Wilderness (accessible by horseback or small airplane). During winter months *Wing Ridge Ski Tours* (541–426–4322; www.wingski.com) leads experienced skiers on hut-to-hut ski tours in the snowy Wallowa Mountains.

In this far-flung region of high mountains, winter snows, alpine fir, rushing rivers, and deep canyons, a gray wolf in early February 1999 decided to pay the Beaver State a visit from neighboring Idaho. With just her radio collar as a passport but with no snowmobile, pickup truck, or sport utility vehicle and with no skis, snowboard, or snowshoes, this lone female wolf known as B-45 apparently swam across the Snake River. Later, B-45 was sighted west of Baker City in the Blue Mountains exhibiting typical wolfish behavior, that of scouting an elk herd for prey. After much public and private debate between the area's ranchers and numerous environmentalists, and with state and federal agencies in the middle, B-45 was captured and returned to her native Idaho.

## OTHER SITES IN THE PACIFIC NORTHWEST

**Columbia Gorge Interpretive Center**
Stevenson, Washington
(509) 427–8211
Presents history of the gorge; contains an enormous Indian fishwheel, a gigantic vintage Corliss steam engine, ancient artifacts, and research library.

**Makah Cultural and Research Center**
Neah Bay, Washington
(360) 645–2711
Interprets the Makah tribe and displays artifacts from Ozette, an ancient coastal village.

**Nez Percé National Historical Park**
Spalding, Idaho
(208) 843–2261
Features tours and programs that focus on Nez Percé history and culture.

**Shoshone–Bannock Tribal Museum**
Fort Hall, Idaho
(208) 237–9791
Displays a fine collection of photos and artifacts.

**Whitman Mission National Historic Site**
Walla Walla, Washington
(509) 522–6360
Fine museum and outdoor sites interpret the Cayuse and missionary conflicts of the 1840s.

**Yakama Nation Cultural Heritage Center**
Toppenish, Washington
(509) 865–2800
Interprets the culture and traditions of the Yakama Nation.

Travelers visiting this wild and scenic area of northeastern Oregon who also are interested in animal issues can contact the following sources for current information about the Northern Rocky Mountain Wolf Recovery Program and about other animals of the wild such as black bears, mountain goats, and mountain lions: Oregon Natural Desert Association, www.onda.org, (503) 525–0193; U.S. Fish & Wildlife Service, La Grande region, (541) 963–2138. If you would like to have firsthand experience of the great outdoors in the area, call *Joseph Fly Shoppe* (541–432–4343) or *Eagle Cap Fishing Guides* in Joseph (800–940–3688) to arrange a history, natural-history, birding, or fishing tour. You might even spot another visiting wolf or a coyote.

To explore on your own, during summer months, and with a sturdy four-wheel-drive vehicle, ask about the condition of the gravel road up to *Hat Point,* elevation 6,982 feet, with its showstopping views of the Snake River and its canyon, which is 1,276 feet deep, and Idaho's Seven Devils Mountains, over 9,000 feet in elevation. The spectacular viewpoint is accessed about 25 miles from Imnaha (restaurant, limited groceries, seasonal motel, and no gasoline), which is located about 30 miles northeast of Joseph via Highway 350 and skirting Little Sheep Creek. A number of years ago, residents of this tiny, unincorporated village barbecued five bears and fried 150 rattlesnakes for a gigantic

Bear and Rattlesnake Feed. "But we ran out by early afternoon," says Dave Tanzy, proprietor of the rustic Imnaha Store and Tavern built in 1908. "We shoulda had six bears."

For more traditional vittles in the Joseph-Enterprise area, check out *Mountain Air Cafe* (541–432–0233) and *Old Town Cafe* (541–432–9898), both on Main Street in Joseph; *Wildflour Bakery* (541–432–7225), also on Main Street, for breads, cinnamon rolls, and tasty breakfast and lunch fare; *Vali's Alpine Deli & Restaurant* (541–432–5691) on Wallowa Lake Highway, just outside Joseph; and *Cloud 9 Bakery* (541–426–3790) on Courthouse Square in Enterprise for lunches and delectable bakery treats.

The farthest northeastern corner of the state, in the high Wallowa Mountains and Eagle Cap Wilderness, was once home to Chief Joseph and the Nez Percé Indians. To experience a historical section of the Nez Percé country, ask for directions to *Nee-Me-Poo Trail* (meaning "route to freedom"), located about 15 miles north of Imnaha (the last 10 miles are best negotiated with high-clearance vehicles; no vehicles pulling trailers). Here you can walk in the footsteps of Chief Joseph and his people. Chief Joseph, in 1879, said, "The earth is the mother of all people, and all people should have equal rights upon it . . . let me be a free man . . . free to travel. . . ."

# Places to Stay in Northeastern Oregon

## BAKER CITY

**Best Western Sunridge Inn**
Sunridge Lane
(877) 867–4343

**Eldorado Inn**
695 Campbell Street
(800) 537–5756

## GRANITE

**The Log Lodge at Granite**
1525 McCann Street
(541) 755–5200

## JOHN DAY

**Best Western
John Day Inn**
315 West Main Street
(541) 575–1700

## JOSEPH

**The Bronze Antler
Bed & Breakfast**
309 South Main Street
(866) 520–9769

## LA GRANDE

**Pony Soldier Inn**
Highway 82/Interstate 84
interchange
(541) 963–7195 or
(800) 634–7669

**Quail Run Motor Inn**
2400 Adams Avenue
(541) 963–3400

**Stange Manor
Bed & Breakfast**
1612 Walnut Street
(888) 286–9463

# Places to Eat in Northeastern Oregon

## BAKER CITY

**Geiser Grand Restaurant
& Saloon**
1996 Main Street
(541) 523–1889

Mad Matilda's
Coffeehouse
1917 Main Street
(541) 523–4588

**ELGIN**

Bare Naked Beans
Espresso
Highway 82
(541) 437–1709

**HEREFORD**

Eldorado Ditch Co.
Restaurant
(541) 446–3447

**JOHN DAY**

Java Jungle
142 East Main Street
(541) 575–2224

The Snaffle Bit
Dinner House
U.S. Highway 395
(541) 575–2426

**JOSEPH**

Mountain Air Cafe
Main Street
(541) 432–0233

Wildflour Bakery Cafe
Main Street
(541) 432–7225

**LA GRANDE**

Benchwarmers Pub & Grill
210 Depot Street
(541) 963–9597

Highway 30 Coffee Co.
1302 Adams Avenue
(541) 963–6821

Joe & Sugars
1119 Adams Avenue
(541) 975–5282

**MILTON-FREEWATER**

Old Town Restaurant
513 North Main Street
(541) 938–2025

Ron's Place Cafe
1014 Main Street
(541) 938–5229

**NORTH POWDER**

Uncle Willy's Burgers
190 E Street
(541) 898–2444

## HELPFUL TELEPHONE NUMBERS AND WEB SITES FOR NORTHEASTERN OREGON

Baker County Visitor and
Convention Bureau
(800) 523–1235

Grant County Visitor Center
(800) 769–5664
www.grantcounty.cc

La Grande/Union County
Visitor Center
(800) 848–9969
www.visitlagrande.com

Milton-Freewater Visitor Center
(541) 938–5563
www.mfchamber.com

Oregon Natural Desert Association
(541) 330–2638
www.onda.com

Oregon road conditions
(800) 977–6368
www.tripcheck.com

Pendleton Visitor Center
(541) 276–7411 or (800) 547–8911
www.pendleton-oregon.org

U.S. Forest Service
La Grande Ranger District
(541) 963–7186

Wallowa County Chamber of
Commerce and Visitor Center
(800) 585–4121
www.wallowacountychamber.com

Wallowa–Whitman National Forest
Wallowa Mountains Visitor Center
(541) 426–5546

## PENDLETON

**The Bread Board**
141 South Main Street
(541) 276–4520

**Main Street Diner**
349 South Main Street
(541) 276–1952

**Pendleton Coffee Roasters**
428 South Main Street
(541) 276–2242

**Rooster's Restaurant**
1515 South Gate
(541) 966–1100

## PRAIRIE CITY

**Uptown Girls Coffee, Bakery, & Gifts**
225 South Front Street
(541) 820–4292

# Portland and Environs

## Downtown and Old Town

In the late 1840s **Portland** was a small clump of log cabins on the banks of the Willamette River, where riverboats laden with people and supplies scuttled back and forth between Fort Vancouver (near present-day Vancouver, Washington) and Oregon City, some 20 miles upriver. Early settlers chopped down stands of tall Douglas fir along the riverbanks to make room for those first small cabins, and the place was called The Clearing. Later the tree stumps were whitewashed to prevent folks from stumbling over them after dark, and the nickname Stumptown emerged.

During the 1850s and 1860s, steamboats appeared, and Stumptown became a full-fledged town with a new name decided by the toss of a coin. Now, a century and a half later, the greater Portland area is a large region containing three of the most populated counties in the state—Multnomah, Washington, and Clackamas—and offering visitors a variety of mountains and rivers, vineyards and wineries, museums and historical sites, and contemporary homes and vintage farms as well as theaters, zoos, festivals, gardens, unique shops, eateries, bed-and-breakfast inns, and hostelries.

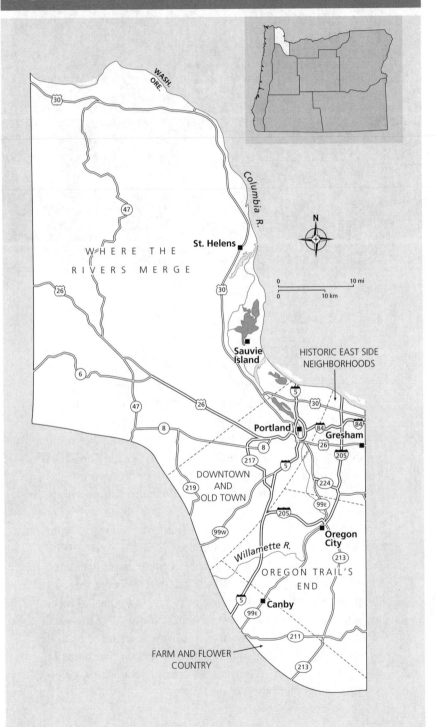

WASH.
ORE.

Columbia R.

St. Helens

N

WHERE THE
RIVERS MERGE

0          10 mi
0      10 km

Sauvie
Island

HISTORIC EAST SIDE
NEIGHBORHOODS

Portland

Gresham

DOWNTOWN
AND
OLD TOWN

Willamette R.

Oregon
City

OREGON TRAIL'S
END

Canby

FARM AND FLOWER
COUNTRY

The city proper and its far-flung environs are now situated on both sides of the broad ***Willamette River,*** stretching east toward Mount Hood, west into the Tualatin Hills toward the Tualatin Valley and Coast Range, and south toward Lake Oswego, West Linn, and historic Oregon City. The Willamette flows into the mighty Columbia River just a few miles northwest of the downtown area. The whitewashed stumps are long gone, but today's visitor will find broad avenues and fountains, parks and lovely public gardens, and, of course, nearly a dozen bridges spanning the Willamette to connect the east and west sides of town.

One of the best ways to get acquainted with the Beaver State's largest city is to take a walking tour of the Historic Old Town area, where Stumptown began. First, stop by the Portland Visitor Information Center at Pioneer Courthouse Square, lower level (503–275–8355; www.travelportland.com), for helpful brochures and maps. The square is located between SW Sixth Street and Broadway at Yamhill Street in downtown Portland. Then slip into your walking shoes and head 6 blocks west, down to the paved esplanade along the Willamette River.

Incidentally, travelers who like to walk can inquire at the visitor center to get the current schedule of walks with a hale and hearty group, an international group of volksmarchers—walking aficionados—that began in Germany, then came to the United States. For further information visit www.walk oregon.org and contact local groups such as East County Wind Walkers and Rose City Roamers.

For a shoreside view of the river, first while away an hour or so at ***River-Place,*** located on the west riverbank near the heart of the downtown area. It

## TOP HITS IN PORTLAND AND ENVIRONS

**The Classical Chinese Garden**
Portland

**Crystal Springs
Rhododendron Garden**
Portland

**Hawthorne Bridge**
Portland

**Historic Sellwood neighborhood**
southeast Portland

**Japanese Garden**
Portland

**Nob Hill neighborhood**
northwest Portland

**Northeast Broadway neighborhood**
Portland

**St. Johns Bridge**
Portland

**Washington Park Rose Gardens**
Portland

contains condominiums and offices, restaurants—one of them floating right on the water—and delis, gift shops and boutiques, the European-style **RiverPlace Hotel** (503–228–3233; www.riverplacehotel.com), and a large boat marina. There are comfortable benches for sitting and watching myriad activities, both on the water and ashore. On blue-sky days, lunching at one of the round tables outdoors is a pleasant option.

On almost any day you can see energetic members of the **Portland Rowing Club** sculling on the river in sleek shells that hold from two to four rowers; one of the best times to watch, though, is at 5:00 A.M., when some of the most devoted rowers scull across the river's early morning, glasslike surface. When the group formed in 1879, it was called the Portland Rowing Association; by 1891 the North Pacific Association of Amateur Oarsmen had been established by active rowing clubs in Portland and as far away as Vancouver, British Columbia, and Coeur d'Alene, Idaho.

## trivia

In 1887, when the first Morrison Street Bridge opened across the river in the heart of the downtown area, the toll was 5 cents per human pedestrian, pig, or sheep and 10 cents for a cow or horse.

World War II brought an end to rowing in Portland for about thirty years, until the early 1970s, when a group of former college oarsmen organized a group called Station L, composed of master oarsmen and college-club crews from both Reed College and Lewis and Clark College. Given the former dusty, leaking boathouse and empty racks, the sport in Portland has come far—the spiffy new racing shells have found not only a permanent home on the new docks at RiverPlace but many ardent participants and enthusiastic spectators as well.

Two women's crews from the Portland Rowing Club won national championships in Seattle in 1986, and rowers now congregate from all over the Northwest to compete in the annual Portland Regatta in mid-April. At this event, both men and women vie for the racing cups, and there are competitions for juniors as well.

You can watch the races from RiverPlace Marina or from the grassy sloping lawn at **Tom McCall Waterfront Park,** just next to the RiverPlace Hotel. Following the races there's usually a water-ski extravaganza that features barefoot waterskiing, ski jumping, human pyramids, swivel-ski ballets, and adagio doubles. All in all, the goings-on make for a fun day on the historic Willamette River, where Stumptown began. If you'd like to explore learning to row the sleek racing shells yourself, stop for information at the Rowing Shop, near the marina shops and delis.

To continue your walking tour, head north from RiverPlace and Waterfront

Park on the esplanade along the seawall. During Portland's annual **_Rose Fes-tival_,** held the first three weeks in June, the seawall is filled with ships of all sizes and lengths, hailing from U.S. Navy and Coast Guard bases as well as Canadian ports, and some can be toured during the festival. At SW Ankeny and First Avenues, stop to see the **_Skidmore Fountain,_** one of the city's first pub-lic fountains. It was donated by a local druggist "for the benefit of the horses, men, and dogs of Portland." **_New Market Theatre,_** at 50 SW Second Street, is now full of specialty shops but was built in 1872 as both a market and a the-ater—sopranos sang arias on the second floor while merchants sold cabbages on the first. And at the north end of the Central Fire Station is a small museum

## Portland's Bridges: History across the Willamette

Portland is a mecca for bridge lovers, according to Henry Petroski, writer, bridge admirer, and chairman of the civil and environmental engineering department at Duke University, Durham, North Carolina, and echoed by fellow writer and Portland bridge aficionado Sharon Wood, author of *The Portland Bridge Book.* Sharon interviewed Henry several years ago, and her article was published June 24, 1996, in the *Oregonian.* Here are some intriguing facts about Portland's bridges from these two unabashed bridge lovers:

Some twelve bridges span the Willamette River between Oregon City and the St. Johns area, north of downtown Portland. Eight of these bridges are situated within ¾₀ mile of one another in the heart of the downtown area:

**Broadway Bridge** (1913): Open to pedestrian traffic, it was designed by Ralph Modjeski, principal engineer for the major railroads and cities of the United States.

**Burnside Bridge** (1926): The bridge's opening mechanism was designed by Joseph Strauss of Golden Gate Bridge fame.

**Fremont Bridge** (1973): A large span towering over the central downtown area and just above historic Union Railroad Station and railroad tracks.

**Hawthorne Bridge** (1910): Designed by John Waddell, the oldest operating vertical lift bridge in the United States.

**Marquam Bridge** (1966): A high curving span of concrete that allows wide views of RiverPlace Marina and shops.

**Morrison Bridge** (1887, 1958): One of the city's best pedestrian bridges; connects with the downtown Esplanade walkway.

**Ross Island Bridge** (1926): A graceful aqueduct-style bridge.

**Steel Bridge** (1912): Designed by John Waddell, a roadway and railway bridge and the only double-deck bridge in the world with decks capable of independent movement.

devoted to firefighting and containing vintage fire engines; find it just across from Ankeny Park and the Skidmore Fountain.

At the **Architectural Preservation Gallery,** on NE Second and Couch Streets, you can see changing exhibits of historic building fragments, paintings, and old photographs; you can also visit the **Portland Police Museum,** housed in the same site. The **Pioneer Courthouse,** at SW Fifth and Yamhill, was built in 1869, making it the oldest public building in the Pacific Northwest. Just across the street from the courthouse, detour through **Pioneer Square,** an enormous, block-wide square almost in the heart of the city; colorful outdoor events are held here throughout the year.

The **Park Blocks,** constructed on land set aside in 1852 for a city park, stretch from SW Salmon Street south and slightly uphill to the Oregon Historical Center, the Portland Art Museum, and the campus of **Portland State University.** Here you'll find shady places to walk, rest, and watch the pigeons, and you may well encounter roving musicians or street performers from such local theater groups as Artists Repertory, New Rose, Storefront, and Firehouse, along with the ever-present college students, museumgoers, and people watchers.

The **Oregon Historical Center** (503–222–1741; www.ohs.org), at 1200 SW Park Avenue, comprises a fine museum of changing exhibits, a historical research library, a gift shop, and a bookstore. The museum is open Tuesday through Saturday from 10:00 A.M. to 5:00 P.M. and on Sunday from noon to 5:00 P.M.

## Other Portland Bridges of Interest

The Interstate 205 Bridge, a short span just north of the Oregon City Bridge, carries the bulk of freeway traffic around the east flank of the city.

The old Oregon City Bridge, part of old Highway 99E, spans a section of the Willamette River closest to Willamette Falls and the Willamette Falls Locks at Oregon City, about 10 miles south of the downtown area.

The most impressive and aesthetically pleasing bridge is located about 5 miles north of the downtown area—St. Johns Bridge. Built in 1931, it is one of only three suspension bridges in Oregon. It was designed by David Steinman, who also designed the Mackinac Bridge in Michigan.

The narrow Sellwood Bridge connects Macadam Avenue (Highway 14), heading south to Lake Oswego, with the historic Sellwood-Moreland neighborhoods, located just a couple of miles from the downtown area.

## TOP ANNUAL EVENTS IN
## PORTLAND AND ENVIRONS

**Antique Spinning Wheel Showcase**
Aurora; mid-March
(503) 678–5754

**Fiesta Cinco de Mayo**
Portland; May
(503) 275–8355, www.cincodemayo.org

**Portland Rose Festival**
Portland; early June
(503) 275–8355, www.rosefestival.org

**Chamber Music Northwest**
**Summer Festival**
Portland; mid-June
(503) 223–3202, www.cmnw.org

**Lake Oswego Festival of the Arts**
Lake Oswego; July
(503) 636–3634, ww.lake-oswego.com

Located directly across Park Blocks from the Historical Center, the ***Portland Art Museum*** (503–226–2811) contains an excellent permanent exhibit of Northwest Coast Indian art and artifacts; museum and gallery lovers can also inquire here about the numerous small galleries sprinkled throughout the downtown area. If you're in the area in late fall, when the tall, leafy trees in the Park Blocks are ablaze with bright yellow, orange, and red autumn hues, consider attending one of the ***Wednesday Evening Jazz Concerts*** held in the indoor sculpture court at the art museum; the concert program starts around the third week in October. The museum is open Tuesday through Saturday from 10:00 A.M. to 5:00 P.M. and Sunday from noon to 5:00 P.M.

For an impromptu snack in the Park Blocks, pick up picnic items at ***Metro on Broadway,*** near Broadway and Salmon Street, just a couple of blocks south of Pioneer Square, or at ***South Park Seafood Grill & Wine Bar*** (503–326–1300), on Ninth and Salmon Streets. Should you walk through the lower downtown area on a weekend, stop by the colorful ***Saturday Market,*** situated under the west end of the Burnside Bridge, just north of the Skidmore Fountain between SW First Avenue and SW Ankeny Street and near ***Waterfront Park.*** Here you can stroll through a variety of booths that offer an array of Oregon and Pacific Northwest goods, from pottery, wood, and leather to jewelry, candles, and handwoven items. From open-air food stands you can choose tasty, ready-to-eat meat and veggie items.

If you're ready to leave the bustle of downtown and enjoy a lazy afternoon in the outdoors, visit cool, shady ***Forest Park,*** one of the largest urban parks in the United States. The 4,700-acre park begins just a few blocks from down-

## Portland: A Mecca for Walkers, Joggers, In-Line Skaters, and Bikers

We once had a mayor who rode his bicycle to work. He also, on occasion, wore lederhosen. And he sported a full beard and handlebar moustache. Then we had another mayor (an emigrant from the East Coast), and she often wore sporty walking tennies and usually rode the bus downtown to her office in City Hall.

Living in a great outdoor city, most Portlanders enjoy walking, jogging, in-line skating, or biking, in all sections of the city. You'll see business folks doing lunchtime or after-work runs. Families with youngsters, teens and their buddies, and grandparents and seniors—folks of all ages—thoroughly enjoy the out-of-doors on weekdays and weekends, rain or shine! Paved walkways extend along the Willamette River seawall on both sides of the river adjacent to the downtown area. More walkways range south of nearby RiverPlace along the river, heading toward the John's Landing area.

Outdoor aficionados can get helpful information and walking maps from the visitor information center at Pioneer Courthouse Square (503–275–8355). Folks can also get a helpful three-county bike map by contacting the Bicycle Transportation Alliance (503–226–0676, www.bta4bikes.org).

town, off West Burnside Street and adjacent to **Washington Park International Rose Test Gardens** and the gorgeous **Japanese Garden.** The easy Wildwood Trail can be accessed either near the Japanese Garden or from the **World Forestry Center,** near **The Oregon Zoo,** just west of Washington Park.

Portland's mild and moist weather offers an extraordinary haven for wonderful year-round gardens. The city offers gardens for strolling, for romantics, for families, and for serious botanic buffs. Gardens especially suited for families include **Washington Park Rose Gardens,** 400 SW Kingston Avenue (503–823–3636 for the garden and 503–227–7033 for the garden gift shop; www.portlandparks.org). At the perimeter of this splendid garden above the downtown area, you will find shady lawn spaces to picnic with views of the city and the Cascade Mountains to the east. Also enjoy strolling the International Rose Test, the Miniature Rose collection, and the Gold Medal Award Roses sections of the gardens. The 8,000 roses—500 varieties—bloom all summer, with peak bloom time in June and July. The park and gardens encompass four acres and are open daily until dusk; it is most crowded on warm summer weekends.

Located just below Washington Park is the historic **Nob Hill neighborhood,** an assortment of interesting northwest Portland shops, boutiques, and eateries that range along Twenty-first and Twenty-third Avenues just north of Burnside Street.

Visit the city's newest garden, the *Classical Chinese Garden* (503–228–8131; www.portlandchinesegarden.org), located at NW Third and Everett Streets in Portland's Chinatown area. Behind thick, white walls encompassing the entire city block, stroll decorative pebble and rock paths, walk across small bridges, gaze at reflections on the central pond, and peek into meditative courtyards and wooden teahouses. Splendid views unfold with every step and reveal an aesthetic fusion of mature trees, bamboo, flowering ornamentals, and ancient rocks. This contemplative garden is open daily, April through October, from 9:00 A.M. to 6:00 P.M., and November through March from 10:00 A.M. to 5:00 P.M.

*Crystal Springs Rhododendron Garden*, located on SE Twenty-eighth Avenue, 1 block north of Woodstock Boulevard (503–771–8386; www.rhodies .org), is a seven-acre wooded glen where visitors will find dozens of Northwest tree and shrub species, small waterfall and stream plantings, and impressive stands of mature rhododendrons, including many that reach 25 to 30 feet in height. The best color displays occur April through June. Meander around the waters of Crystal Springs Lake and across the lake's boardwalk to find park benches with views of the water and nearby Eastmoreland Golf Course.

Gardens especially loved by serious botanic garden lovers include *The Berry Botanic Garden*, at 11505 SW Summerville Avenue (503–636–4112; www.berrybot.org). Visitors see and stroll through a unique six-acre species garden developed by early Portland plantswoman Rae Selling Berry at her

## Spring Flower and Bulb Bonanza

The following is a list of the best times to see specific spring flowers in bloom, by month:

**March:** Common crocus in purple, lavender, yellow, and white; early tulips; grape hyacinth; bluebells; windflower; flowering pink currant; pale yellow winter hazel; weeping cherry; magnolia tree species

**April:** Trumpet daffodils like yellow King Alfred and white Mount Hood; checkered lily in exotic purple and green; fragrant purple, white, and pink hyacinth; Dutch iris with flowers in purple to yellow range; bright yellow Oregon grape; forsythia and quince; Japanese flowering cherry tree species

**May:** Azaleas; rhododendrons; wisteria; late tulips; crown imperial fritillaria; daffodil paper whites; Persian buttercup; poppy anemone in bright red, violet, blue, and white

**June:** Bearded Siberian and Japanese iris; giant allium, regal, tiger, and croft lilies; baby gladiolus; glorious roses: miniature, florabunda, hybrid tea, grandiflora, and climbers

# Romantic Gardens for Strolling

There is nothing quite like a beautiful and scenic garden to bring couples of all ages out-of-doors, especially in the springtime, summer, and fall. One's romantic instincts seem heightened by the wonderful scents of old and new roses; by colors and textures of other flowers, ornamental shrubbery, and trees; and by the musical sounds of a bubbling stream or small waterfall cascading down a rocky incline. The following are my favorite gardens in the city for romantic walks and for intimate tête-à-têtes with loved ones:

**Crystal Springs Rhododendron Garden**
(503) 771–8386
The best time to visit here is in the morning or in the early evening when families with crowds of children have departed. The view from the bridge, of willow trees with their graceful branches overhanging the lake, is especially romantic.

**Elk Rock Garden**
11800 SW Military Lane
At the Bishop's Close (Episcopal Diocese), formerly the eleven-acre estate of Scotsman Peter Kerr, pathways beckon visitors around wide expanses of lawns, trees, and shrubs, including pink dogwood, elegant magnolias, Japanese cherry, rhododendron, and azaleas. In early spring, around mid-May, climb steps behind the manor house to see a magnificent old wisteria vine with long drapes of pale lavender blossoms that grows across a rocky ledge. Other pathways in this fine estate garden lead across a wood bridge, around a stream and pond area planted with iris and ferns, and on to upper views of the Willamette River at the south section of the grounds; native wildflowers grow in this section. There are no public facilities here; the garden is open until dusk year-round and is beautiful in all four seasons. Head south from downtown on Macadam Avenue (Highway 43 to Lake Oswego), turn downhill on SW Military Road, and take an immediate right onto Military Lane to the garden entry. It is rarely crowded; early evening strolls are wonderful.

home in the southwest hills. In addition to native plants, alpine species, and more than 145 rhododendron species, the garden, now tended by volunteers, offers outstanding collections of primula and lily species from the western United States. The days and hours are restricted; call to make an appointment to visit and to obtain directions to the garden. *Leach Botanical Garden,* 6704 SE 122nd Avenue (503–823–9503) is cooperatively sponsored by Leach Garden Friends and the City of Portland Bureau of Parks and Recreation. This nine-acre garden glen and house, Sleepy Hollow, was once home to John and Lilla Leach. The couple's extensive botanical collections have been restored, and these include a native woodland garden, bog garden, riparian zone, shaded rock garden, sunny rock garden, display collections, and Leach discoveries sec-

### The Grotto Gardens
(503) 254–7371; www.thegrotto.org
This is a peaceful and quiet woodland sanctuary of garden rooms, statuary, shrines, and reflection ponds high atop a basalt cliff on the city's northeast side. Open year-round; access entrance from Sandy Boulevard at NE Eighty-fifth Avenue. The gardens and gift shop are open daily; those interested can inquire about the daily Mass schedule held outdoors or in the Chapel of Mary. The gardens are lighted during the Christmas holiday season. Visit early or late in the day.

### The Japanese Garden
(503) 223–1321; www.japanesegarden.com
Immerse yourself in five traditional garden styles of ancient Japan in this five-and-one-half-acre garden gem, including Shukeiyen, the natural garden; Rijiniwa, the tea garden; Chisen-Kaiyui-Shiki, the strolling pond garden; Seki-Tei, the sand and stone garden; and Hiraniwa, the flat garden. Enjoy wide views of the city and mountains from the bluff area near the garden pavilion. Park near the tennis courts at the Washington Park Rose Gardens and walk the winding path up to the Oriental-style wood entry gate. Visit early or late in the day and midweek for the most solitary strolls.

### Ladd's Addition Rose Blocks
(503) 823–3636
Located off SE Hawthorne Boulevard at SE Sixteenth and Harrison Streets, this garden features old rose varieties planted in formally designed beds that fill 4 blocks surrounding Ladd's Circle. This is one of Portland's oldest neighborhoods. You won't find crowds of people here.

### The Shakespeare Garden at the Washington Park Rose Gardens
Tucked in the southeast corner behind a high brick wall, this garden offers a colorful assortment of poppies, lavender, and rosemary combined with clusters of other lush annuals and perennials. Several flowering tree species in this garden room offer especially grand bloom displays in early spring. Visit early in the morning or in the evening when the crowds are gone.

tion. The Oregon Fuchsia Society maintains a test garden for hardy fuchsias on the upper terrace. Access this fine Northwest botanical garden from the Foster Road exit off Interstate 205, continuing east to 122nd Avenue and turning south to the parking area. The garden is open daily until dusk.

Along 10 miles of trails in nearby *Hoyt Arboretum,* you can try your hand at identifying Douglas fir, Jeffrey pine, broad-leaved maple, hemlock, red cedar, and grand fir, as well as cherry, ash, madrona, and Indian plum. Spectacular in the spring are native wildflowers, including trillium and buttercups. More than 110 different species of birds and more than 50 species of animals have been identified in Forest Park and the arboretum. Browse the Web site at www.hoyt arboretum.org.

Pick up arboretum trail maps and informational literature at **Hoyt Visitor Center,** at 4000 SW Fairview Boulevard (503–823–3655; www.hoytarboretum .org). Ask about guided tours through the 175-acre arboretum, which contains some 600 species of trees from all over the world. Information about other guided tours, nature walks, and interesting day trips in the area can also be obtained from the staff at the Portland Parks and Recreation office, 1120 SW Fifth Avenue, Suite 1302 (503–823–2223; www.portlandparks.org) and from the Metro Regional Parks and Greenspaces Department, 600 NE Grand Avenue, Portland (503–797–1850; www.metro-region.org).

To experience another nearby city forest, this one in southwest Portland near Lewis and Clark College, in splendid second-growth Douglas fir, call the friendly park staff and volunteers at **Tryon Creek State Park** (503–636–9886). Ask about hiking and bicycle trails and about current nature programs. The park's annual Trillium Festival is celebrated the first weekend in April.

One of the most charming hostelries right in the heart of the downtown area, just up Broadway from Pioneer Square, is the **Heathman Hotel.** It's also

## Uptown Street Names Revisited

In the trendy Nob Hill district, just up Burnside Street from the downtown area, you can get close to early Portland's movers and shakers by noting the alphabetically arranged street names; this naming was done in 1891. Here are a few selected historical notes on the streets' namesakes (from *Portland Names and Neighborhoods* by historian Eugene Snyder):

**Burnside Street:** Named for David Burnside, pioneer flour merchant; he reportedly operated at First and B Streets in the roughest section of the waterfront.

**Couch Street:** Named for Captain Couch (pronounced Kooch), the district's founder.

**Davis Street:** Named for Anthony L. Davis, the city's first justice of the peace.

**Flanders Street:** Named for Capt. George Flanders, shipmate, business partner, and brother-in-law of Captain Couch.

**Hoyt Street:** Named for Capt. Richard Hoyt, 1851 pioneer who organized the Columbia Steam Navigation Company.

**Johnson Street:** Named for Arthur H. Johnson, a meat merchant who had his store in the New Market Theater building; he also operated a slaughterhouse at NW Twenty-third and Flanders.

**Lovejoy Street:** Named for attorney Asa L. Lovejoy, co-owner of the original donation land claim where Portland's early townsite was situated.

located next door to the *Arlene Schnitzer Concert Hall* (503–248–4335), the *Portland Center for the Performing Arts* (www.pcpa.com), and the South Park Blocks. Making its debut in the jazzy 1920s, the Heathman Hotel served Portlanders and travelers for nearly fifty years before it began showing its age.

When you find this classy gem of a hotel, you'll discover one of the traditions that road-weary travelers especially appreciate: a genuinely friendly and helpful staff. Enjoy afternoon tea in the grand Tea Court, looking just as it did in 1927, including its paneling of polished eucalyptus, or try a cold beverage, along with late-afternoon hors d'oeuvres, in the nearby marble and mirrored bar or in the intimate mezzanine lounge.

Then settle into leather armchairs in the hotel's casual restaurant. Here guests can sample the chef's award-winning Northwest cuisine—including freshly cooked entrees from the ocean, farms, and fields—during each of the four seasons. The guest rooms and suites are comfortable nests decorated in warm earth tones, accented with soft English chintzes covering rattan sofas, armchairs, and queen-size beds. Green plants add a fresh, outdoorsy touch. For

**Overton Street:** Named for William Overton, co-owner with Lovejoy of the land claim; Overton stayed one year, then sold out and departed Portland for other destinations.

**Pettygrove Street:** Named for Francis W. Pettygrove, who bought Overton's claim for $50 in goods; Pettygrove became the town's first promoter.

**Thurman Street:** Named for G. William Thurman, assistant manager of Pacific Postal Telegraph in Portland.

**Vaughn Street:** Named for George W. Vaughn, merchant and Portland mayor in 1855.

**No women allowed:** I can't help but notice the lack of women's names in this august lineup of alphabetical street names in northwest Portland (even the ones not included here were all male). Where were the ladies? And how about the poets, writers, playwrights, and directors? How about the educators? How about the concert pianists, jazz musicians, and actors? How about the gardeners and horticulturists? And the early suffragettes? A number of Northwest names surface; for example, Abigail Scott Duniway (early activist and publisher), Georgiana Burton Pittock (she hosted the city's first rose show), Lilla Leach (horticulturalist), Rae Selling Berry (plantswoman), Hazel Hall (poet and writer), and Mother Joseph (early Catholic educator). Nevertheless, when you visit the eclectic Nob Hill district, which ranges between Burnside and Vaughn Streets and between Twenty-first and Twenty-third Avenues, you will most likely mingle happily with all of the above categories of folks—from both sexes. The area abounds in great coffee and espresso shops, good cafes and restaurants, and enough specialty shops and boutiques to keep one entertained and busy for days. It is great fun all hours of the day and early evening. The only discordant note is finding a parking place—try the side streets above NW Twenty-third Avenue.

## OTHER ATTRACTIONS WORTH SEEING IN PORTLAND AND ENVIRONS

**Oregon Museum of Science and Industry**
Portland
www.omsi.edu

**Pearson Air Museum, Fort Vancouver Historic Site and British Gardens**
Vancouver, Washington
(800) 832–3599

**Salmon Run Bell Tower**
Esther Short Park
Downtown Vancouver, Washington

**Swan Island Dahlias** and **Flower Farmer and Phoenix & Holly Railroad**
Canby

additional information and reservations, contact the staff at the Heathman Hotel, SW Broadway at Salmon Street (503–241–4100; www.heathmanhotel.com).

Try yet another small, elegant hotel, such as **Hotel Vintage Plaza** at 422 SW Broadway (503–228–1212; www.vintageplaza.com). You won't find boring, look-alike rooms in this charming hostelry; rather, guests find excellent antique reproductions, eclectic fabrics, and unusual prints, giving each room a distinctive personality. You could, however, order the special Recipe for Romance, which includes a warm greeting from the valet who parks your car, a luxurious deluxe guest room, rose petals sprinkled over your sheets at turndown, scented bath salts, plush terry robes, and a bottle of chilled champagne. The hotel's restaurant, Pazzo Ristorante (503–228–1515), offers great Italian entrees and a good wine list.

Music and theater lovers can also check out summertime offerings, some outdoors. For example: **Your Zoo and All That Jazz,** in July and August (503–226–1561; www.oregonzoo.org). When you get to town, pick up a copy of *Willamette Week* for current listings of stage, theater, gallery, and film offerings, as well as bistro and restaurant listings and reviews.

For current information call the Portland Visitors' Association at (800) 962–3700 or log onto www.travelportland.com.

# Where the Rivers Merge

For another pleasant excursion head north and west of downtown via Twenty-third Avenue to access U.S. Highway 30, and then drive about 10 miles to **Sauvie Island,** a pastoral area lying along the confluence of the Willamette River from the south and the Columbia River from the east. The small island was settled in the late 1840s, and at one time some forty dairy farms were scattered about it. The southern half now contains strawberry and raspberry fields, fruit orchards, and vegetable farms; many Sauvie Island farmers offer their homegrown fruit and produce in open-air stands all summer and into early autumn.

After crossing the Sauvie Island Bridge onto this flat, oblong island that is loved by weekend bicyclers, enjoy meandering along the quiet roads that nearly encircle the terrain. Take a detour to **Oak Island** for some serious bird-watching, canoe on tiny Sturgeon Lake or quiet Multnomah Channel, or bring your bicycle and pedal around the quiet byways. The northern half of the island—where Oak Island and Sturgeon Lake are located—remains a native wetlands area, the **Sauvie Island Wildlife Refuge.** Hundreds of birds migrating along the busy Pacific Flyway make pit stops here twice each year to rest and refuel.

Meriwether Lewis and William Clark also passed near this area on their trek to the Northwest during the early 1800s. On November 3, 1805, Clark, while camped along the Columbia River and feeling somewhat disgruntled, wrote in his journal that the party couldn't sleep, "for the noise kept up during the whole of the night by the swans, Geese, white & Grey Brant, Ducks, & c on a small Sand Island . . . They were imensely numerous, and their noise horid."

With the aid of binoculars, you'll probably spot Canada geese, snow geese, white-fronted geese, assorted ducks, and smaller birds and wildlife. Without binoculars, however, you'll often see many larger birds, such as marsh and red-tailed hawks, vultures, tundra swans, sandhill cranes, and blue herons. During winter a population of about thirty bald eagles roosts in an old-growth forest some miles away, leisurely commuting to Sauvie Island at sunrise to spend the day.

Because something like 500,000 acres of U.S. "wetlands"—a composite description for ponds, lakes, and sloughs and their adjacent grasslands and meadows loved by waterfowl, other birds, and wildlife—are being drained and filled each year, the number of birds using the Pacific Flyway has changed dramatically since the days of the Lewis & Clark expedition. For helpful information about efforts to conserve wetlands in the Portland area, including a schedule of bird-watching treks to Sauvie Island and other nearby wildlife habitats, contact the education director, or Mike Houck, an urban naturalist, at the **Portland Audubon Society,** located at 5151 NW Cornell Road (503–292–6855; www.audubonportland.org). Better yet, stop by the society's visitor center on your way from downtown Portland, via Lovejoy Street (head west), for maps and bird-watching lists before continuing out to Sauvie Island. The Sauvie Island Wildlife Refuge office at 18330 NW Sauvie Island Road can be reached at (503) 621–3488. The refuge office is open Monday through Friday, 8:00 A.M.

to 5:00 P.M. (but closed noon to 1:00 P.M.). Stop here to purchase the refuge parking permit.

While you're exploring Sauvie Island, stop at the *James Bybee House and Agricultural Museum,* ca. 1850, at Howell Territorial Park (503–797–1850; www.metro-region.org). In the pioneer orchard you can inspect 115 varieties of apple trees; in the restored farmhouse you can see vintage furnishings and, on the second floor, a wonderful children's room; and in the side yard you can have a picnic amid the collection of old, scented roses. Poke into the huge barn to see pioneer farm equipment, sacks of grain, and old-time wagons. The pungent aroma of hay and grain always reminds me of visiting a grandparent's farm in the country.

Reaching the farmstead is simple: After crossing narrow Multnomah Channel on the Sauvie Island Bridge from US 30, follow the signs to 13801 NW Howell Park Road and turn down the lane to the large parking area. The Bybee House is open June through Labor Day, Wednesday through Sunday, from noon to 5:00 P.M. The Wintering-In festival takes place on the last Saturday in September and offers freshly pressed cider, demonstrations of pioneer handicrafts, and a sale of old photographs, as well as games for children, live music, and tours of the Bybee House.

Promoting outdoor experiences for women and youngsters, *Becoming an Oregon Outdoors Woman,* a program developed through the Oregon Department of Fish and Wildlife, offers fun workshops in, for example, turkey

James Bybee House and Agricultural Museum

hunting, fly fishing, pheasant hunting, duck hunting, and archery for girls and boys ages eight to thirteen. Other experiences are offered in areas such as canoeing and boating; camping and outdoor cooking; wilderness survival and wildlife identification; fly fishing and basic fishing; crabbing and clamming; archery and shotgun/rifle shooting; and big game, upland bird, and waterfowl hunting. For the most current schedule, contact the Oregon Department of Fish and Wildlife, (503) 947–6000, ext 5; www.dfw .state.or.us (click on Information & Education).

You could also stay the night on the island by arranging pleasant quarters with views of the Columbia River at **Westlund's River's Edge Bed & Breakfast,** 22502 NW Gillihan Road, Portland (503–621–9856; www.rivers edge-bb.com).

If time allows, continue west out US 30 about 12 miles farther, to **St. Helens,** to enjoy a panoramic view from the historic waterfront area of this ca. 1844 city. Follow Columbia Boulevard through downtown and find **Columbia View Park** just next door to the courthouse, then walk down a few steps to watch the powerboats, sailboats, and barges on the river. For tasty bistro fare stop at **Dockside Steak & Pasta,** 343 South First Street (503–366–0877). **The Wild Currant Cafe,** 201 South First Street (503–366–9099), offers breakfast and lunch daily. Pop into **Fresh Start Espresso,** 58499 Columbia River US 30 in downtown St. Helens, for espresso drinks and bakery goodies.

# Historic East-Side Neighborhoods

Enjoy visiting a bevy of secondhand stores and antiques shops in **Historic Sellwood neighborhood,** via Macadam Avenue and Sellwood Bridge, located just south of the downtown and Old Town areas. This old neighborhood, with its small homes and tidy lawns, skirts the Willamette River's east bank near the Sellwood Bridge and **Oaks Park.** Amble along SE Thirteenth Avenue, stopping for lunch or tea and dessert at one of the many delis or small restaurants in the area, or take a picnic down to the park along the river, just north of the Sellwood Bridge. You can also visit nearby Oaks Park to see and ride the refurbished **Oaks Park Carousel,** which survived four Willamette River floods—in 1948, 1964, 1974, and 1996. Then, at nearby Westmoreland Park you can watch youngsters and oldsters sail their small boats on the large pond. You'll find comfortable benches for sitting and enjoying the view all along the west side of the pond. Access **Westmoreland Park** just off Bybee Boulevard near Twentieth Avenue.

From Westmoreland Park continue east on Bybee Boulevard, where you'll pass **Eastmoreland Public Golf Course** (503–775–2900) and circle around to SE Woodward Street and Twenty-eighth Avenue (along the way notice the vintage homes of Eastmoreland shaded by enormous old trees). Detour onto Twenty-eighth Avenue for a block or so to find the entrance to lovely **Crystal Springs Rhododendron Garden.** Spend an hour or so walking through this special place, where you'll marvel at fifty-year-old rhododendrons; walk a boardwalk across the lake with its plethora of ducks, waterbirds, and songbirds; and watch golfers across the water playing the "front nine" at Eastmoreland Golf Course.

Wish you had brought a picnic lunch to eat at one of the benches along Crystal Springs Lake? Well, stop first at ***Otto's Sausage Kitchen and Meat Market,*** just up the hill past Reed College, at 4138 SE Woodstock Boulevard (503–771–6714; www.ottossausagekitchen.com), to collect sandwiches, salads, chips, imported cheeses, imported and domestic ales, muffins, cookies, coffee,

## Tee Off! Fore! Favorite Golf Courses in Oregon

Although I have golfed at fine private golf courses in my native Oregon, I remain firmly a public-golf-course aficionado. I love public golf courses, especially during less busy midweek times. And I especially like to find and support little-known golf courses, small gems tucked away in nooks and crannies throughout the state. I hope you'll toss your golf clubs in the car and enjoy finding your own golf-course gems as well. Here is my current list of personal favorites; call well ahead for tee times. Greens fees rating per nine holes, weekdays: $ (economical), $6.00 to $12.00; $$ (moderate), $13.00 to $17.00; $$$ (pricey), $18.00 to $25.00 and over.

**PORTLAND ENVIRONS AND MOUNT HOOD RECREATION AREA**

**Broadmoor**
northeast Portland
(503) 281–1337, $

**Charbonneau**
near Wilsonville
(503) 694–1246, $$

**Colwood National**
northeast Portland
(503) 254–5515, $$

**Eastmoreland**
southeast Portland
(503) 775–2900, $

**Gresham Golf Links**
Gresham
(503) 665–3352, $

**Heron Lakes-Greenback**
northeast Portland
(503) 289–1818, $

**Lake Oswego Municipal**
Lake Oswego
(503) 636–8228, $

**Oregon City Municipal**
Oregon City
(503) 518–2846, $$

**Red Tail**
southwest Portland near Beaverton
(503) 646–5166, $

**Resort at the Mountain**
Pine Cone and Thistle, the old original eighteen holes (formerly Bowman's) on the east side
(503) 622–3151, $$$

**Rose City**
northeast Portland
(503) 253–4744, $

**Sandalie East**
near Wilsonville
(503) 655–1461, $

**OREGON COAST**

**Gearhart Golf Links**
north of Seaside on the north coast
(503) 738–3538, $$

and lattes. Otto's has been making great sausages since 1929 and is open Monday through Saturday from 9:30 A.M. to 6:00 P.M.

Then wend your way over to the ***Hawthorne neighborhood*** by turning north onto Thirty-ninth Avenue at Woodstock Boulevard. On Hawthorne Boulevard, between Fortieth and Twentieth Avenues, you'll find a restored area of

**Neskowin**
south of Tillamook on the north coast
(503) 392–3377, $$

**Sunset Bay**
west of Coos Bay and north of
Charleston on the south coast
(541) 888–9301, $$

**WILLAMETTE VALLEY, CENTRAL
CASCADES, AND SOUTHERN OREGON**

**Fiddler's Green**
Eugene
(541) 689–8464, $

**Grants Pass Golf Club**
Grants Pass
(541) 476–0849, $$

**Laurelwood**
Eugene
(541) 687–5321, $$

**McNary**
Salem
(503) 393–4653, $$

**Tokatee**
east of Eugene-Springfield
(800) 452–6376, $$

**CENTRAL AND EASTERN OREGON**

**Crooked River Ranch Golf Course**
near Redmond and Terrebonne
(541) 923–6343, $$

**Kah-Nee-Ta Resort Golf Course**
Warm Springs
(541) 553–1112, $$

**Kinzua Hills**
Fossil
(541) 763–3287, $

**Juniper Golf Course**
Redmond
(541) 548–3121, $$

**MOST SCENIC GOLF COURSES,
MY FAVORITES**

**Broadmoor**
northeast Portland

**Colwood National**
northeast Portland

**Crooked River Ranch**
near Redmond-Terrebonne

**Eastmoreland**
southeast Portland

**Juniper Golf Club**
Redmond

**Resort at the Mountain**
the original nine holes east side, Welches

**Tokatee**
Blue River east of Eugene-Springfield

**MOST AWESOME HOLE**

Number 12 at Mountain View, Boring (east of Portland)—tee up on a bluff nearly 200 feet above the green; the narrow fairway is edged thickly with shrubs and trees

interesting shops, delis, restaurants, and boutiques. Stop by **Dragonfly Gardens,** near Twenty-second, for a good selection of plants and garden-related goodies; snoop through the **Hawthorne Coffee Merchant,** near Thirty-fifth Avenue, for gourmet coffees, teas, and candies; or have lunch at **Bread and Ink Cafe** (503–239–4756) near Thirty-sixth Avenue. For a real treat stop in at **Grand Central Bakery** (2230 SE Hawthorne Boulevard; 503–232–0575) for outstanding cinnamon rolls, scones, and espresso as well as the rustic Italian breads for which the bakery has become famous: thick, crusted, free form, and very chewy, made by slow-rise and long-fermentation processes. Among the greatest hits are the Como loaf, rustic baguette, Sole Mio, sour white round, and rosemary roll. Detour next to Belmont Street and Thirty-fourth Avenue, just a few blocks north, to visit another recently renovated neighborhood. Check out colorful **Zupan's Market,** which extends along the entire block. **Stumptown Coffee Roasters** is nearby at 3356 SE Belmont Street (503–232–8889).

Continue east on Hawthorne Boulevard and drive up 600-foot **Mount Tabor** for a view of the city from atop one of Portland's extinct volcanic cinder cones. For the best view wind up to the top, where you'll be sheltered beneath towering Douglas fir, their long branches swaying in the gentle breezes like graceful ballerinas. Picnic tables are located in shaded or sunny spots here and there, and you can hike around the park for views of snowcapped Mount Hood, to the east.

You can also discover comfortable places to spend the night on the east side of town. Among the coziest, **Georgian House B&B** (503–281–2250; www.the georgianhouse.com); **Portland's White House** (503–287–7131; www.portlands whitehouse.com); and **The Lion & the Rose Victorian B&B** (503–287–9245; www.lionrose.com)—all fine bed-and-breakfast inns located in this area.

Park on any side street near Fifteenth Avenue and enjoy walking and browsing the trendy **Northeast Broadway neighborhood**—dozens of great shops, delis, coffeehouses, cafes, and galleries range from NE Tenth to NE Twentieth Avenues. Also nearby are the Memorial Coliseum, the **Rose Quarter,** and the **Convention Center,** where sports and other public events are held throughout the year.

# Oregon Trail's End

Those blue-sky afternoons often beckon young and old alike to the **Willamette River,** just as they did when the first pioneers arrived and settled near the base of the falls at Oregon City. In the late 1800s the Willamette River was the "main street" for life in the Willamette Valley: People traveled by riverboats and stern-wheelers, produce and supplies were shipped in and out by steamboats, and Oregon's principal cities started as river towns and steamboat landings. No

## Oregon Plum Cobbler Cake

½ cup butter, softened          ½ tsp. cinnamon
¾ cup sugar                     1 cup buttermilk
1 egg, beaten                   1 tsp. vanilla
2 cups flour                    1 tsp. grated lemon peel
1½ tsp. baking soda             2 cups chopped, fresh, peeled plums
½ tsp. salt                     sweet cream

*Topping:* ⅓ cup sour cream, mixed with 2 tbs. brown sugar

Cream together butter and sugar. Add egg and beat. Sift dry ingredients together and add alternately with buttermilk to the creamed mixture. Add vanilla and lemon peel. Gently blend in chopped plums, which have been lightly floured to absorb extra juice. Pour into 9-inch by 9-inch pan; sprinkle topping over batter and bake at 350 degrees for 40 to 50 minutes. Serve with sweet cream and a sprinkling of cinnamon.

fewer than seven major cities are located along the river, and more than half the people in Oregon live within 10 miles of the Willamette; in fact, more than 60 percent of all Oregonians live within the Willamette River Basin.

One of the best ways to cool off and see this historic area from a different perspective is to take a boat ride upriver about 18 miles, south toward Lake Oswego, West Linn, Milwaukie, Gladstone, and Oregon City. The boat proceeds south from downtown Portland, first maneuvering under the ***Ross Island Bridge,*** and then continues upriver past tiny Ross Island toward the Sellwood area. Sunlight sparkles from the moving water, and the city skyline recedes in midafternoon's golden light. The air smells fresh and clean.

Cruising upriver at a comfortable speed, the boat may pass a flotilla of small sailboats engaged in a race. White sails catch the wind, and sunlight turns them brightly translucent. Tinkly music from the ***Oaks Park Carousel*** wafts across the water as the boat passes under the ***Sellwood Bridge,*** continuing south toward the small communities along both banks of the river and to Willamette Falls at Oregon City.

A profusion of greenery passes by—cool canopies of trees, shrubbery, and mosses clinging to basaltic ledges and rocky walls here and there on both east and west banks of the river. The boat cruises past waterside homes; a small pontoon plane crouches at its dockside resting place; water-skiers glide past on wide skis; and great blue herons—Portland's official bird—catch the wind overhead, often in the company of seagulls who have flown in from the coast some 80 miles west.

# Best Historic Neighborhoods for Browsing and Shopping in Portland and Environs

Within the past ten years or so, Portland has rediscovered its wonderful old neighborhoods. They're being transformed from tired streets with straggly shrubbery, run-down houses, and empty storefronts to vibrant avenues for browsing, shopping, walking, jogging, bicycling, in-line skating, and generally hanging out. I never tire of snooping into old and new shops and finding cozy places to hole up with friends over cups of espresso or hot steaming lattes, great hamburgers or healthy pastas, delicious salads, and desserts. These shops include every sort of enthusiastic local entrepreneur and every sort of business—from antiques, collectibles, and vintage or new clothing to trendy kitchen boutiques, flower and garden shops, havens for books and magazines and cigars, and shops for backyard bird lovers and for pet lovers. Here are my favorite neighborhoods, those that extend warm welcomes to travelers as well as native city folks.

### WEST SIDE

**Multnomah Village:** Located between Capitol Highway and Multnomah Boulevard from SW Thirty-first to SW Fortieth Avenues. From Interstate 5 north take exit 296B (Multnomah Boulevard), turn right on Thirty-fourth, and then right onto Capitol Highway. From Interstate 5 south take exit 294 (99W/Barbur Boulevard), right at Huber, and left at Capitol Highway. This neighborhood is eclectic, funky, and has a few good coffee shops and several good eateries.

**Nob Hill District:** Located uptown between NW Twenty-first and NW Twenty-third Avenues and extending north from West Burnside Street to Vaughn Street. Access from downtown by heading west on West Burnside Street. This is an eclectic, funky, trendy, and fun neighborhood with great eateries.

**Pearl District:** Located downtown between NW Tenth and NW Thirteenth Streets and extending north from West Burnside to NW Hoyt Street. This vibrant renovated historic area is hopping with new shops and cafes.

At *Clackamette Park,* near Gladstone and Oregon City, peer over the railing to see where the smaller Clackamas River quietly enters the Willamette. The boat passes beneath the I–205 and old Oregon City bridges, toward the falls.

The boat maneuvers around to the entrance to *Willamette Falls Locks,* the early settlers' solution to the problem of navigating the river at this point. Someone jumps onto the dock and yanks the rope, which, in turn, activates a light and horn alerting the lock tender. If there's no tugboat coming through the locks from upriver, your boat will be next in line.

## EAST SIDE

**Hawthorne Boulevard:** From downtown head east over the Hawthorne Bridge and continue east; the heart of the area extends from about SE Twentieth to SE Thirty-ninth Avenues. This neighborhood is very laid back, funky, and fun and has a few good eateries. Detour north over to SE Belmont Street and SE Thirty-fourth Avenue to visit the new, sleek, and trendy Zupan's Market. Detour at SE Twentieth Avenue and head south a few blocks to inspect the Ladd's Addition Gardens near the Ladd's traffic circle; formal rose gardens in adjacent diamond-shaped beds and lush groupings of rhododendrons and azaleas are planted in the circle itself.

**Historic Sellwood:** From downtown head south on Macadam, passing John's Landing shops and continuing to and crossing the Willamette River via the Sellwood Bridge. Head east to SE Thirteenth Avenue for the first group of shops; then head north on SE Thirteenth around to Milwaukee Avenue for more shops. This area is much loved by antiques buffs and also offers excellent bakeries, coffee shops, and restaurants.

**Northeast Broadway:** From downtown head east over the Broadway Bridge and continue east on NE Weidler Street to NE Twentieth Avenue; turn left to NE Broadway. The area extends from NE Twentieth Avenue down to about NE Twelfth Avenue. There is an unusual variety of shops and several good eateries and coffee shops.

## OUTER EAST SIDE

**North Main Avenue in Gresham:** From downtown take the MAX train out to the end of the line in Gresham, or drive the scenic route heading east across the Ross Island Bridge and onto Powell Boulevard, continuing about 10 miles out to Gresham. Park near the City Park on Powell Boulevard near Roberts Street and walk across to Main Avenue; the area ranges several blocks along Main Avenue and extends to Second, Third, and Fourth Streets. This neighborhood features great shops and excellent restaurants including Bocelli's, Jazzy Bagels, Sunny Han's Wok & Grill, and Thai Orchid.

The giant wooden doors soon open wide, and the boat moves into the first of the four watery chambers. The lock master waves from the small station, keeping track of the gates and traffic on a television monitor while relaying instructions to a second lock tender in the upper station. It takes about thirty minutes to reach the upper Willamette River channel above the falls with the help of the historic locks. Constructed in 1872 by Chinese laborers, these locks have operated since 1873. In 1974 the project was placed on the National Register of Historic Places, and in 1991 the American Society of Civil

Engineers, Oregon Section, designated the locks a national civil engineering landmark. *NOTE:* Midweek, after 5:00 P.M., is the best time to enter the locks without waiting; delays can run thirty or forty minutes on a busy summer weekend.

Its passengers warmed by the late-afternoon sun, the boat then cruises upriver a couple of miles before returning through the locks to the lower channel and heading downriver, past Clackamette Park and waterside homes. A great blue heron balances long, spindly legs on a rock outcropping, and the city reappears, a surreal image of thick vertical lines on the sunset horizon.

***Stern-wheelers*** resurrected from yesteryear are once again cruising up both the Willamette and the Columbia Rivers. To join one of the cruises on either river, check with the stern-wheeler *Rose,* which makes frequent trips (503–286–7673). For smaller charter boats inquire at the visitor center in downtown Portland (503–275–8355).

If you would like to visit the Willamette Falls Locks (503–656–3381) and arranging a boat ride isn't feasible, you can drive from downtown Portland south via Macadam Avenue and Highway 43 through Lake Oswego to West

## Portland Institutions— Time-Tested Favorites

Herewith is a selected list of those places—locales, shops, eateries—that have been around the Portland area a long time and generally do not fit the description of "here today, gone tomorrow."

**The Bomber Restaurant**
13515 SE McLoughlin Boulevard
(503) 659–9306
World War II memorabilia galore
and good eats

**Caro Amico Italian Cafe**
3606 SW Barbur Boulevard
(503) 223–6895
delicious old-style Italian food since
the 1940s

**Clear Creek Distillery**
1430 NW Twenty-third Avenue
(503) 248–9470
owner Stephen McCarthy specializes in
pear, apple, and plum brandies; in
grappa, marc, and kirsch; tours and
tastings by appointment

**Dan & Louis Oyster Bar**
208 SW Ankeny, downtown in Old Town
(503) 227–5906
serving great oysters, fish-and-chips, clam
chowder, and other seafood since 1907

**Darcelle XV**
208 NW Third Avenue
(503) 222–5338
renowned local female impersonator
review with glamour, glitz, and outrageous
comedy

**International Rose Test Gardens at
Washington Park**
uptown off SW Burnside at 400 SW
Kingston Avenue
open from June through September (don't
miss it)

Linn. Drive under the I–205 bridge, continue to the redbrick building housing West Linn City Hall and Police Department, and look for the sign—just before crossing the old Oregon City Bridge—that says WILLAMETTE FALLS LOCKS AND ARMY CORPS OF ENGINEERS. Don't give up—it's well worth the effort to find this out-of-the-way gem. Park nearby and follow the paved walk and series of concrete stairs that lead down to the public viewing area.

Just for fun, spend a couple of hours on dry land watching tugboats, barges, pleasure boats, and perhaps a party of canoes pass through the four lock chambers. The lock tenders are a congenial lot and are usually pleased to answer questions about the historic locks; there is a large grassy area with shade trees, picnic tables, and sunny spots. The public restrooms are wheelchair accessible. A small historical museum on the grounds offers detailed information and wide-angle photographs of the construction of the four lock chambers; it is open daily during summer months from 9:30 A.M. to 8:00 P.M.

To visit the tiny community of Willamette, the most historic part of West Linn, head west on the frontage road, Willamette Falls Drive, winding above the locks and the Willamette River for a couple of miles. Here you'll find a cou-

**JaCiva's Chocolate and Pastry Shop**
4733 SE Hawthorne Boulevard
(503) 234–8115
decadent miniature chocolate cakes
to die for

**The Pittock Mansion**
3229 NW Pittock Drive
uptown off West Burnside above
Washington Park
(503) 823-3624
French-style heritage mansion built by
newspaper publisher Henry Pittock and his
wife, Georgiana Burton Pittock; wide views
to the Cascade Mountains; wonderful any
time of year, but especially in spring and
when decorated for the holidays

**Portland Saturday Market**
between SW First Avenue and Naito
Parkway and from the Burnside Bridge
through Ankeny Park
(503) 222–6072
open-air crafts market features some 400
local artists, craftspeople, and cooks; it's
very funky and great fun

**Rheinlander German Restaurant**
5035 NE Sandy Boulevard
(503) 288–5503
a fun evening of German food and music

**Rich's Cigar Store**
820 SW Alder Street, downtown
(503) 228–1700
periodicals and tobacco, imported steins
and flasks, and the best selection of
domestic and foreign newspapers and
magazines in the state

**The Ringside Restaurant**
2165 West Burnside Street, downtown
(503) 223–1513
strictly steaks and onion rings since
the 1940s

ple of antiques shops, several good eateries and coffee shops, and a large city park along the river (great spot for a picnic).

Just east, after you've crossed the Willamette River from West Linn via the old Highway 99 **Oregon City Bridge,** you'll find historic **Oregon City,** which boasts the distinction of being the first incorporated city west of the Rocky Mountains. In the winter of 1829–30, however, there were just three log houses here, and the following spring, the first vegetables—potatoes—were planted. Apparently the local Native Americans resented this infringement on their territory and reportedly burned the houses. A flour mill and a sawmill, constructed near the falls in 1832 by the British Hudson's Bay Company, made use of the first waterpower in the territory.

The emigration over the Oregon Trail in 1844 added several hundred folks to Oregon City's population. The provisional government body, formed in 1843 at Champoeg, on the banks of the Willamette River south and west a few miles, chose Oregon City as its seat; the first provisional legislature assembled here in June 1844, at the Rose Farm.

By 1846 Oregon City contained some seventy houses and about 500 citizens. In January 1848 Joe Meek carried the request of the provisional legislature for territorial status to President James K. Polk in Washington, D.C. Meek returned in March 1849 with the newly appointed territorial governor, Joseph Lane. Oregon City was made the territorial capital and remained so until 1852, when the seat of government was moved to Salem, some 50 miles south, in the heart of the Willamette Valley.

To begin your tour, stop first at the **End of the Oregon Trail Interpretive Center** (503–657–9336; www.endoftheoregontrail.org), located near Washington and Abernethy Streets—you can't miss the three gigantic pioneer wagons with their white canvas tops. You'll take a guided tour that illustrates and explains the rigorous, 2,000-mile journey from Independence, Missouri, to Oregon City—the land route across the prairies, mountains, and deserts to The Dalles, including the float on crudely made barges down the swift and dangerous Columbia River. Later, the alternate Barlow Trail route was forged over Mount Hood. Of the 300,000 emigrants who undertook this formidable trek, some 30,000 died on the way and were buried along the trail. The interpretive center is open Monday through Saturday from 11:00 A.M. to 4:00 P.M. and Sunday from noon to 4:00 P.M. The center also offers visitor information (800–424–3002; www.historicoregoncity.org and www.mthoodterritory.com) about the Oregon City and Clackamas County area.

Next, pick up the *Historic Walking Tour* brochure and map, park on Main Street near the Clackamas County courthouse, and walk a few blocks to the **Oregon City Municipal Elevator,** accessing it via the lower entrance, on Railroad Avenue at Seventh Street. You'll take a thirty-second vertical ride up the face of the 90-foot basalt cliff—the city is built on two levels. The elevator—one of only four municipal elevators in the world—replaced the old Indian trails and pioneer paths that originally led from the river's edge to the top of the basalt bluff.

The first elevator, which took three minutes to travel up and down, was powered by water. It was constructed in 1915—much to the chagrin of citizen Sara Chase, who objected to its location in front of her Victorian mansion. Not only did Sara never use the municipal elevator, but she had a heavy wrought-iron fence erected so that "none of those elevator people" could trespass on her property. On the interior wall of the observation area atop the elevator, you can see an artist's painting of the Chase mansion.

Walk south a few blocks along the upper **Promenade** (it's also wheelchair accessible) for a spectacular view of Willamette Falls. Imagine what the area must have been like before the settlers arrived, before power lines and buildings, before bridges and freeways and automobiles. Actually, the first long-distance transmission of electricity in the United States happened here—from Oregon City to Portland—in 1888.

The early Native American families fished for salmon along the forested riverbanks amid stands of Douglas fir, the roar of the falls ever present. The falls cascade some 42 feet over several basaltic ledges in the middle of the wide river. You can sit at any of the public benches along the Promenade, basking in the late-afternoon sun while imagining a bit of Oregon history.

Continuing a few blocks north and east, visit the historic **McLoughlin House** (503–656–5146; www.mcloughlinhouse.org and www.nps.gov/mcho), at 713 Center Street, which is open Wednesday through Saturday from 10:00

McLoughlin House

A.M. to 4:00 P.M. This was the home of Dr. John McLoughlin, a dominant figure in not only the Hudson's Bay Company but also the early development of the region. Appointed chief factor, or superintendent of trade, of the British company in 1824, the tall, white-haired, cane-carrying man ruled over the entire Columbia country before the Oregon Trail migration began in 1843.

Under orders from the Hudson's Bay Company, McLoughlin established the first settlement at Oregon City and, later, moved here from Fort Vancouver, across the Columbia River, when he resigned from the company in 1845. Incidentally, reconstructed Fort Vancouver and its splendid reclaimed British-style vegetable, herb, and flower gardens are well worth a visit. There is a stockade, as well as living-history programs in the kitchen quarters, baking quarters, general store, blacksmith shop, and main house, which are all provided by National Park Service staff and volunteers. **_Fort Vancouver National Historic Site,_** open daily, is located just across the Columbia River from Portland, at 612 East Reserve Street, Vancouver, Washington (800–832–3599; www.nps.gov/fova). Born in the Canadian province of Quebec, McLoughlin became a U.S. citizen in 1851 and spent his later years operating his store, gristmill, and sawmills near the base of Willamette Falls at Oregon City.

McLoughlin's house, a large clapboard-style building with simple, dignified lines, was saved from demolition and moved from its original location along the Willamette River near the falls up to the top of the bluff and placed in what is now McLoughlin Park at Seventh and Center Streets. On the lovely grounds are large rhododendrons, clumps of azaleas, and old roses, and to the rear of the house sits a moss-covered fountain, shaded by tall Douglas firs and trailing ivy. You can attend the annual Candlelight Holiday Tour in early December and the Family Festival in August.

Also stop to see splendid exhibits of pioneer quilts, early fashions, and river and steamboat memorabilia at the Clackamas County Historical Society's **_Museum of the Oregon Territory,_** located on a bluff just above the Willamette River and Willamette Falls, at 211 Tumwater Street (503–655–5574; www.historicoregoncity.org).

Another rural loop from Oregon City offers a ramble into the eastern section of Clackamas County, reaching into the foothills of the Cascade Mountains. Take the Park Place exit from I–205 and turn left at the first light, toward Park Place. Settle into the slow lane and wind along Clackamas River Drive toward Carver. Rather than crossing the river here just yet, continue east on Springwater Road; then just beyond the boat-ramp entrance, turn right and proceed for about a quarter mile to the **_German Methodist Church_** and the **_Baker Cabin,_** located at the corner of Hattan and Gronlund Roads.

The small church, built around 1895, sits like a tidy little dowager under tall firs surrounded by well-kept grounds. Walk the gravel drive to the far end of the grassy area to inspect the Baker Cabin, which dates from 1856. Notice the old grapevine, with its enormous main trunk, which must have been planted around the same time as the cabin was built. The logs were hand-hewn into square-shaped timbers that deftly interlock at the four corners. Tiny ferns and wild-flowers grow from crevices in the old rock fireplace chimney at the west end of the cabin. For information about the annual Pioneer Bazaar and other events open to the public, contact the Baker Cabin Historical Society (503–631–8274).

Now backtrack to the Carver bridge, cross the Clackamas River, and go far-ther off the beaten path by taking Highway 224 east about 15 miles toward Estacada.

For history buffs, your next stop is the ***Philip Foster National Historic Farm*** (503–637–6324; www.philipfosterfarm.com), located just off Highway 224 at 29912 SE Highway 211, Eagle Creek. Offering living-history programs during the year, this site provides a nostalgic look at the 1840s, when Philip and Mary Foster ran a general store, restaurant, and resting place for Oregon Trail pioneers on the final leg of their trek to the West. You'll see Mary's lilac tree blooming in the front yard; it was planted in 1843, having survived the arduous journey "around the horn" from Calais, Maine. Mary, bless her heart, cooked meals for some 10,000 emigrants during those early trail years. And she

## OTHER ATTRACTIONS WORTH SEEING IN PORTLAND AND ENVIRONS

**Philip and Mary Foster National Historic Farm**
Eagle Creek
(503) 637– 6324
open Friday through Sunday from
11:00 A.M. to 4:00 P.M.

**Pittock Mansion**
northwest Portland
(503) 823-3624

**The Rose Farm**
Oregon City
(503) 656–5146
call for current hours

**The Vancouver National Historic Reserve**
(including Officers Row, Fort Vancouver Historic Site, British Gardens, and Pearson Air Museum)
Vancouver, Washington
(800) 832–3599, www.nps.gov/fova
open daily year-round (except major holidays)

**Old Aurora Colony Museum and Aurora National Historic District**
Aurora
(503) 678–5754

raised nine children and tended the orchards and gardens as well. On the last Saturday in September, stop by the farm to take in the annual Cider Squeeze and Harvest Festival.

In the small community of Estacada look for **Harmony Bakery** (503–630–6857) tucked away at SW Second and Wade Streets. Here you can join a diverse group of local folks who meet to drink coffee, eat freshly made bagels, and, of course, have a good morning or afternoon chat about the weather and the state of the world's affairs. A bagel with cream cheese to go is still just 50 cents, or you could order the omelet with spicy hash-brown potatoes, vegetarian fare, or more traditional sandwiches and burgers. The restaurant is open daily for breakfast and lunch from 7:00 A.M. to 3:00 P.M.

From Estacada continue south another 15 miles or so via Highway 211 to Molalla to discover **Pacific Northwest Live Steamers** (503–829–6866), a miniature railroad park set in Shady Dell Park near Molalla. Congenial volunteer engineers, members of the Pacific Northwest Live Steamers Club, run miniature trains on some 6,000 feet of track from noon to 5:00 P.M. on the second and fourth Saturday and on Sunday, May through October. There's a shady picnic area here as well. To get to the park from Highway 211, drive into Molalla and turn south at the Y-Grocery and proceed for about ½ mile, then turn west onto Feyrer Park Road to Shady Dell Park.

Riding with the kids in one of the small open-air cars behind your "Sunday engineer" is reminiscent of one's childhood days, dreaming of choo-choo trains, clanging bells, and whistle blasts. Two long toots signal "start" or "release brakes"; a long and a short mean "warning"; three shorts when a train is stopped designate "back up"; and one long whistle indicates the train is approaching a station. The miniature engine huffs and puffs steam from a tiny smokestack, just like its full-size original counterpart: the sleek steam locomotive that replaced horse-drawn wagons as well as Pony Express riders and helped to settle the West.

In recent decades, these mechanical marvels have all but disappeared, especially the steam locomotives, although many full-size models are also being restored and put back into service for nostalgic weekend trips; examples are the **Mount Hood Railroad** in Hood River (541–386–3556; www.mthoodrr .com); the **Sumpter Valley Railroad** in Sumpter, near Baker City (541–894–2362 or 541–894–2268; www.svry.com); and the **Oregon Coast Explorer** in Tillamook (800–685–1719; www.potb.org/oregoncoastexplorer).

You could linger overnight in the small community of Molalla by calling the innkeepers at **Prairie House Inn** at 524 East Main Street (503–829–8245). The large prairie-style farmhouse with its deep wraparound porch has been restored as a comfortable bed-and-breakfast inn with four guest rooms on the second floor. Breakfast is served in the cozy dining area with such treats as freshly made muffins, gourmet frittatas, and seasonal fruits served along with steaming hot coffees and teas. From Molalla it's an easy trek to Mount Angel, Silverton, and the Salem area.

# Farm and Flower Country

From Molalla you can complete your rural loop back to the Portland area by heading west on Highway 211 to Woodburn and turning north on old Highway 99E through Hubbard to Aurora, Canby, and back to Oregon City. Old Highway 99, which divides into two sections, 99E and 99W, as it winds through Willamette Valley towns, was the first paved north-south route (it followed sections of the early stagecoach route) linking all cities and towns along the Willamette River and south into the Umpqua and Rogue River valleys. From my childhood in the 1940s, I remember trips on Highway 99 that took seven "long" hours of driving from Grants Pass, in southern Oregon, to Portland.

Although travelers can now whiz up and down sleek Interstate 5, covering the same distance in about four and a half hours, once in a while it's nice to get off the freeway and ramble along sections of old Highway 99 and its rural tributaries. It's a nostalgic trek into yesterday for native Oregonians, one generously shared with visitors.

Pull off Highway 99E in Aurora to visit the *Aurora National Historic District* and the *Old Aurora Colony Museum* (503–678–5754; www.aurora colonymuseum.com), which inhabits a large, refurbished ox barn on Second Street. The colony's history began in the Harmony Colony in Pennsylvania,

## A Stitch Here and There— Historic Quilt Patterns

| | |
|---|---|
| Broken Dishes | Nine Patch |
| Double Wedding Ring | Sun Bonnet Sue |
| Dresden Plate | A Wild Goose Chase |
| Log Cabin | Bow Tie |

Quilt lovers can obtain further information about historic quilts from the Mennonite Quilters by calling the Aurora Colony Museum, (503) 678–5754. You can also see living-history programs, including quilting, candle making, and soap making at the historic Stauffer-Will Farm near Aurora. Contact the Aurora Colony Museum for the current schedule of events.

from which William Keil, a German tailor, physician, and preacher, and his followers emigrated to found the town of Bethel, Missouri, near the start of the Oregon Trail.

Some of the historic landmarks have vanished over the years, but many of the buildings remain, including the ox barn that houses the museum, a small log cabin, a washhouse, and a machine shed; there's also an assortment of farm machinery, and a lovely miniature garden, the **Emma Wakefield Herb Garden.** The colony was well known for its fine cooking and music; its brass band entertained at community festivities and events. In the museum you'll see many of the brass instruments, including the *schellenbaum,* a rare bell tree.

The museum has an excellent collection of historic quilts made by various women of the community, and many of these quilts are displayed throughout the year. In early March take in the popular **Spinner's Festival,** held at the ox barn museum. The museum complex is open Tuesday through Saturday from 10:00 A.M. to 4:00 P.M. and is closed during January.

Antiques buffs can browse more than two dozen shops in Aurora. Try **Main Street Mercantile,** 21610 Main Street (503–678–1044), for antiques and collectibles; **Home Again,** 21631 Main Street (503–678–0227), for Americana and primitives; and **Amish Workbench Furniture,** 14936 Third Street NE (503–678–7799), for Amish handcrafts. **Sunnyside Mercantile,** 21641 Main Street (503–678–3064), offers early country Americana, folk art, and espresso, and **For You Only Deli & Gifts,** 21620 Main Street (503–678–2830), puts out tasty lunch fare and homemade desserts. For coffee, espresso drinks, and tasty baked goods, try **Joe's Java** on Highway 99 (503–678–1594) and **The Hen House,** 21317 Highway 99 in Aurora (503–678–1630).

As you head north toward Canby from Aurora, you can take another side ramble by turning east onto Barlow Road and proceeding about 4 miles to **St. Josef's Winery** at 28836 South Barlow Road (503–651–3190). Owners Lilli and Josef Fleischmann decided to trade the bakery business for wine making more than twelve years ago. The tasting room is open daily from noon to 5:00 P.M.

As you head back toward Canby on Barlow Road to Highway 99E, notice the large fields of tulips and other bulbs that bloom during mid-April. In these far southern reaches of Clackamas County, the rich alluvial soils from ancient rivers support more than a hundred nurseries, where growers raise everything from annuals and perennials to ornamentals and fruit stock, and acres of lush green turf grass.

Most of the nurseries are the wholesale variety, shipping to destinations throughout the United States, but a few are open to the public. Near Canby, just a few miles west of the downtown area at 995 NW Twenty-second Avenue, visit **Swan Island Dahlias** (503–266–7711) and wander through some forty-three acres of the gorgeous perennials that bloom in late summer, beginning in August and lasting until the first frost, sometime in mid- to late October.

This large nursery has been operated by the Gitts family since the 1950s, and dahlias have been part of the Canby area since the late 1940s. The farm features more than 250 dahlia varieties, with blooms ranging from 12 or more inches in diameter to those of tiny pompons, at less than 2 inches across.

From Canby you can get to Swan Island Dahlias via Ivy Street to Second Street, then Holly Street to Twenty-second Street. During the farm's indoor Dahlia Show, usually held the first or second weekend of September, you can watch professional designers fashion the vibrant blooms into creative arrangements. If you miss that event, you can still stroll through the blooming fields, beginning in August, Monday through Friday from 9:00 A.M. to dusk.

If your golf clubs are in the trunk, consider playing nine holes at the par 3 **Frontier Golf Course,** 2965 North Holly Street in Canby (503–266–4435). It's open daily March through November.

If the kids or the grandkids are along, stop at the nearby **Flower Farmer and Phoenix & Holly Railroad,** located at 2412 North Holly Street (503–266–3581; www.flowerfarmer.com). Train rides to the farm's Pumpkin Patch in October are a special treat. The open market stand is loaded with the freshest seasonal varieties of corn, beans, tomatoes, peaches, and the like; the indoor gift shop offers a fine selection of dried flowers and fresh flowers from the fields. It's open May through November from 10:00 A.M. to 6:00 P.M. Ask if the nearby **Canby Ferry** is running; if so, take the five-minute ride across this section of the Willamette River. From here you can drive west toward Sandelie Golf Course and access I–5 at nearby Wilsonville.

To delve into more history of the area, stop at the **Canby Depot Museum** (503–266–6712) at the north edge of town. The museum, maintained by the Canby Area Historical Society, is housed in the oldest railroad station owned by the C&C Railroad. The restored building is just off Highway 99E at the Fairgrounds exit and is open Thursday through Sunday from 1:00 to 4:00 P.M. Also, be sure to poke into the charming restored caboose located a few steps from the museum's entry door. To inquire about the old-fashioned **Clackamas County Fair,** one of the best late-summertime events in the area, contact the Canby Visitor Center at 266 NW First Street, Canby (503–266–4600).

## Places to Stay in Portland and Environs

### PORTLAND

**The Governor Hotel**
SW Tenth Avenue
at Alder Street
downtown
(503) 224–3400

**Hotel Lucia**
400 SW Broadway
downtown
(877) 225–1717

**Red Lion Inn**
1021 NE Grand Avenue
near the Rose Quarter
(503) 235–2100

**Residence Inn by Marriott**
1710 NE Multnomah Street
(503) 288–1400

## Places to Eat in Portland and Environs

### GRESHAM

**Sunny Han's Wok & Grill**
(casual)
305 North Main Avenue
(503) 666–3663

## HELPFUL TELEPHONE NUMBERS AND WEB SITES FOR PORTLAND AND ENVIRONS

**Clackamas County Historical Society**
(503) 655–5574
www.historicoregoncity.org

**Gresham Area Visitors Association**
(503) 665–1131
www.greshamchamber.org

**Metro GreenScene Regional Center**
(503) 797–1850
www.metro-region.org

**Oregon City and Clackamas County Visitor Center**
(800) 424–3002
www.mthoodterritory.com

**Oregon Historical Society**
(503) 222–1741
www.ohs.org

**Portland Oregon Visitor Association**
(503) 275–8355
www.travelportland.com

**Portland Parks and Recreation**
(503) 823–2223
www.portlandparks.org

**St. Helens Visitor Center**
(503) 397–0685, www.shschamber.org

**Troutdale Area & Columbia Gorge Visitor Center**
(503) 669–7473
www.westcolumbiagorgechamber.com

## MILWAUKIE

**The Bomber Restaurant**
(casual)
13515 SE McLoughlin
Boulevard
(503) 659–9306

## PORTLAND

**Assaggio**
(fine dining)
7742 SE Thirteenth Avenue
Historic Sellwood
(503) 232–6151

**Cadillac Cafe**
1801 NE Broadway
(503) 287–4750

**Cameo Cafe East**
8111 NE Sandy Boulevard
(503) 284–0401

**Elephant's Delicatessen**
115 NW Twenty-second
Street
(503) 299–6304

**Fireside Coffee Lodge**
1223 SE Powell Boulevard
(503) 230–8987

**Island Cafe on the River**
250 NE Tomahawk
Island Drive
(503) 283–0362

**McCormick & Schmick's Harborside and Pilsner Room**
(fine dining)
0309 SW Montgomery Street
RiverPlace Marina
(503) 220–1865

**Otto's Sausage Kitchen**
4138 SE Woodstock
Boulevard
(503) 771–6714

**Papa Hayden**
NW Twenty-third Avenue
(503) 228–7317

**The Rose and Thistle Restaurant & Pub**
(casual)
2314 NE Broadway
(503) 287–8582

**Wilf's Restaurant and Piano Bar at Union Station**
(fine dining)
NW Sixth and Irving Streets
(503) 223–0070

**Zell's An American Cafe**
1300 SE Morrison Street
(503) 239–0196

## SCAPPOOSE

**Mark's on the Channel**
(fine dining)
34326 Johnson Creek
Landing
(503) 543–8765

## ST. HELENS

**Dockside Steak & Pasta**
343 South First Street
(503) 366–0877

**St. Helens Cafe**
298 South First Street
(503) 397–1692

**Wild Currant Cafe**
201 South First Street
(503) 366–9099

# Columbia River Gorge and High Cascades

## Scenic Columbia River Gorge

Although much of the original winding highway, clinging alongside the Columbia River Gorge since 1915, has deteriorated or become part of streamlined Interstate 84, visitors can enjoy two good-size segments of the historic **Columbia River Scenic Highway** east of Portland between Troutdale and The Dalles.

Before heading east into the Columbia Gorge, particularly if you've not eaten, consider stopping in **Troutdale** to find the **Powerhouse Pub** and the **Black Rabbit Restaurant,** two eateries at **McMenamins Edgefield** (503–669–8610). It is located at 2126 SW Halsey Street, just south of I–84 at the Wood Village exit. The pub's juicy hamburgers are legendary; in the more formal restaurant you might order such Northwest fare as salmon with hazelnut butter or clams steamed in ale. If time allows, tour the twenty-five-acre complex that, in the early 1900s, housed the fully self-contained Multnomah County Poor Farm. Now completely restored, including a perennial and herb garden and small vineyard, the complex includes bed-and-breakfast lodging, meeting rooms, a winery and wine-cellar pub, an outdoor barbecue and picnic area, and a theater for showing vintage movies.

# COLUMBIA RIVER GORGE AND HIGH CASCADES

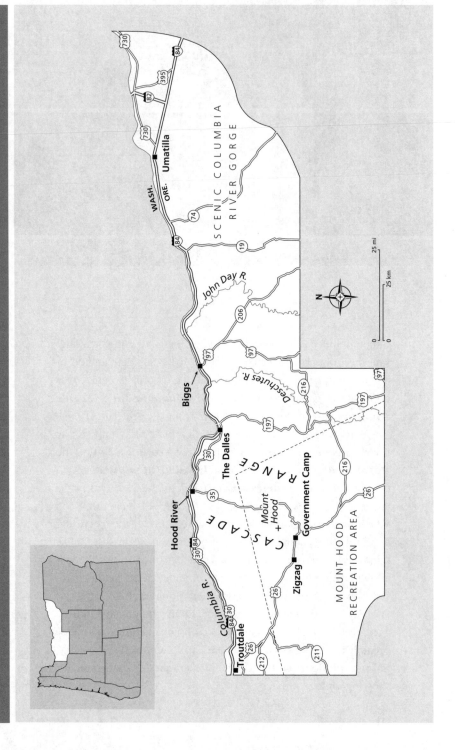

The small community of Troutdale is fast becoming a pleasant destination for antiques buffs, with fun shops such as ***Nostalgia Antiques & Collectibles*** (503–661–0123) and ***Troutdale Antique Mall*** (503–674–6820). After shopping for antiques, you can also browse in several gift shops such as ***The Troutdale General Store*** (503–492–7912); ***Front Porch Originals*** (503–492–2667); ***Celebrate Me Home*** (503–618–9394); and ***Art, Ink, & Letters*** (503–465–0055), located on the second floor of Celebrate Me Home. All these establishments are located on Troutdale's main street, the Historic Columbia River Highway. Park down by the Troutdale Rail Depot Museum and enjoy!

***Jack's Snack 'N' Tackle*** (503–665–2257), near Glenn Otto Park just east of the downtown Troutdale shops, offers deli sandwiches, espresso, and fishing supplies. If time allows, however, ease into ***Cafe Bono's*** (503–491–1200) also on Troutdale's main street and enjoy breakfast, lunch, or dinner with an Italian flair.

Should you pause in Troutdale over the weekend, see if the historic ***Harlow House Museum,*** at 726 East Historic Columbia River Highway (503–661–2164), is open. The farmhouse was built in 1900 by the Harlow family; Capt. John Harlow founded the town. Generally open Saturday and Sunday from 1:00 to 4:00 P.M., the house is cared for by the Troutdale Historical Society. Period furnishings fill the nooks and crannies of the old house, its cupboards spill over with dry goods and period wallpapers, and there may be exhibits of teapots and accessories, early fashions, and quilts. For additional information about the area, contact the staff at the West Columbia Gorge Visitor Center (503–669–7473) in Troutdale, open daily except Sunday from 8:00 A.M. to 5:00 P.M.

Railroad buffs can plan to stop and browse a nice collection of memorabilia at the ***Troutdale Rail Depot Museum,*** located at 473 East Columbia River Highway (503–661–2164). Originally built in 1882, the depot was one of the earliest stations along the Columbia River route. It's open June through October, Wednesday through Sunday from 1:00 to 4:00 P.M.

## TOP HITS IN COLUMBIA RIVER GORGE AND HIGH CASCADES

**Historic Clackamas Lake Ranger Station**
off US 26, east of Government Camp

**Historic Columbia River Highway**
starting at Troutdale

**Mosier Tunnels Trail**
Mosier–Hood River

**Timberline Lodge**
Government Camp

Punctuated with a dozen or more cascading waterfalls and enough hiking trails to keep outdoor buffs busy for weeks, the **_Historic Columbia River Highway_** offers a relaxed alternative to busy I–84. To access the first section of the old highway, detour from the freeway at the Lewis and Clark State Park exit east of Troutdale, just across the Sandy River.

## Once Upon a Time, Forty Million Years Ago . . .

I never tire of the story of the Columbia River Gorge; it starts with the volcanic peaks strung along the crest of the Cascade Mountain Range like a long necklace. We learn that eons ago their fires erupted, leaving lava and mudflows up to 2 miles thick. Although moss, lichen, wildflowers, and trees now obliterate much of the ancient volcanic activity, most everyone can learn how to identify the solidified flows stacked one on top of another along the cliffs throughout the gorge.

The next chapter in the formation of the gorge started about 15,000 years ago, near the end of the last ice age. A warming trend melted thick icefields, causing gigantic floods up to 1,200 feet deep, and these carved the river corridor, scoured steep cliffs, and left many streams hanging high above the bed of the river. These bubbling creeks and streams cascade down the basalt cliffs, creating a large concentration of waterfalls, particularly in the western section of the gorge.

Those forty-seven seventh-graders we took on field trips in the early 1970s learned how to identify and name all the waterfalls and also the varied ecosystems in this panorama, which extends from Troutdale east toward The Dalles some 80 miles away—from moist, green Douglas fir forests to pine and oak woodlands and on to the arid and sagebrush hills of the eastern section. Everyone had a clipboard, a journal, and a checklist. It was such fun, especially when we hiked up the trail at Multnomah Falls or carefully negotiated the rocky creek at narrow Oneonta Gorge to see geology up close and personal. My hope is that you, too, will take the kids, the grandkids, and the grandparents to go explore the scenic Columbia River Gorge.

For helpful information browse the Web site for the Columbia Gorge National Scenic Area, www.fs.fed.us/r6/columbia. It contains links to cultural history, geology, recreation reports, mountain-bike trails and roads, hiking trails, hiking trail of the month and trail conditions, backcountry preparation, campgrounds, fall colors, endemic wildflowers, waterfalls, education and interpretive programs, gorge views and maps, special-use permits, and volunteer opportunities. There are also links to Mount Hood National Forest and to Gifford Pinchot National Forest on the Washington side of the gorge. Travelers are also invited to stop by the Columbia River Gorge National Scenic Area/USDA Forest Service Visitor Center, 902 Wasco Avenue, Suite 200, Hood River (541–308–1700).

## TOP ANNUAL EVENTS IN COLUMBIA RIVER GORGE AND HIGH CASCADES

**Hood River Valley Blossom Festival**
Hood River; mid-April
(800) 366–3530

**Northwest Cherry Festival**
The Dalles; late April
(541) 296–2231

**All Indian Rodeo**
Tygh Ridge, Dufur; mid-May
(541) 296–2231

**Old-Fashioned Ice Cream Social**
Troutdale; early June
(503) 661–2164

**Annual Gorge Hiking Weekend**
Columbia River Gorge; mid-June
(503) 241–3762

**Cowboy Pancake Breakfast**
Camp Howe, Carson, Washington
late June
(509) 427–9427

**Trout Lake Festival of the Arts**
Trout Lake, Washington; mid-July
(509) 493–3630

**Fort Dalles Junior Rodeo**
The Dalles Rodeo Grounds; late July
(541) 296–2231

**Hood-to-Coast Relay**
Timberline Lodge to Seaside
(watch for slow traffic); late August
(503) 292–4626 or
www.hoodtocoast.com

**Hood River Valley Harvest Fest**
Hood River; mid-October
(800) 366–3530

**Wine and Art Festival**
Resort at the Mountain, Welches
mid-November
(503) 622–3005

Or, from Troutdale, continue east and south on the Historic Columbia River Highway and follow it as it parallels the bank of the Sandy River and loops several miles south, then angles east through a sun-filtered canopy of big-leaf maples and Douglas fir, climbing gradually to the small community of Corbett. Just east of Corbett, pull into the *Women's Forum Park,* at *Chanticleer Point,* for one of the best panoramas of the Columbia River Gorge and the wide Columbia River, which separates Oregon and Washington.

The view is almost too vast to absorb. You'll see the massive stone Vista House perched atop *Crown Point* just a couple of miles distant; the silver ribbon of river shimmering some 750 feet below; then 800-foot *Beacon Rock,* a volcanic monolith about 25 miles upstream on the Washington side of the river; and the Union Pacific railroad tracks and I–84, narrow ribbons paralleling the mighty river. For a pleasant overnight stay with the added pleasure of blufftop views of the Columbia River and the gorge, contact Ed and Phyllis Thiemann at *Brickhaven Bed & Breakfast,* 38717 East Historic Columbia River Highway in Corbett (503–695–5126). A cozy gathering room offers deep overstuffed chairs, brick fireplace, grand piano, video library, and nonstop views from wide windows. Two guest rooms with shared bath offer king or queen beds, English country decor, TV/VCRs, and more spectacular views of the river, the gorge, and Cascade Mountains. A full country breakfast includes hot entrees and homemade jams and breads. "We're close to Vista House and to Multnomah Falls," says Phyllis, "and guests often like to detour from here for a scenic drive up to Larch Mountain as well."

You could bring a picnic and beverages and travel the **Larch Mountain Road** about 10 miles up to the top of the mountain, where you'll find picnic tables set in cozy wooded glens and short trails out to wide vistas of the gorge. *NOTE:* The road to the top usually opens by June and closes with the first snows. Take sweaters and warm windbreakers, as temperatures can be brisk at this 1,500-foot elevation. From here backtrack down Larch Mountain Road to return to the Historic Columbia River Highway.

Samuel Hill, a Washingtonian and a lover of roads, inspired the building of the Columbia River Highway. Combining forces with Samuel Lancaster, the consulting engineer, and Portland businessmen Simon Benson and John Yeon, Hill not only envisioned the economic and tourist potential of such a road but appreciated the aesthetic and natural beauty of the gorge as well. The highway was dedicated and opened in 1915 in order to lure the state's turn-of-the-twentieth-century motorists as well as travelers en route to the 1915 Panama Pacific Exposition in California.

In the design of this first major highway in the Northwest, Lancaster incorporated graceful stone bridges, viaducts, stone walls, tunnels, and stone benches. He had been inspired by a trip to Europe with Sam Hill for the purpose of studying the historic Roman roads there. Alongside the Columbia River the ancient trail of deer, Native peoples, and those first fur trappers was replaced with the functional yet beautiful highway that clung so closely to the gorge's lush moss-and-fern-covered and tree-laden outcroppings.

Stop at the parking area at **Crown Point Visitor Center** at **Vista House** for more camera clicking and history recollecting; the impressive stone structure was dedicated in 1918 as a monument to the pioneers and early settlers of Oregon. Passing Shepperd's Dell, continue on to **Wahkeena Falls** (*Wahkeena* is an Indian word for "most beautiful"), where you'll find more parking and a large picnic area. Wahkeena tumbles and cascades in a series of frothy falls; dainty wildflowers bloom around rocks and in mossy crevices.

**Multnomah Falls,** just east of Latourell and Wahkeena Falls, is the most spectacular in the Columbia River Gorge, cascading in a long drop of 620 feet

# Waterfall-Watching 101

The more than seventy-five waterfalls on the Oregon side of the Columbia River Gorge come in all shapes, sizes, widths, and lengths. They cascade down rocky inclines, fall across basalt ledges, separate and fan over other large rocks, spray over rocky terraces, and plunge straight down in lacy drapes. Waterfall-watchers can learn to classify the eight main forms: block, cascade, fan, horsetail, plunge, punchbowl, segmented, and tiered. Here is a short list of examples easily identified along the Historic Columbia River Highway.

**Block falls:** Dutchman Falls, along upper Multnomah Creek, is an example of this type, which often pours over a wide rocky ledge.

**Cascade falls:** Upper Multnomah Falls, on Multnomah Creek, is an example of this type, which tumbles across a wide rocky area.

**Fan falls:** Fairy Falls, located about a mile from the trailhead of Wahkeena Trail #420, is a example of a fan falls, which is similar to horsetail falls but fans more broadly at its base.

**Horsetail falls:** Horsetail Falls and Oneonta Falls are good examples of this type, which drops vertically with a slight fanning toward the bottom.

**Plunge falls:** Multnomah Falls and Latourell Falls are good examples of this type, which plummets straight down in a long, watery ribbon.

**Punchbowl falls:** Punchbowl Falls, on Eagle Creek Trail, is the model; at the end of the 2 $\frac{1}{10}$ mile trail you will find a viewpoint and a comfortable bench on which to sit and enjoy this spectacular type of falls, which cascades from a narrow opening in the water source, usually a stream, and falls into a pool.

**Segmented falls:** McCord Creek Falls, on the Elowah Falls trail east of the Multnomah Falls, is a good example of this type, which typically separates into several parts over rocky areas.

**Tiered falls:** Bridal Veil Falls and Wahkeena Falls are good examples. This type of falls separates into distinctive tiers at different levels as it cascades from the top and downward.

*NOTE:* Along the route are numerous places to pull off and park; some falls are reached by short trails, while others are close to the highway. There are parks, campgrounds, and good places to picnic. Keep an alert eye on young children in your party and be wary of automobile and bicycle traffic along the busy and narrow highway. This old highway does not offer the wide shoulders that modern highways usually have. Summer weekends are busiest; try to visit midweek for a more peaceful sojourn. For helpful information and trail maps, stop at the Forest Service information counter at Multnomah Falls Lodge. Or visit the Web site www.fs.fed.us/r6/columbia, which provides information about the Columbia River Gorge National Scenic Area as well as trails to the waterfalls, directions, and more.

from the basaltic gorge rim. It's one of the highest waterfalls in the United States. If time allows, walk the easy trail to the upper bridge for a close encounter with the cascading water, accompanied by its swishing roar and cool mist.

An easy, though somewhat steep, trail continues from the bridge up to the rim for a top-of-the-falls, panoramic view of the world below. It's well worth the 2⁶⁄₁₀-mile round-trip trek, especially midweek, when you'll encounter fewer tourists. Take along some water or another beverage, and keep an eye out for poison oak, which lurks here and there along the trail's edge; the leaves look like a miniature oak leaf, and almost everyone is allergic to every part of the plant.

At the base of the falls, linger to visit rustic *Multnomah Falls Lodge,* also constructed in 1914–15, where breakfast, lunch, and dinner are served in a lovely atrium dining room; there is also a snack bar, a gift shop, and a Forest Service Visitor Center. Call (503) 695–2376 for dinner or Sunday brunch reservations.

# Backcountry Hiking in the Gorgeous Columbia River Gorge

Travelers will find more than 200 hiking trails in the Columbia River Gorge, and these are especially suited for spring, summer, and fall treks. Forest Service rangers suggest the following preparation for everyone, regardless of how experienced they are with backcountry hiking into the forest:

Always inform someone not traveling with you of your complete route.

Carry these essentials: whistle, map, compass, a flashlight with extra batteries and bulb, waterproof matches, fire starter, first-aid kit, pocket knife, hat and sunburn protection, extra water for every member of the group, trail food, and adequate clothing.

Folks today often carry cell phones with them as well, which can be quite helpful if you need assistance. If possible, learn the basic skills of backcountry orienteering with map and compass. Beginning hikers should choose short trails near established areas or, an even better option, join a guided hike. Check with local ranger stations for trail maps and for information about guided nature hikes. To research current information, start with the excellent Columbia Gorge Scenic Area Web site, www.fs .fed.us/r6/columbia, and call Portland Parks and Recreation (503–823–5132) for current lists of guided treks.

My favorite summer afternoon hike? That would be the McCord Creek Trail at Elowah Falls. The trailhead is located east of Multnomah Falls near Ainsworth State Park. Take a small picnic and beverages and enjoy munching while sitting on the large flat rocks at the upper falls. It's about a 2-mile hike to the upper falls.

East of Multnomah Falls, and still on the Historic Columbia River Highway, is **Oneonta Gorge.** Oneonta Creek bubbles through the narrowest of high, mossy chasms here, and those who don't mind getting their feet wet can walk up the shallow creek to the cascading falls. Hikers are asked to be cautious of large boulders, however, which can dislodge and cause injury. Just east, a trail at **Horsetail Falls** leads behind the upper falls, crossing Oneonta Creek right before the water plunges over the rim in a frothy ribbon.

For helpful trail maps and hiking information, go to the Zigzag Forest Service Ranger Station, 70220 East U.S. Highway 26, Zigzag (503–622–3191). The ranger station is open year-round, Monday through Friday from 8:00 A.M. to 4:30 P.M. You can also find maps at Forest Service visitor centers located at Multnomah Falls Lodge (503–695–2372) and at Dolce Skamania Lodge (509–427–2528), just east on Washington Highway 14 on the Washington side of the river (access via Bridge of the Gods at Cascade Locks).

If your visit coincides with the busy summer crush of traffic on the narrow Historic Columbia River Highway and you want to get away from the crowds, continue east toward **Ainsworth State Park.** Instead of pulling onto I–84 at this point, stay to the right on the frontage road that parallels the freeway and continue just a half mile or so to a large parking area and the **Elowah Falls–McCord Creek** trailhead. Bask in the sun on large rounded rocks at the lower falls—take a left at the trail's first fork—or relax in sun-filtered shade on large rocks at the upper falls. Both hikes are easy—less than 2 miles in length—and the views of the falls and gorge are spectacular, particularly on the upper falls route. These quiet, peaceful walks are far removed from the crowds and allow a focused interlude with the incredibly beautiful gorge habitat.

If time permits, don't miss this trek into history, geology, and plant life that numerous wildlife and conservation groups are working to protect. From the Native Plant Societies of Oregon and Washington to local chapters of the Audubon Society, the Sierra Club, and The Nature Conservancy, as well as the Friends of the Columbia River Gorge, the USDA Forest Service, the Mazamas, the Trails Club of Oregon, the American Alpine Club, and the Historic Preservation League, thousands of folks are dedicated to the task of preserving the fragile and irreplaceable as well as historical habitats within the Columbia River Gorge. Contact Friends of Columbia River Gorge (503–241–3762; www.gorge friends.org) about the annual **Gorge Hiking Weekend,** which offers group hikes of various lengths and terrain in the western section of the gorge in mid-June. Contact the Forest Service Visitor Center at Multnomah Falls Lodge (503–695–2372) to ask about day hikes into old-growth Douglas fir forests in the Mount Hood National Forest, such as Multnomah Creek, Upper Multnomah

Loop, Bell Creek, Herman Camp Loop, Herman Creek, North Lake Loop, Indian Springs Loop, Lost Lake Loop, Lost Lake Old-Growth Trail, Lost Lake Butte, and Jones Creek. *NOTE:* On all hikes in the gorge, be sure to wear sturdy shoes; stay on the established trails; and pack along water, an emergency trail kit, camera, and binoculars. There is poison oak in the gorge, so be wary of the small oak-shaped leaves.

Lots of folks, including kids, are learning about the sport and skill of orienteering, finding one's way through natural terrain. The sport combines land navigation using a map and compass with running or walking through a natural area. Local groups offer clinics, workshops, seminars, and field meets. Each meet, including national and international championships, offers shorter courses with navigation geared to beginners as well as more challenging courses. "Orienteering is also a popular sport in Europe," says one aficionado of the craft. For current information on local offerings, check the Pacific Northwest Orienteering Web site, www.pnwo.org. Proper gear for orienteering forays includes long pants, sunscreen, a hat, water, food, extra clothing, bug spray for ticks and other assorted critters, and a whistle for everyone in your group (just in case someone gets lost).

Other folks are learning about the many edible wild plants in the region from John Kallas, a guru of edible wild food with a doctorate in nutrition from Michigan State University. He says Oregon is the nirvana of edible vegetation. But he also cautions folks about what not to eat; one such no-no is the wild iris. How about making pudding out of acorns, muffins from cattail flour and blackberries, even vinaigrette from Oregon grape? For information on current field trips, contact John Kallas at Wild Food Adventures in Portland (503–775–3828; www.wildfoodadventures.com), or contact Portland Parks and Recreation (503–823–2223).

Or, you could just enjoy identifying and photographing the wildflowers and native plants of the gorge while walking the trails. For native plant lists and helpful information on best times to view blooming wildflowers, visit the Zigzag Ranger Station, 70220 East US 26 (503–622–3191). Avid wildflower buffs and those who are interested in learning more about the native plants of the gorge are invited to attend the Guest Speaker Series, which takes place at Skamania Lodge in Stevenson, Washington, on Sunday afternoons during March, April, and May. Check the informative Web site, www.fs.fed.us/r6/columbia, or call the Forest Service Information Center at the lodge (509–427–2528) for current information. Fall colors in the gorge are supreme during late October and early November, with big-leaf maple, cottonwood, Oregon ash, and leafy shrubs all changing to brilliant hues.

Connect with I–84 near McCord Creek, continuing east toward Bonneville Dam and Cascade Locks. First detour to see **Bonneville Dam,** the first hydro-electric dam constructed on the Columbia River. Built in 1937 and dedicated by President Franklin Roosevelt, the dam offers underwater views of salmon and steelhead as they swim up the fish ladders to reach the upper section of the river. There are locks for use by riverboats, a children's playground, and large

## Selected Columbia River Gorge Historic Events

**1792:** Capt. Robert Gray and his crew sail up the river from the Pacific Ocean

**1805:** Lewis and Clark expedition passes through the gorge on its way to the Pacific Ocean

**1811:** Pacific Fur Company is established at Astoria with early fur trading in the gorge

**1825:** The British Hudson's Bay Company establishes Fort Vancouver near the site of Vancouver and Portland

**1832:** Nathaniel Wyeth leads the first group of white settlers through the gorge

**1836:** The first steamship, *Beaver,* laden with supplies, makes its way from the mouth of the Columbia River at Astoria to Fort Vancouver

**1841:** The first Oregon Trail families and their goods are floated down the treacherous river on flat riverboats to Fort Vancouver

**1845:** The Barlow Toll Road is cut through thick forests on the south flank of Mount Hood, providing an alternate route to the Willamette Valley

**1851:** The first mail is delivered in the gorge to the post office at the Lower Cascades

**1878:** Construction begins on Cascade Locks; it is completed in 1896

**1879:** Fishwheels begin operating on the Columbia River

**1915:** The Historic Columbia River Highway is completed

**1926:** The Bridge of the Gods is completed at Cascade Locks

**1938:** Bonneville Dam, the first federal dam on the river, is completed and is dedicated by Franklin D. Roosevelt

**1986:** The Columbia River Gorge National Scenic Area is established, protecting 253,500 acres of the gorge on both sides of the river

**2000:** A 51-mile section of the Historic Columbia River Highway is designated a National Historic Landmark

shallow pools for seeing the enormous Columbia River sturgeon. These light gray, leathery-looking fish reach lengths of 5 feet and longer.

Just east of the dam, exit at Cascade Locks for a good assortment of hamburgers, soups, salads, and desserts at the *Charburger Restaurant* (541–374–8477) and enjoy a view of the Columbia River as well. In a cottonwood-shaded park along the river, just a few blocks east of the restaurant, the *Port of Cascade Locks Marine Park* has a small historical museum, situated in one of the original lock masters' houses, that offers an extensive photo and artifact collection. It's open daily, afternoons, June through September 1. On the grounds you can also take a look at the first rail steam engine, the *Oregon Pony*, used on a 4-mile stretch of track, Oregon's first railroad, constructed in 1858. During summer the 145-foot stern-wheeler *Columbia Gorge* takes visitors on two-hour tours up and down the river, boarding from the Marine Park dock. For current information call Port of Cascade Locks Visitor Center at (541) 374–8427.

In 1875, army engineers recommended building a canal to circumvent the dangerous rapids at both Cascade City and The Dalles; the work was completed in 1896. Before then passengers and cargo were unloaded and moved overland on the 4-mile track to a safer point on the river, where they were reloaded on a different steamboat for the continuing journey. Later, bridges connected the two sides of the Columbia River at Cascade Locks, Hood River, The Dalles, Biggs, and Umatilla.

If time allows, cross the historic *Bridge of the Gods* from Cascade Locks to the Washington side of the river, turning west on Washington Highway 14 for a few miles to *Beacon Rock.* A steep, safe trail with steps here and there leads to the top of this volcanic remnant. On a bright sunny day, you can sit rather comfortably on large flat rocks atop the monolith to enjoy great views of the gorge upriver to the east and downriver to the west.

When you return east on WA 14, continue a couple of miles beyond the bridge toward Stevenson, turning north in just a quarter mile or so to visit *Dolce Skamania Lodge* (509–427–7700 or 800–221–7117). It overlooks the gorge to the east, on the Washington side of the Columbia River. The rustic Cascadian-style lodge (which has an enormous lobby/lounge with a gigantic rock fireplace) offers overnight accommodations, an eighteen-hole golf course, tennis courts, walking and horseback-riding trails, a gift shop, an indoor swimming pool, and a natural-rock outdoor whirlpool spa. A restaurant and lounge both take advantage of all that marvelous scenery. And don't miss a visit to the *Columbia Gorge Interpretive Center* (509–427–8211; www.columbiagorge .org), located just below the lodge at 990 SW Rock Creek Drive. It also commands a grand view of the river and gorge toward the east. Inside you'll see the replica of an enormous Indian fishwheel and a gigantic old Corliss steam engine, once used in logging, that still actually works. The interpretive center and its splendid collection of artifacts and reference materials is open daily.

Return to the Oregon side and I–84 via Bridge of the Gods, heading east again. Detour at Hood River, about 18 miles east of Cascade Locks, and wind down to the *Hood River Boat Basin and Marina Park* to watch dozens of men and women ply the Columbia's rough waters on sailboards that sport sails of bright rainbow colors. This particularly windy stretch of the river from Cascade Locks through Hood River and The Dalles to Rufus has become a mecca for the intrepid sailboarders. With their oblong boards firmly attached atop cars and vans, these enthusiasts return like flocks of migrating birds, beginning in April and remaining through September.

In mid-July the *Gorge Games* feature adrenalin-pumping competition in numerous lively outdoor events—from sailboarding, paragliding, kayaking, and kite-skiing to snowboarding, mountain biking, and rock climbing. For entry information (for hardy daredevils and those in top physical condition), spectator information, or a schedule of events, check with the Hood River Visitor Center, located near the marina at 405 Port Way Avenue (800–366–3530; www .hood river.org). Helpful information and brochures can also be obtained from the Columbia River Gorge National Scenic Area office, 902 Wasco Avenue in Hood River (541–308–1700; www.fs .fed.us/r6/columbia).

For a glimpse into Hood River's interesting past, plan to visit the *Hood River County Historical Museum*—located at 300 East Port Marina Drive (541–386–6772) near Port Marina Park—where exhibits of Native American culture, pioneer history, lumbering, and fruit-growing memorabilia are displayed. The museum is open April through October, Monday through Saturday from 10:00 A.M. to 4:00 P.M. and Sunday from noon to 4:00 P.M.

Speaking of fruit, if travels bring you to the area in early spring, plan to take in the annual *Hood River Valley Blossom Festival* during the

Sailboarding on the Columbia River

third weekend of April, when thousands of pear, apple, and cherry trees are in glorious bloom in the Hood River Valley. Local tours through the orchards, along with arts-and-crafts fairs, quilt sales, antiques sales, and open houses at fruit-packing establishments, wineries, and fire departments, are among the eclectic round of activities that take place throughout the weekend. For the current Fruit Loop map and brochure, contact the Hood River Visitor Center at (800) 366–3530.

One of the best offerings is a nostalgic train ride on the **Mount Hood Railroad**'s Fruit Blossom Special, which winds through the flowering orchards to Parkdale and Odell. The old railroad, which began in 1906 as a passenger and freight line, was resurrected in 1987, when a group of enterprising Hood River–area citizens purchased it from the Union Pacific Railroad. Several 1910–26 Pullman coaches have been restored and are pulled by two General Motors/EMD GP-9 locomotives built in the 1950s. For current information contact the Mount Hood Railroad, 110 Railroad Avenue, Hood River (541–386–3556; www.mthoodrr.com).

For overnight accommodations check with the staff at the refurbished **Hood River Hotel,** at 102 Oak Street (800–386–1859; www.hoodriver hotel.com) in the uptown area near the railroad depot. Renovated in the early 1990s, the four-story redbrick structure offers twenty-six guest rooms to Columbia River Gorge travelers. Breakfast, lunch, and dinner are available in the hotel

## Hood River's Fruit Loop Trail

At these and other open-air markets open from June through September, you'll find a variety of Hood River Valley fruits, berries, nuts (including colossal chestnuts), and tasty baked goods. (For maps and info log onto www.hoodriverfruitloop.com.)

**Alice's Orchard**
1623 Orchard Road, Hood River
(541) 386-5478

**Draper's Farm**
6200 Highway 35, Parkdale
(541) 352-6625

**Gorge Fruit & Craft Fair**
Hood River County fairgrounds, Odell
mid-April and mid-October
(541) 354-2865

**Hood River Saturday Market**
Fifth and Cascade Streets, Hood River

**Nutquacker Farms**
3435 Neal Creek Road, Hood River
(541) 354-3531

**Rasmussen Farms**
3020 Thomsen Road, Hood River
(541) 386-4622
www.rasmussenfarms.com

restaurant, **Pasquale's Ristorante,** open daily from 7:00 A.M. to 10:00 P.M.; guests are served a continental breakfast.

Travelers can find a number of welcoming bed-and-breakfast inns in the area—equally good places to bed down for the night. **Panorama Log Lodge Bed & Breakfast,** located 3 miles from Hood River at 2290 Old Dalles Road (888–403–2687; www.panoramalodge.com), offers three guest rooms with outrageous views of Mount Hood and the Columbia River Gorge. Another cozy bed-and-breakfast is tucked away at 46650 East Historic Columbia River Highway: **Bridal Veil Lodge Bed & Breakfast,** in the hamlet of Bridal Veil (503–695–2333). At **Lakecliff Bed & Breakfast,** 3820 Westcliff Drive (541–386–7000; www.lakecliffbnb.com), guests find cozy rooms, gas log fireplaces, and wide views of the Columbia River. For current information about other comfortable bed-and-breakfast inns in the area, contact the Hood River Visitor Center (800–366–3530) or the Hood River Bed & Breakfast Association (541–386–6767).

If you decide to detour from Hood River south toward Parkdale and the Mount Hood Recreation Area, **Sage's Cafe & Coffee House** at 202 Cascade Street (541–386–9404) is a good place to stop for made-to-order deli sandwiches, salads, soups, and special desserts. The restaurant is open daily.

Also welcoming travelers are **6th Street Bistro & Loft** at 509 Cascade Street (541–386–5737); **Hood River Bagel Company,** 13 Oak Street (541–386–2123); and **Divots Clubhouse Restaurant,** 3605 Brookside Drive (866–386–7770), offering good eats and great views of Mount Hood and Mount Adams at Indian Creek Golf Course.

If, as many Oregonians do, you love live local theater, see www.gorge.net for the current play schedule at the **CAST Performing Arts Theatre** or call the Waucoma Bookstore (541–386–5353).

Plan to visit **Oregon's International Museum of Carousel Art,** located at 304 Oak Street, Hood River (541–387–4622), which is open Wednesday through Sunday from noon to 4:00 P.M. You'll see some 135 colorfully restored carousel animals, including horses, tigers, and dragons.

You might now head into the eastern section of the Columbia River Gorge, taking I–84 for about 20 miles to The Dalles. On the way, stop to walk or bike a scenic section of the old Columbia Gorge Highway for about ¾ mile to the **Mosier Tunnels,** now open only to hikers and bikers. The twin open-air tunnels, closed since 1946, stretch 400 feet along a cliff that overlooks the river—the view is awesome. Access the eastern section of the Mosier Tunnels trailhead by driving east on I–84 from Hood River for 5 miles, taking exit 69. Proceed a few blocks from here to U.S. Highway 30, and as you enter Mosier immediately

## Historical Tidbits from 1805 and Eons Before

Explorers Meriwether Lewis and William Clark, in 1805, as well as the French fur trappers and Native peoples who preceded them, knew the Columbia River and its swift currents intimately. They navigated its rapids and 4- to 6-foot waves in dugouts hand-hewn from large Douglas fir trunks.

This mighty river, whose humble beginnings are traced north to the Canadian Rockies in British Columbia, has been tamed for both navigation and flood control by a series of power-generating dams. But before this, those Native peoples who lived here—the Yakamas, Warm Springs, Umatilla, and Nez Percé—fished the river for salmon at Celilo Falls near The Dalles. Tribes from all over the Northwest came to this area to trade for dried, smoked salmon. Remnants from enormous and ancient trade sites have been uncovered, one in particular near Stevenson on the Washington side of the river—I think it must have been a lively combination of farmers' market, arts-and-crafts market, Saturday-night dance, and giant community potluck!

turn left onto Rock Creek Road and climb ½ mile up to the Mark Hatfield trailhead parking area. From here walk back down the road for about 2 blocks to access the newly paved Mosier Tunnels trail; there is handicap parking here. Because of the 5 percent gradual but consistent grade on the ¾-mile route, take along plenty of water when you hike this trail. Maps and additional information can be obtained at the Twin Tunnels Visitor Center in Hood River (541–387–4010). To get to the center from Hood River, take exit 64 and go south for a few blocks; then turn east onto US 30 and continue east 1 mile.

For additional refreshments before or after your hike to the tunnels, slow down on your way through the tiny community of Mosier and stop at **Route 30 Roadside Refreshments** (541–478–2525), open April to October, daily from 9:00 A.M. to sunset. Hikers and bikers swear by the espresso, fruit smoothies, and ice cream cones. For a tasty lunch try **Wildflower Cafe** (541–478–0111) on Main Street, open Wednesday to Sunday. From Mosier wind east on the last section of the old highway and stop at scenic **Rowena Plateau** and at **Tom McCall Preserve** to see carpets of wildflowers and more panoramic views of the Columbia River. This 15-mile stretch of the old scenic highway joins I–84 at The Dalles. If you decide to stay overnight in the area, however, call the friendly folks at **The Mosier House Bed & Breakfast,** a large restored Victorian now on the National Register of Historic Places, at 704

Third Avenue (541–478–3640). There are three comfy guest rooms on the second floor with large shared baths, plus a master suite with a private bath. The innkeepers serve tea and tasty baked goods in the afternoon and a full gourmet breakfast in the morning.

Over the years the power-generating dams built on the Columbia River gradually obliterated both the historic rapids and the ancient fishing grounds of Native peoples. An example is the famous Celilo Falls, which was near the site of **The Dalles Dam.**

For information about visiting the dam, stop at The Dalles Area Visitor Center at 404 West Second Street (541–296–2231 or 800–255–3385). Also inquire about the area's festivals, such as the **Celilo Wyam Salmon Feast** in early April, the **Cherry Festival** in mid-April, the **Tygh Valley All Indian Rodeo** in mid-May, the **Fort Dalles Rodeo** in mid-July, the historic **Dufur Threshing Bee** in early August, the **Gorge Cities Windsurfing Blowout** in mid-August, and the **Wasco County Fair** at the end of August.

To better understand the historical significance of this area, visit the **Fort Dalles Historical Museum** (541–296–4547), at 500 West Fifteenth Street, located in the only remaining building, the Surgeons Quarters, at 1857 Fort Dalles. The charming carpenter Gothic structure is listed on the National Register of Historic Places, and the museum is open daily March through October.

Ask, too, about the self-guided walking or driving tour of historic homes and buildings and for directions to **Sorosis Park,** located above the city and offering a magnificent viewing spot and a rose garden at the top of the bluff. From the viewing area notice the large bend in the Columbia River. By the point where the river reaches The Dalles, the Douglas fir–clothed western section of the gorge has changed to another elevation, above 2,000 feet, to the sunny eastern high desert. Now the rounded, hunched hills are sparsely clad, and in nearby canyons, sagebrush and bitterbrush bloom splashes of yellow in the spring and early summer. Rolling wheat country extends east and north of The Dalles up into Wasco, Moro, and Grass Valley, and thousands of cherry trees blossom each spring in nearby orchards as well.

To learn more about the history of the gorge and its settlement, visit the **Columbia Gorge Discovery Center** and the **Wasco County Historical Museum,** 5000 Discovery Drive in The Dalles (541–296–8600); access the museum complex via exit 82 from I–84, just west of The Dalles city center. You and the kids travel back in time to an early-nineteenth-century town and can board a side-wheeler, make your own canning label, or dress up in vintage clothing. The museum complex and Basalt Rock Cafe are open daily from 10:00 A.M. to 6:00 P.M. except for major holidays.

In The Dalles you can stop at **Holstein's Coffee Co.,** 811 East Third Street (541–298–2326), for cinnamon rolls, espresso, and lattes; at historic **Baldwin Saloon,** 204 Court Street (541–296–5666), for great service and meals that get raves from locals; and at **Cousins Restaurant & Saloon,** 2116 West Sixth Street (541–298–2771), for down-home cookin'. Diners are greeted with a friendly "Hi, cousin," from waiters dressed in black slacks, white shirts, and black vests. The bar stools in the cafe section are fashioned of stainless steel milk cans with round seats covered in black vinyl; the Formica table tops are of whimsical black-and-white cowhide patterns.

Short excursions on the near Washington side of the Columbia River include the impressive European-style **Maryhill Museum** (509–773–3733), east on WA 14, where you can see an extensive collection of vintage chess sets, a sampling of Rodin sketches and sculptures, and a splendid restored collection of French designer mannequins (miniatures) dating back to postwar 1945. The museum's **Cafe Maryhill** offers deli-style lunches and outdoor seating over-looking the Columbia River. For fresh produce and crafts, stop by the **Maryhill Saturday Market** at 65 Maryhill Highway on Saturday, 10:00 A.M. to 5:00 P.M., June to October. **Maryhill Winery** (877–627–9445), located just west of the museum, offers samples of its wines, such as pinot noir, merlot, zinfandel, and chardonnay. The handsome mahogany bar in the tasting room was sal-vaged from the Fort Spokane Brewery. The winery is open daily from 10:00 A.M., and it has an arbor-shaded patio that invites picnics and overlooks the scenic gorge and the river. The winery's 4,000-seat outdoor amphitheater offers music events during the summer (www.maryhillwinery.com); bring your fold-ing chairs and blankets. For other wineries and tasting rooms in the region, log onto www.yakimavalleywine.com.

From The Dalles take another pleasant side trip into the rural past, by heading south on U.S. Highway 197 just 13 miles to the tiny farming commu-nity of **Dufur.** You're definitely in the slow lane now. Gently rolling wheat fields, the color of golden honey, extend for miles in all directions. Several tall grain elevators punctuate the wide blue skyline. You see Mount Hood's snowy peak to the west. There is no freeway noise, just quantities of fresh, clean air and friendly smiles from local residents. You ease into the rhythm of the farm-land.

You can pause in the small farm community of Dufur and hunker down at the nearby **Dufur Pastime Cafe,** 25 South Main Street (541–467–9248), for breakfast, lunch, and dinner. The cafe is open daily except Monday. You can pick up snacks and beverages at the town grocery store and also see the large stuffed cougar on display there.

From Dufur continue about 30 miles south on US 197 through Tygh Valley to Maupin and the **Deschutes River Recreation Area.** In addition to many campgrounds and places to fish, including fly fishing, you could bed down in rustic comfort at **Imperial River Company Lodge** (541–395–2404; www .deschutesriver.com), on the banks of the Deschutes. The owners specialize in one- to three-day rafting trips (with gourmet meals) on this popular stretch of the river. **The Oasis Resort,** 616 Mill Street in Maupin (541– 395–2611), offers cabins, the Oasis Cafe, fishing guide services, and "the world's smallest fly-fishing museum." Additional information about the area can be obtained from the Maupin Visitor Center, located in a small log structure at the edge of town (541–395–2599).

# Mount Hood Recreation Area

**Mount Hood,** an imposing, snow-covered, andesite volcano rising some 11,235 feet from the forested Cascades, easily dominates the skyline to the south of Hood River and is always seen on clear days from Portland, 50 miles to the west. Newcomers, as well as those of us who have lived in Portland and in the Columbia River Gorge area most of our lives, all naturally claim the mountain as our personal property.

One of the most scenic routes to the mountain is accessed from Hood River at the exit near Port Marina Park. Along Highway 35 you'll encounter the venerable, snowcapped peak around many bends while winding up through the Hood River Valley's lush orchards. When driving through the area in the fall, detour at **Sappington Orchards** or at **Apple Valley Country Store** to sample fresh apple cider and purchase homemade applesauce and gift packages of delicious apples and pears. The orchards are located at 3187 Highway 35, about 6 miles from Hood River; visitors are welcome to stop in daily from September 15 to December 15.

Apple Valley Country Store is situated a few miles west, to Odell, then north on Odell Highway to Tucker Road. A popular nosh-and-shop, the organic farm is located at 2363 Tucker Road (541–386–1971; www.applevaleystore .com). It's open daily March through December. You'll feel that you've stepped back in time as you browse the store's wares, from corn relish and spiced peaches to huckleberry preserves and apple cider.

A good choice for dinner along Highway 35 is to detour onto Cooper Spur Road and stop at **Cooper Spur Inn** (541–352–6692; www.innatcooperspur .com) at 10755 Cooper Spur Road; this is about 23 miles from Hood River. Sitting snugly on the eastern flank of Mount Hood, this log cabin–style steak house is noted for serving logger-style portions of food in its rustic mountain atmosphere. It's open Wednesday to Sunday from 5:00 to 9:00 P.M.

During snowy winter months, **Cooper Spur Ski Area**, at 11000 Cloud Cap Road (541–352–7803; www.cooperspur.com), just up the road from the inn, is a great place for families and beginners to enjoy skiing on easy terrain. Here you'll encounter just 500 vertical feet of terrain, 4,500-foot top elevation, with one rope tow and one T-bar. For cross-country buffs there are about 10 kilometers of groomed Nordic trails. Another excellent area for beginning skiers and for the kids is **Summit Ski Area** (503–272–0256; www.summitskiarea.com) in Government Camp, on the southwest flank of the mountain. The top elevation is 4,306 feet, with a 306-foot vertical drop. There is a good inner-tubing hill here, as well as a 10K Nordic track for cross-country skiing.

Legend passed down by Native peoples says that Mount Hood was at one time a mighty volcano known as Wy'east, a great chief turned into a mountain, spouting flame and hurling boulders skyward in anger. The first recorded white people to visit the area, members of the British Royal Navy, saw the mountain in 1792 from their vessel while sailing on the Columbia River. A British naval officer named it Hood, after his admiral. The earliest white folks to trek over the slopes of Mount Hood were most likely French fur trappers, in about 1818; botanist David Douglas, in 1833; and a few other hardy souls who followed the main deer and Indian trails connecting the east and west sides of the mountain.

For a good bit of history and a helpful map of the first emigrant road across the Cascades along those ancient Indian trails, pick up a copy of *The Barlow Road,* available from the Zigzag Ranger Station, 70220 East US 26 (503–622–3191).

The **Barlow Road,** opened in 1845, completed the Oregon Trail as a land route from Independence, Missouri, to the Willamette Valley. This alternate land route to Oregon City on the Willamette River became a major entry into western Oregon for those who wanted to avoid the dangers or costs of floating down the Columbia River from The Dalles to Fort Vancouver.

Samuel K. Barlow, his family, and others literally chopped the crude wagon trail through the thick evergreen forest on the southeast and southwest flanks of Mount Hood to a location between Government Camp and Rhododendron. Following roughly the same route, Highway 35 winds past Cooper Spur Ski Area and intersects with US 26 just south of the busy **Mount Hood Meadows Ski Area** (503–337–2222; www.skihood.com). Historic Government Camp is about 6 miles west. (You can also head southeast at this point, toward Warm Springs, Kah-Nee-Ta Resort, and central Oregon.)

As you make your way to Government Camp, stop at **Trillium Lake** and

# Mount Hood Ski Area Information

**ON THE INTERNET**

www.skibowl.com
(at Government Camp)

www.skihood.com
(Mount Hood Meadows)

www.timberlinelodge.com
(Timberline Lodge and Ski Area)

**FOR UPDATED SNOW REPORTS
AND CONDITIONS**

**Cooper Spur Ski Area**
north of Hood River via Highway 35
(541) 352–7803

**Mount Hood Meadows Ski Area**
south of Cooper Spur via Highway 35
(503) 337–2222

**Mount Hood Ski Bowl**
at Government Camp off US 26
(503) 222–2695

**Summit Ski Area**
at Government Camp off US 26
(503) 272–0256

**Timberline Ski Area**
6 miles above Government Camp
off US 26
(503) 222–2211

**CROSS-COUNTRY SKIING,
SNOWSHOEING, SNOWMOBILING
INFORMATION**

**Mount Hood Recreation Area
Visitor Center**
on US 26 at Welches
(503) 622–4822; www.mthood.info

**Zigzag Ranger Station**
on US 26 at Zigzag, between
Welches and Rhododendron
(503) 622–3191
www.fs.fed.us/r6/mthood

**OUTDOOR RECREATION CLASSES,
GROUP LESSONS, OVERNIGHT AND
DAY TRIPS**

**Outdoor Recreation, Portland Public
Parks & Recreation Department**
(503) 823–5132

take a look at the remnants of the Barlow Trail and *Summit Meadows,* which is where the emigrants camped. The Forest Service access road, from US 26, is just opposite the *Snow Bunny Ski Area*—a great place for families with small children—a few miles west of the Highway 35 junction. Near the large meadow you can find a small pioneer cemetery and the site of one of the early tollhouses.

At this site once stood early pioneer Perry Vicker's log cabin, barn, lodge, and shingled tepee. Vicker also built, across the north edge of the meadows, a corduroy road—a type of early road constructed by laying small tree trunks side by side. Such roads became familiar surfaces for horse-drawn wagons and, later, for the first automobiles. Needless to say, traveling in those early days was a distinct challenge and more often than not included moving branches, or even fallen trees, off the roadway in order to continue the journey.

Hike or drive down to Trillium Lake for a picnic and stay in one of the nearby campgrounds: one right on the lake and the other, *Still Creek Campground,* along the creek just north of the pioneer graves and Summit Meadows. During July and August you'll probably find delicious huckleberries along Still Creek; during winter folks clamp on cross-country skis and trek across the snowy meadow and onto the same roads all the way around the picturesque frozen lake. This is a lovely, and easy, trek not to be missed, especially on a crisp blue-sky day.

Then, too, you can enjoy this forested area in the warm spring, summer, and fall months, finding a cluster of small lakes in which to swim, canoe, row, and fish. These small lakes are also great places to camp away from the crowds: Timothy Lake, Little Crater Lake, Clackamas Lake, Summit Lake, Clear Lake, Trillium Lake, and Frog Lake. For information on the lakes and campgrounds, call the Zigzag Ranger Station (503–622–3191). Ask about visiting days for the *Historic Clackamas Lake Ranger Station,* now listed on the National Register of Historic Places. The complex dates from 1933, when it was constructed by members of the Depression-era Civilian Conservation Corps. You'll see two wood-frame houses built for the district ranger and his assistant, a gas station, a road-and-trails warehouse, a mess hall, a blacksmith shop, a pump house, a barn, and a fire warehouse. The buildings are beautifully crafted and enhanced with fine stonework. The complex is open, depending on snow conditions, from Memorial Day weekend to mid-September, Thursday through Monday from 9:00 A.M. to 5:00 P.M. There's also a scenic 2-mile hike that starts at the ranger station. At an elevation of 3,400 feet, there are about forty-five campsites here, drinking water, and vault toilets. Most of the narrow roads traveling to the lakes from US 26 are paved and can accommodate small RVs.

In historic Government Camp sleep snug and warm at *Falcon's Crest Inn Bed & Breakfast* (503–272–3403), at an elevation of 4,000 feet, and imagine what sleeping outdoors in a covered wagon might have been like. Innkeepers Bob and Melody Johnson pamper guests with special treats, the sort those emigrants probably never experienced at Perry Vickers's tollgate cabin just up the road at Summit Meadows. Try evening aperitifs and appetizers served in the comfortable Great Room, warmed by an enormous woodstove; then a gourmet dinner, if you wish, a prix fixe affair; and finally a morning tray, set just outside your door, of steaming-hot coffee and freshly baked muffins, often with both orange and cranberry butters. Breakfast at the dining table, with its ample window views, may consist of waffles with a strawberry compote, a special

## Mount Hood's Early Climbers

According to records at the Oregon Historical Society library, the earliest settlers to climb Mount Hood, on July 11, 1857, were members of a party from Portland led by Henry L. Pittock, who published the *Oregonian* newspaper. Henry later assisted in forming the long-standing mountain lover's club, Mazamas, based in Portland. In 1867 two women, Frances Case and Mary Robinson, climbed the mountain wearing traditional Victorian long skirts! Another notable mountaineer, Elijah Coalman, first climbed Mount Hood at age fifteen, in 1897. He later became the first fire lookout on top of the mountain in 1914, and in 1915 he built the first shelter at the summit. Elijah must have thrived on deep snow, chilling winds, and icy crevasses, for he climbed Mount Hood nearly 600 times and stayed on as lookout until 1930.

mushroom quiche, or a cheesy omelet, along with seasonal fruits, juices, and coffee or herbal teas.

In the early 1900s pioneer guide Oliver Yocum built a hotel at Government Camp, and it survived until 1933, when a fire destroyed it. Within ten years after the Barlows' pioneering route over the shoulder of **Mount Hood,** the mountain became a much-sought-after landmark, instead of a formidable nuisance, and for more than a century and a half it has drawn city dwellers to its slopes year-round.

As early as 1890, skiers and climbers flocked to the snowy slopes of Mount Hood. And in those days it took folks at least two days' travel to get from Portland to the mountain. Until a graded road was constructed to Government Camp in the 1920s, the last day's trek during winter months was via snowshoes from Rhododendron. In 1924 the first hotel at timberline was built by the Forest Service, near the present Timberline Lodge. Serving as emergency shelter during summer and winter, the original lodge was about 8 by 16 feet, with several additional tents nearby. Mountain lovers brought their own blankets, rented a mattress, and got a meal.

Today, however, you can sleep in more luxurious comfort at this 6,000-foot level by checking in at one of the state's oldest mountain inns, **Timberline Lodge** (503–622–7979; www.timberlinelodge.com), located just 6 miles up the mountain from Government Camp. Construction of the lodge was approved in 1935 by President Franklin Roosevelt as a project of the Works Progress Administration during the Great Depression. A contingent of more than 250 Northwest artisans—carpenters, stonemasons, woodcarvers, metalworkers, painters, weavers, and furniture makers—created in two years a magnificent lodge that looks like the rough-hewn castle of a legendary Norse mountain king.

The lodge was dedicated by President Roosevelt in September 1937 and officially opened to the public in February 1938. Fires crackled in six fireplaces arrayed around the massive hexagonal chimney structure, 14 feet in diameter, constructed with 400 tons of native stone, and rising 92 feet in the peak, as a parade of some 150 guests registered for the opening weekend. Today you can hear FDR's voice crackling from a vintage recording—a portion of his dedication speech—as you walk through the *Rachel Griffen Historic Exhibition Center* on the refurbished main-entry level.

Just imagine, however, in the not-too-distant past, skiers grouped about those massive entry-level fireplaces, drying their ski socks and munching sack lunches before heading back to the snowy slopes. Nowadays all skiers use the Wy'East Day Lodge just across the upper parking area.

Most of the fifty-nine guest rooms at venerable Timberline Lodge are one of a kind, with carved headboards, patchwork quilts, and hooked rugs. Everything was made by hand—some of the original curtains, from dyeing old army uniforms and blankets. The original fabrics and weavings, along with the Native American, pioneer, native wildflower, and animal motifs, have all been restored and repaired through the painstaking efforts of the *Friends of Timberline.* The person who initiated the fine restoration of Timberline Lodge in the 1950s is longtime mountain lover Richard Kohnstamm. Above the second-floor lounge and restaurant is a quaint, hexagonal balcony with small alcoves, some with benches and desks offering a place to write letters or read. To the north, floor-to-ceiling windows frame spectacular Mount Hood.

If time allows, plan to have breakfast, lunch, or dinner with a view in the lovely and rustic *Cascade Dining Room,* located on the second floor in Timberline Lodge; reservations are required for dinner (503–622–0700). Breakfast is served from 8:00 to 10:00 A.M., lunch is served from noon to 2:30 P.M., and dinner is served from 5:30 to 8:00 P.M. Other places to eat inside the lodge include the informal Blue Ox Deli, open daily from noon to 7:00 P.M. during the summer season, and the cozy Ram's Head Bar, open daily from 11:00 A.M. to 11:00 P.M.

In the early 1940s the state highway commission decided upon a great experiment: to keep the section of narrow road between Welches and Government Camp open throughout the entire winter. Winter sports enthusiasts were exhilarated. They flocked to the mountain, and the pilgrimage to Mount Hood has never ceased. For information about alpine and Nordic skiing areas, as well as the names of expert instructors and mountain-climbing guides, contact the *Mount Hood Area Visitor Center,* 65000 East US 26, Welches

## OTHER ATTRACTIONS WORTH SEEING IN COLUMBIA RIVER GORGE AND HIGH CASCADES

**Cascade Cliffs Winery
and Tasting Room**
Wishram, Washington

**The Dalles Dam Tour Train**
The Dalles

**Huckleberry Festival and Barlow
Trail Days**
Mount Hood

**Tollgate Campground**
Rhododendron

**Wind River Cellars and Tasting Room**
Husum, Washington

(503–622–4822; www.mthood.info). *NOTE:* Do not entertain the notion of climbing Mount Hood—or any other mountain in the high Cascades—without expert guidance, preparation, and assistance.

If you visit the *Mount Hood Recreation Area* from July through September—summer on the mountain—use your copy of *The Barlow Road,* which has a clearly marked map, along with a copy of the Mount Hood National Forest map, and explore to your heart's content on well-marked Forest Service roads. Both maps can be obtained at the Zigzag Ranger Station, just below Toll Gate Campground and Rhododendron, 70220 East US 26 (503–622–3191).

While you're there, ask for current information about summer and fall day hikes in the area. In the nearby *Salmon Huckleberry Wilderness* is the easily accessed *Salmon River National Recreation Trail.* The Salmon River Gorge, with its many waterfalls, is a picturesque area of volcanic plugs, pinnacles, and forested cliffs. The trail lies several hundred feet above the river, except for the lower 2½-mile section.

Ask for directions to the *Hidden Lake Trail,* located just 6 miles east of the Zigzag Ranger Station. In early to mid-June you'll find the lakeside section of the trail punctuated with masses of pale pink blooms from the stately native rhododendrons.

In addition, the 2-mile *Mountaineer Trail,* located higher on the mountain, is an especially good hike for families. Passable from August through October, this trail is on the east side of Timberline Lodge and climbs through gnarled alpine fir beyond the timberline to *Silcox Hut,* at the 7,000-foot level. Silcox Hut offers dormitory-style lodging for small groups. For information call Timberline Lodge at (503) 622–7979. On the hike you'll have splendid panoramic

# Tree, Shrub, and Animal Species in the Mount Hood National Forest

(Information source: USDA Forest Service)

**Above 6,000 feet:** White-bark pine and mountain hemlock, trees being very sparse at this elevation; heathers and juniper; raven, rosy-crown finch, and Clark's nutcracker

**5,000 to 6,000 feet:** Mountain hemlock, subalpine fir, and whitebark pine; big huckleberry, pink and red heather; wolverine and golden-mantled ground squirrel

**3,000 to 5,000 feet:** Douglas fir, noble fir, Pacific silver fir, western and mountain hemlocks, western white pine, lodgepole pine, and Engelmann spruce; rhododendron, huckleberry, vine maple, dwarf Oregon grape, salal, Cascades azalea, and fool's huckleberry; Clark's nuthatch, gray jay, great gray owl, grouse, and sandhill crane

**Below 3,000 feet:** Douglas fir, western hemlock, western red cedar, red alder, and big-leaf maple; rhododendron, vine maple, dwarf Oregon grape, salal, wild hazel, devil's club, and salmonberry; spotted owl

**LOCALLY EXTINCT ANIMAL SPECIES**

**Gray wolf:** The last one was shot in the northern Cascades in the 1940s.

**Grizzly bear:** Wildlife experts surmise they were in the northern Oregon Cascades and were hunted out by early trappers and settlers.

**Mountain goat:** American Indian elders from the Warm Springs tribes say their ancestors hunted the goats on the mountain. Diseases from domestic sheep brought by Europeans could easily have destroyed the population.

**ENDANGERED ANIMAL SPECIES**

Northern spotted owl, bull trout, California wolverine, and Townsend's western big-eared bat

**THRIVING ANIMAL SPECIES**

Black bear, cougar, deer

For further information and to contact regional Forest Service staff members, check the helpful Web site www.fs.fed.us/r6/columbia.

views of Mount Jefferson, Three Sisters, and Broken Top to the south and east and, on a clear day, of the Coast Range some 85 miles to the west. The trail, though quite steep in some places, is easy to navigate during summer months and takes about two hours round-trip.

If you're more than a bit adventurous and a rugged outdoors type of person in good physical condition, consider camping a couple of days at *Five Mile Butte Fire Lookout,* located west of Dufur at the 4,600-foot elevation level in the *Mount Hood National Forest.* In a 14-foot-square rustic cabin-shelter atop a 30-foot wood tower, campers have the ultimate room with a view—a stunning 360-degree panorama of Cascade mountain peaks, alpine and Douglas fir forests, and the rolling wheat fields of central and eastern Oregon. Lots of stairs? Yes, but the view is worth it! The lookout is available from November through May; campers need to bring in their own water and be prepared for snow and very cold weather. For current information and regulations, contact the Barlow Ranger Station in Dufur (541–467–2291). Ask, too, about *Valley View Cabin* in the nearby Badger Creek Wilderness. It's at a lower elevation and open year-round.

If you decide to take a snack or a picnic along on your mountain hikes, stop at *Subway Sandwiches* on US 26 in Zigzag before leaving the area and heading east, climbing toward Laurel Hill, Government Camp, or Timberline. For tasty coffee and espresso drinks, stop at *Mountain High Espresso* (503–622–6334), next to Mount Hood Foods grocery in Rhododendron.

For lovely handmade gifts and willow furniture along with note cards, candles, and casual sportswear, stop and browse through the many treasures offered by Susie Welch at *Heart of the Mountain Gifts and Treasures* at 67898 East US 26 in Welches (503–622–3451). Open daily to 5:30 P.M. Pause for lunch at *The Soup Spoon* (503–622–0303), located at the rear of the gift shop. The daily-special soups are delicious, and the desserts are enticing. On sunny days you can eat at tables on the deck under big umbrellas. Open Tuesday through Saturday from 11:00 A.M. to 4:00 P.M.

For a delicious supper pull over at *Don Guidos Restaurant* (503–622–5141) in Rhododendron, just east of Welches and Zigzag. Owners Doug and Anne Kinne have renovated the interior of the old Log Lodge, long known to skiers and mountain dwellers. Inside, notice the large polished logs with their original horsehair chinking. Winter hours are 5:00 to 9:00 P.M. Thursday through Sunday and 5:00 to 9:00 P.M. daily during summer months.

Since bedding down at lower elevations may be just as appealing as sleeping in the clouds at Government Camp or Timberline, consider *Old Welches Bed and Breakfast Inn* (503–622–3754; www.mthoodlodging.com), located just below Zigzag on Welches Road, across from the old front nine of the original Bowman's Resort (now a classy resort, with the golf course expanded to thirty-six holes). Judi Mondun and her family have restored Jennie Welch's home, and they especially welcome bed-and-breakfast travelers who appreciate a sense of history.

Nearby, innkeepers Coni and Terry Scott at *Hidden Woods Bed & Breakfast,* near Brightwood (503–622–5754; www.thehiddenwoods.com), welcome mountain visitors to a charming log cottage. Up the log stairway are two sleeping spaces, the largest with a queen lodgepole pine feather bed to die for. A sumptuous five-course breakfast is served next door in the Scotts' 3,000-square-foot log home. If the cottage is not available when you call, you could contact the innkeeper at nearby *Brightwood Guest House Bed & Breakfast* (888–503–5783; www.mounthoodbnb.com) for a romantic retreat amid tall Douglas fir and with a miniature pond, private deck, small kitchen, and sleeping loft with a comfy feather bed.

For a romantic gourmet dinner, try the splendid *Rendezvous Grill and Tap Room* (503–622–6837), in Welches just off US 26. For an informal ski lodge atmosphere, a bit more rustic, try the well-worn but well-loved *Zigzag Inn Restaurant* (503–622–4779), just east of Welches and near the Zigzag Ranger Station. And, to order a tasty latte or espresso, and casual food fare, stop at *Mount Hood Roasters* (503–622–1389), located just off US 26 at milepost 41 in Welches. Hours are 7:00 A.M. to 8:00 P.M. daily.

Summer visitors can take in *Sandy Mountain Days* (503–668–4006), held in the community of Sandy, just down the mountain from Welches and Brightwood, toward Gresham and Portland. Highlighting the mid-July festival are, in addition to a carnival and parade, the international Bed Race finals, a wine fair and feast, the annual *Black Powder Shoot,* and a gathering of about 150 Northwest artists and craftspersons who display, demonstrate, and sell their wares in shady *Meining Memorial Park.*

While visiting Meining Memorial Park, stroll through the lovely garden designed for the blind; it contains a variety of scented herbs and an assortment of perennials and annuals of different textures.

Should you be in the area during the fourth weekend of April, around April 25, ask about the All-You-Can-Eat Sportsman's Breakfast, which is held at the Sandy Fire District 72 Main Station, 17460 Bruns Avenue, just off US 26. Trading their fire hoses for frying pans and griddles, the volunteer firefighters cook up a few thousand eggs and as many pancakes and slices of ham to not only herald the beginning of the traditional trout-fishing season but also to earn funds for a number of local charitable causes. The fellows and ladies of District 72 Main Station have been cooking up this breakfast feast every year since 1962. For current information about the event, which is open to townsfolk as well as visitors, call the fire district office at (503) 668–8093. It's a great way to meet the friendly local folks over cups of coffee and heaps of pancakes!

# HELPFUL TELEPHONE NUMBERS AND WEB SITES IN COLUMBIA RIVER GORGE AND HIGH CASCADES

**Camping in National Forest Campgrounds**
(877) 444–6777, www.reserveusa.com

**Columbia Gorge Windsurfing Association**
(541) 386–9225

**Columbia River Gorge National Scenic Area Visitor Center**
(541) 308–1700
www.fs.fed.us/r6/columbia

**The Dalles Area Visitor Center**
(800) 255–3385
www.thedalleschamber.com

**Hood River County Visitor Center**
(800) 366–3530
www.hoodriver.org

**Mount Adams Visitor Information**
(509) 493–3630

**Mount Hood Information Center**
off US 26 at Mount Hood
RV Village, Welches
(503) 622–4822
www.mthood.info

**Multnomah Falls Visitor Center**
(503) 695–2372

**Oregon Department of Fish and Wildlife**
(503) 947–6000
www.dfw.state.or.us

**Oregon State Parks and Campgrounds**
(800) 452–5687

**Road conditions and weather reports**
(800) 977–6368
www.tripcheck.com

**Sandy Area Visitor Center**
(503) 668–4006
www.sandyoregonchamber.org

**Skamania County Visitor Center**
(800) 989–9178
www.skamania.org

**West Columbia Gorge Visitor Center**
(503) 669–7473
www.westcolumbiagorgechamber.com

**USDA Forest Service Recreation and Camping information**
(503) 872–2750
www.naturenw.org

**U.S. Fish & Wildlife Columbia River Information**
(503) 657–2000
www.gorge.net/usfws

**Washington/Oregon/Klickitat County Visitor Center at Waving Tree Vineyard**
Goldendale, Washington
(509) 773–6552

**Zigzag Ranger Station**
off US 26 at Zigzag
(503) 622–3191

# Places to Stay in Columbia River Gorge and High Cascades

## BRIGHTWOOD

**Brightwood Guest House Bed & Breakfast**
64725 East Barlow
Trail Road
(888) 503–5783

## CASCADE LOCKS

**Best Western Columbia River Inn**
(541) 374–8777

## THE DALLES

**Best Western River City Inn**
(888) 935–2378

**Columbia House Bed & Breakfast**
525 East Seventh Street
(541) 298–4686

## GLENWOOD WASHINGTON

**Flying L Ranch**
via Hood River Bridge and
northeast of Hood River
(509) 364–3488

## HOOD RIVER–MOSIER

**Best Western Hood River Inn**
(541) 386–2200

**Mosier House Bed & Breakfast**
US 30, Mosier
(541) 478–3640

**Panorama Lodge Bed & Breakfast**
2290 Old Dalles Road
(888) 403–2687

**Pheasant Valley Orchards Bed & Breakfast**
3890 Acree Drive
(541) 386–2803

## MOUNT HOOD– PARKDALE

**Inn at Cooper Spur**
southwest of Hood River via
Highway 35
(541) 352–6692

## SANDY

**Hidden Woods Bed & Breakfast**
19380 East
Summertime Drive
(503) 622–5754

## WELCHES

**Mount Hood RV Village & Cabins**
US 26
(503) 622–4011
(800) 255–3069

**Old Welches Inn Bed & Breakfast**
26401 East Welches Road
(503) 622–3754

# Places to Eat in Columbia River Gorge and High Cascades

## THE DALLES

**Baldwin Historic Saloon & Restaurant**
First and Court Streets
(541) 296–5666

**Basalt Rock Cafe**
Columbia Gorge
Discovery Center
5000 Discovery Drive
(541) 296–8600

## GOLDENDALE WASHINGTON

**Cafe Maryhill**
Maryhill Museum
(509) 773–3733

## HOOD RIVER

**Bette's Place Cafe**
416 Oak Street
(541) 386–1880

**Egg Harbor Cafe**
1313 Oak Street
(541) 386–1127

**Divots Restaurant**
Indian Creek Golf Course
3605 Brookside Drive
(866) 386–7770

Full Sail Tasting Room
& Pub
506 Columbia Street
(541) 386–2247

Sage's Cafe & Coffee
House, Lunch Deli
202 Cascade Street
(541) 386–9404

**MAUPIN**

The Oasis Cafe
616 Mill Street
(541) 395–2611

**MOSIER**

Route 30 Roadside
Refreshments
US 30
(541) 478–2525

Wildflower Cafe
US 30 , Main Street
(541) 478–0111

**RHODODENDRON**

Mountain High Espresso
next to Mount Hood Foods
(503) 622–6334

**SANDY**

Calamity Jane's
Hamburger Parlour
Restaurant
US 26
(503) 668–7817

The Oregon Candy Farm
48620 SE Highway 26
(503) 668–5066

**WELCHES**

El Burro Loco Cafe
67211 East US 26
(503) 622–6780

The Soup Spoon, Heart of
the Mountain Gifts
67898 East US 26
(503) 622–0303

Wildwood Cafe
Mount Hood RV Village
US 26
(503) 622–0298

**ZIGZAG**

Zigzag Inn Restaurant
US 26
(503) 622–4779

# The Willamette Valley

## Farms and Vineyards

Eons old, with rivers meandering through and bisecting its green hills and rich alluvial soils, the Willamette Valley was surely a welcome sight to the weary pioneers fresh off the Oregon Trail. Out of those abundant soils grew many farms in the 1840s and 1850s and, much later, the hundreds of orchards, nurseries, gardens, and vineyards that continue to thrive in this moist and mild zone between the high Cascade and lower Coast Range mountains and the Pacific Ocean.

This gentle region, now scattered with cities, towns, hamlets, and inviting side roads that skirt Interstate 5 and old Highways 99E and 99W, was also home to the Calapooya Indians. For thousands of years they roamed throughout the broad valley, digging tiny bulbs of the purple camas in early spring, picking juicy blackberries in late summer, and hunting deer and fishing its rivers and streams nearly year-round. If you visit in mid-May, you'll see waves of purple camas blooming along roadsides in meadows throughout the valley.

To get acquainted with this large region, which lies like an enormous green carpet between the mountains and the

# THE WILLAMETTE VALLEY

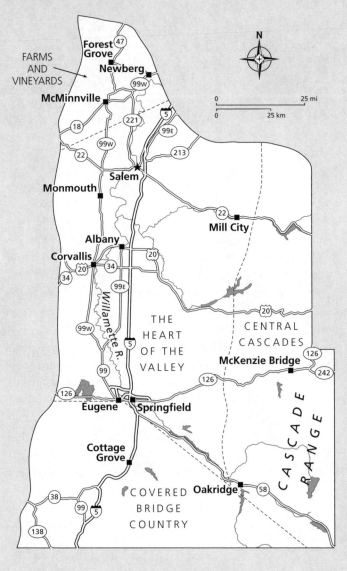

FARMS AND VINEYARDS

Forest Grove
47
Newberg
99w
McMinnville
18
221
5
99w
99E
22
213
Salem
Monmouth
22
Mill City
Albany
Corvallis
34
20
20
34
99E

THE HEART OF THE VALLEY

CENTRAL CASCADES

99w
Willamette R.
5
McKenzie Bridge
126
242
99
126
126
126
Eugene
Springfield
Cottage Grove
COVERED BRIDGE COUNTRY
Oakridge
58
38
99
5
138

CASCADE RANGE

N

0          25 mi
0          25 km

ocean, first head south from Portland on I–5 past Wilsonville to ***Champoeg State Park*** (503–678–1251). This 567-acre park preserves the historic site of the May 2, 1843, meeting at which valley settlers, by a narrow vote, established the first organized territorial government in the Northwest. George Abernethy was elected the territory's first governor. Champoeg was later an important stage-coach stop, trading post, and river landing for steamboats.

From 1850 to 1916 more than fifty steamboats took on passengers, mail, and produce and traversed both the lower and upper sections of the Willamette River south from Portland and Oregon City. To skirt the wide cascading Willamette Falls at Oregon City, the boats, after 1873, navigated the four chambers of Willamette Falls Locks, on the West Linn side of the river, reaching the upper stream. Regular stops included landings at Champoeg, Salem, Albany, Corvallis, and, finally, Eugene, some 100 miles south. The river was the region's "main street" in those days.

On the Saturday of Labor Day weekend, plan to bring a picnic and take in ***Farmstead Day*** at Champoeg State Park, where you and the kids can see colorful living-history activities. The blacksmith fires up his forge, apples are crushed to make cider and apple butter, butter is churned, and wheat is milled in the ca. 1843 Manson barn. You can also tour the nearby Heirloom Kitchen Garden and see the old Champoeg townsite. You can linger overnight in this scenic spot, in the state park campground section, which offers camping and

## TOP HITS IN THE WILLAMETTE VALLEY

**Ballad Town U.S.A.**
Forest Grove

**Champoeg State Park**
Wilsonville

**Cooley's Iris Gardens**
Silverton

**Covered bridges in Linn and Lane Counties**

**Deepwood Estate Gardens and Bush House Gardens**
Salem

**Hendricks Park Rhododendron Garden**
Eugene

**Mary's Peak Auto Tour**
Corvallis

**McKenzie Pass Scenic Drive and Dee Wright Observatory**
McKenzie Bridge

**Mission Mill Village and Thomas Kay Woolen Mill**
Salem

**Mount Angel Abbey**
Silverton

**Mount Pisgah Arboretum**
Eugene-Springfield

**The Oregon Garden**
Silverton

RV sites along with six comfy yurts and six log cabins. For state campground reservations call (800) 452–5687.

Before continuing south toward the state capital, meander over to **New-berg, McMinnville,** and **Forest Grove** to see where many of the old orchards were planted, where new fields of wine grapes are taking root, and where fine old homes are living new lives as tasting rooms or bed-and-breakfast inns. Hundreds of acres are planted with premium wine grapes, and scores of small wineries process the fruit into more than 100,000 gallons of vinifera wines and into thousands of gallons of premium fruit and berry wines. With helpful maps, strike out on your own to visit many wineries and tasting rooms.

To plan a self-guided tour, pick up the handy map at the Washington County Visitors' Association, 5075 SW Griffith Drive, Suite 120, Beaverton (800–537–3149; www.countrysideofportland.org). The locations of these wineries and vineyards range from Beaverton and Newberg out to Hillsboro, McMinn-ville, and Forest Grove. Ask, too, for a copy of the annual *Things to See and Do,* containing detailed maps for visiting vineyards throughout the state.

If you head out toward the Hillsboro area from Portland or Beaverton via U.S. Highway 26 (the Sunset Highway), plan to stop at the **Helvetia Tavern** (503–647–5286), on Helvetia Road just beyond where the road dips under the railroad trestle, about 2 miles north of the highway. Your reward for finding this local gem will be hamburgers the size of dinner plates and fresh-cooked french fries—with skins left on—piled all around. Watch the folks play pool, or

## TOP ANNUAL EVENTS IN THE WILLAMETTE VALLEY

**Amity Daffodil Festival**
Amity; mid-March
(503) 835–2181

**Mount Pisgah Wildflower Festival and Plant Sale**
Springfield; May
(541) 747–3817

**Bohemia Mining Days**
Cottage Grove; mid-July
(541) 942–2411

**Da Vinci Days**
Corvallis; July
(541) 757–6363

**Historic House & Garden Tour**
Albany; July
(541) 928–0911 or (800) 526–2256

**Scandinavian Festival**
Junction City; August
(541) 998–9372

**Great Oregon Steamup**
Brooks; early August
(503) 393–2424

join in yourself. And notice the interesting collection of hats hanging from the walls and rafters. The tavern is open for lunch and dinner every day. *NOTE:* The gentle back roads in this area are fine for bicycling, as well; ask about bike maps at the Washington County Visitors' Association.

If the notion of gargantuan burgers sounds too much for lunch, backtrack on the Sunset Highway a couple of miles, exit at Cornelius Pass, and head south for a lunch or dinner stop at the *Cornelius Pass Roadhouse,* located at 4045 Northwest Cornelius Pass Road (503–640–6174). The restaurant and microbrewery is open for lunch and dinner daily from 11:00 A.M. to 10:00 P.M.

Farms are a way of life in the Willamette Valley, where the passing of the four seasons signals familiar chores having to do with plowing, planting, growing, and harvesting. One group of dedicated draft plowmen, members of the Oregon Draft Horse Breeders Association, continue efforts to improve the five major draft-horse breeds still used for plowing in many areas of the United States. Each spring they, along with the Washington County Historical Society and local service organizations, sponsor the annual *Draft-Horse Plowing Exhibition* (503–645–5353).

At the historical society's center, on the Rock Creek Campus of Portland Community College, you can watch some twenty teams of draft horses (and draft mules) in three-horse teams, each with one plow, demonstrate disk harrowing and plowing. All major breeds of the gentle giants are represented, including Belgian, Clydesdale, Percheron, Suffolk, and Shire. Sets of carefully maintained harnesses used 150 years ago and brought to the territory over the Oregon Trail are used with several of the teams.

See demonstrations of blacksmithing, harnessing, shoeing, and wheel-wrighting, as well as plowing. Bring a picnic lunch or purchase fried chicken, barbecued beef, hamburgers, desserts, and beverages at the farmstead village. The exhibition is held the third Saturday in May, from 10:00 A.M. to 4:00 P.M., near the Washington County Historical Museum on the college campus at 17767 NW Springville Road, just north of the Sunset Highway turning off US 26 at the 185th Avenue exit.

Next throw a corkscrew into the picnic basket and head west on Highway 8 from Hillsboro to Forest Grove. Incidentally, Forest Grove is known as *Ballad Town U.S.A.,* where championship barbershop quartets raise melodious voices in old-fashioned harmony each year in early March. Friendly volunteers, and contestants, too, often dress in Gay Nineties garb. The tickets disappear like hotcakes, so for current information you'll want to contact, in advance, the Forest Grove Visitor Information Center, 2417 Pacific Avenue, (503–357–3006; www.fgchamber.org). In addition, ask about a helpful map for self-guided trips to more Washington and Yamhill Counties vineyards and tasting rooms. You could also contact the Willamette County Wineries Association at (503) 646–2985; www.willamettewine.com, or www.oregonwine country.org.

Also located in Forest Grove is *Momokawa Sake Brewery,* 820 Elm Street (503–357–7056). It is the only such brewery in the Northwest and one of seven such breweries in the United States. The tasting room, which has extraordinary flavors of sake, is open Monday through Saturday from noon to 5:00 P.M. For good eats outdoors with friendly pub ambience, try *The Yardhouse* at the ca. 1922 McMenamins Grand Lodge, located at 3505 Pacific Avenue (503–992–9533; www.thegrandlodge.com) at the east edge of Forest Grove. Or at *Maggie's Buns,* 2007 Twenty-first Avenue, near Main Street (503–992–2231), satisfy your sweet tooth, order a cup of coffee or espresso, have a great lunch, and on some Friday nights enjoy a four-course dinner for less than $15.

While rambling through the rolling Yamhill County area, and if time allows, plan dinner and western-style dancing at the *Flying M Ranch,* 23029 NW Flying M Road (503–662–3222), in the Coast Range foothills near Trask Mountain, just west of the historic community of Yamhill. The 17,000-square-foot main lodge is constructed of enormous logs, many of them from the ranch property. Belly up to the 30-foot-long bar, constructed from a Douglas fir trunk that, when felled, was 36 inches across. The hand-carved bar weighs about six tons. The restaurant is open for breakfast, lunch, and dinner Monday through Thursday from 8:00 A.M. to 8:00 P.M., Friday and Saturday until 10:00 P.M., and on Sunday until 9:00 P.M.

From Yamhill take Highway 47 south to Highway 99W and detour west to McMinnville, the largest community in the Tualatin Valley.

## OTHER ATTRACTIONS WORTH SEEING IN THE WILLAMETTE VALLEY

**Lane County Fair**
Eugene

**The Brass Ring Carousel Project and the Carousel Museum**
Albany

**Evergreen Aviation Museum**
McMinnville

**Salem Peace Plaza**
Salem

**Tokatee Golf Club**
Blue River

Lovers of antiques can easily find the nearby community of Lafayette and poke through eight classrooms filled with treasures and memorabilia of all kinds, sizes, and shapes at the *Lafayette Schoolhouse Antiques Mall* (503–864–2720), housed in the ca. 1910 school building at 748 Third Street (Highway 99W). The mall is open daily from 10:00 A.M. to 5:00 P.M.

The monks at nearby *Trappist Abbey* offer for sale their delicious ginger date nut cake, dark fruitcake, and three kinds of creamed honey, including natural, cinnamon, and ginger. From Lafayette turn north on Bridge Street and go 3 miles to the abbey. The gift shop is open Monday through Saturday from 9:00 A.M. to 5:00 P.M. In nearby Amity, at the *Brigittine Monastery,* 23300 Walker Lane (503–835–8080; www.brigittine.org), the monks turn out legendary truffles and gourmet chocolate fudge. Once you're in Amity, located south of McMinnville via Highway 99W, turn right onto Fifth Street and follow the signs about 4 miles to the monastery. It's open Monday through Saturday from 8:30 A.M. to 5:30 P.M.

If you travel through this area around the third weekend in March, plan to stop at Amity Elementary School, 300 Rice Lane (www.amitydaffodil.org), where you can take in the two-day *Amity Daffodil Festival* put on by the kids, teachers, and parents. Eat such tasty vittles as ham, turkey, lasagna, and barbecued pork ribs as well as legendary desserts like apple cobbler, blackberry pie, chocolate cream pie, and New York cheesecake. You can view a variety of daffodil species in bloom and also take a daffodil walk. Proceeds go to the school's art programs and to scholarships.

If you'd like to stay overnight near the antiques and wine country, there are several fine bed-and-breakfast inns to choose from in the McMinnville-Newberg area, among them *Steiger Haus Bed & Breakfast,* an elegant yet rustic-style home near downtown McMinnville and Linfield College (503–472–0821; www.steigerhaus.com); *Historic Mattey House,* nestled in a small vineyard near McMinnville (503–434–5058); or *Wine Country Farm,* with five varieties of growing grapes and Arabian horses (503–864–3446). For more pastoral views, including a resident elk herd, call the folks at the 350-acre *Gahr Farm* (503–472–6960; www.gahrfarm.com) and ask about the cottage that comes with a hearty farm breakfast.

Just next door to Springbrook Hazelnut Farm is *Rex Hill Winery* (503–538–0666), where folks can drop in to taste locally produced wines. While in the tasting room you can also have a gander at the winery's inner sanctum, where the bubbly stuff is carefully created and aged.

For dining, popular choices are *Red Hills Cafe,* for fine Pacific Northwest dishes, 276 Highway 99W, Dundee (503–538–8224), and *Nick's Italian Cafe,* for northern Italian entrees, 521 NE Third Street, McMinnville (503–434–4471). Other options for informal eats in McMinnville include **Cornerstone Coffee Cafe,** 216 NE Third Street (503–472–6622); **The Sage Restaurant,** for tasty lunches in the 1893 Building at 406 East Third Street (503–472–4445); and **Bistro Maison,** 729 East Third Street (503–474–1888). In Newberg stop at **The Coffee Cottage,** 808 East Hancock Street (503–538–5126), for baked treats and great espresso. In nearby Sherwood detour from Highway 99W at Sherwood Boulevard for tea and scones Tuesday to Saturday at **Lavender Tea House,** 340 NW First Street (503–625–4479).

For further information about Yamhill County's fabulous wine country, contact the Newberg Visitor Center, 415 East Sheridan Street (503–538–2014); and the McMinnville Visitor Information Center, 417 Northwest Adams Street (503–472–6196). Ask, too, about the current schedule of plays offered by the **Gallery Players of Oregon** in McMinnville (503–472–2227) and **Theatre in the Grove** (503–359–5349) in Forest Grove.

# The Heart of the Valley

Head toward the state capital by backtracking about 4 miles from McMinnville via Highway 18 to Highway 221, turning south through Dayton into the heart of the Willamette Valley, and crossing the Willamette River on the **Wheatland Ferry,** one of the last three ferries operating on this historic river. These old-fashioned contrivances are really just cable-operated barges. The ride is short, but you're treated to views upriver and downriver while lumbering across, and the kids will love it. Moreover, the price is right—about $1.00 for an auto. The two others in operation are the **Canby Ferry,** found just north and east of Canby, off Highway 99E, and the **Buena Vista Ferry,** located about halfway between Salem and Albany, near the confluence of the Willamette and Santiam Rivers. The usual hours are from 6:00 A.M. to 9:00 P.M. daily. Passengers on bicycles or on foot can usually ride free of charge.

In the early days of the territory, when competition for trade along the Willamette was keen, various boat landings and trading-post sites sprang up on the banks of the river. Just Albany and Corvallis have survived as good-size river towns. Before heading in that direction, though, detour for a look-see at a well-preserved collection of vintage tractors, automobiles, trolleys, and various types of farm equipment at **Antique Powerland** and **Pacific Northwest Truck Museum,** 3995 Brooklake Road NE, in Brooks, just north of Salem (503–393–2424; www.antiquepowerland.com). In early August you can take in the lively **Great Oregon Steamup** here, with the fun of seeing these enormous mechanical wonders in action. There's even a small 1938 Oregon micro-

Wheatland Ferry

brew truck and a small steam-driven sawmill that get fired up and running during the annual event. There are food and beverage booths, too, of course. Visit the museum grounds daily from 10:00 A.M. to 5:00 P.M.

To feast your eyes on acres of stately bearded iris, from stylish yellows and classic blues to exotic purples and seductive pinks, visit the display gardens at two world-renowned central Willamette Valley iris growers. At **Schreiner's Iris Garden,** 3625 Quinaby Road NE, just north of Salem (503–393–3232; www.schreiners.com), two generations of Schreiners have run the business started in the 1920s by Francis Schreiner. He compiled his first *Iris Lover's Catalogue* in 1928. The field irises are rotated yearly on about 200 acres; you can see some of these level fields blooming alongside I–5 as you motor north or south. Stop at the farm during early spring to enjoy the kaleidoscope of colors in the iris display garden and in the flower display barn. Bulbs can be ordered for later shipment.

Then, just east of Salem, near Silverton, folks can discover more renowned iris growers at **Cooley's Iris Gardens,** located at 11553 Silverton Road NE (503–873–5463). In honor of the garden's sixtieth anniversary, in 1990, a deep caramel-pink iris with a red beard was named for grandmother Pauline Cooley. In mid-May you're invited to help celebrate the garden's current anniversary, with special events including a cut flower show that features hundreds of varieties of the bearded blooms as well as tasting wines from local wineries. The display garden is open daily; camera buffs are encouraged to catch the colorful blooms in the early morning dew.

If mystical tulips and luscious daffodils are your love, however, beat a path to the spring blooming fields at **Wooden Shoe Tulip Farm,** at 33814 South

Meridian Road near Woodburn (503–634–2243; www.woodenshoe.com). You and the kids can wander through some forty acres of gorgeous blooms, order bulbs, purchase cut flowers, browse the gift shop, and attend the spring festival in March through the second week in May. On festival weekends you'll find specialty foods, Northwest wines, microbrews, live music, seminars, and wooden-shoe crafters. *NOTE:* On rainy spring days be sure to pack a thermos of hot chocolate, umbrellas, windbreakers, and sturdy shoes, including extra shoes and warm socks for the kids to change into after field forays.

In *Salem,* pause for a walk through the lovely grounds of the state capitol. In early spring, dogwood, azaleas, and rhododendrons bloom about the well-manicured lawns that surround a large fountain. The setting also offers, from atop the capitol dome, a panoramic view of the city and the broad valley where the Calapooya Indians once lived. Inside the rotunda notice the large, colorful murals depicting historical scenes of the territory and Oregon's beginnings.

Nearby, at 1313 Mill Street SE, stroll through **Mission Mill Museum** (503–585–7012; www.missionmill.org), which houses small shops, boutiques, and eateries, as well as the historic **Thomas Kay Woolen Mill,** in operation from 1889 to 1962. The restored mill now contains the Marion County Historical Society collections, and its displays show the process of changing fleece into fabric. The mill is open Monday through Saturday from 10:00 A.M. to 5:00 P.M. Don't miss the great gift shop on the ground level for a good selection of books and historical memorabilia. You can also join in a tour of the woolen mill and the array of historical houses at the village. Be sure to visit the ca. 1841 **Jason Lee House,** the oldest remaining frame house in the Northwest and the structure that served as the territory's earliest Methodist mission. See, too, the **Pioneer Herb and Dye Garden**'s accumulation of old-fashioned herbs and rare dye plants. The garden is located behind the Methodist parsonage.

The woolen mill drew its power from **Mill Creek,** where there are shady places to feed the ducks and reflect upon the not-so-distant past. The Salem Visitor Center (503–581–4325; www.travelsalem.org) is also located here at the village. The large parking area is a good place to leave your car or recreational vehicle while exploring the nearby historic areas by foot.

Just 4 blocks south, from Twelfth to Sixth along Mission Street, are the marvelous gardens at **Bush Pasture Park, Bush Barn Art Center,** and **Bush House,** an 1878, Italianate-style house built by Asahel Bush, a prominent Salem politician and newspaperman.

The sunny rose garden, just west of the house, was planted in the mid-1950s and contains more than a hundred beds. You can see and sniff more than 2,000 roses tended by Salem Parks Department garden staff and volunteers. Don't miss the Tartar Old Rose Collection, beds of some 300 old garden roses representing varieties and species that came across the prairies during the mid-1800s. This outstanding collection includes such varieties as Rosa Mundi, a striped ancient gallica that is one of the oldest roses mentioned in literature; the Mission Rose, a wedding gift to early pioneer missionary Jason Lee and his bride, Annamarie Pittman; and the lovely damask rose, Bella Donna.

Large perennial beds, located near the greenhouse, have been redesigned and replanted with huge peonies and gatherings of delphinium, astilbe, yarrow, and coreopsis, among other favorites. You can also see the espaliered apple trees and a fine collection of flowering trees and shrubs. Many of these varieties were planted in the early 1900s by Northwest landscape designers Elizabeth Lord and Edith Schryver.

The extensive grounds offer grassy areas for picnicking and for playing with the kids; there's also a small playground area near the well-stocked gift shop and art center. Notice, too, the lovely wisteria vine that climbs on the front porch of Bush House; the old vine is draped with a profusion of pale lavender blossoms in mid- to late May. It's a real showstopper. Bush House is open for tours Tuesday through Sunday from noon to 5:00 P.M. during spring and summer months and from 2:00 to 5:00 P.M. during winter months. To check ahead in case hours have changed, call the staff at (503) 363–4714. The grounds and gardens are open daily dawn to dusk.

## Edible Wild Foods: the Purple Camas

Looking like citron and tasting much like sweet potatoes, steamed purple camas bulbs were dried and stored for winter food by Native Americans. Camas flour mixed with ground tarweed seeds or sweet ripe blackberries made a tasty native dish. Cattail and other roots and bulbs were also dried and ground into flour. The wide flat leaves of the skunk cabbage provided handy wrappings.

Folks today are rediscovering what the native peoples knew—how to harvest and cook the edible native plants of the Willamette Valley. This area is a regular nirvana for edible wild munchables! If you're interested in workshops and field seminars that teach which native plants are edible and also which are not edible (the wild iris is a no-no, for example), contact John N. Kallas, Ph.D., Wild Food Adventures (503–775–3828). You can also browse the informative Web site, www.wildfood-adventures.com, for a current list of wild food workshops and field seminars. To search the Internet for similar topics, try these key words: ethnobotany, Native American Indian ethnobotany, plant identification, edible wild plants, ancient Earth skills, outdoor survival skills, edible cuisine, wild cuisine, sea vegetables, wild gourmet garden vegetables, and deep ecology.

Just a few blocks east of Bush House and Bush Pasture Park is **Deepwood Estate,** at 1116 Mission Street SE. This estate has a fine example of a period English garden, which was designed in 1929 by landscape designers Elizabeth Lord and Edith Schryver. Alice Brown, third owner of the elegant 1894 Queen Anne Victorian house, worked with Lord and Schryver to transform sections of her six-acre estate into various garden rooms.

From the large parking area at the rear, walk onto the main grounds to find the old-fashioned fence and gate that enclose the Tea House Garden. Next, walk down stone steps to the formal Boxwood Garden; its ornamental fencing forms a background for the precisely clipped boxwood hedges growing here. Then, walk back up the steps, detour through the intimate ivy archway onto the main lawn area, and stop to inspect the ca. 1905 white wrought-iron gazebo. Don't miss the 250-foot-long bed of elegant perennials along the eastern perimeter of the grounds, which march in colorful profusion from early spring to late fall. You'll also see dedicated garden volunteers working at Deepwood nearly every Monday morning throughout the year.

You can also browse through the adjacent greenhouse, filled with lush tropical palms, ferns, orchids, and begonias. Deepwood Estate grounds and gardens are open daily dawn to dusk. Call (503) 363–1825 for current information on house tours and special events.

**Salem's Riverfront Carousel,** located in Salem Riverfront Park at 101 Front Street NE (503–540–0374; www.salemcarousel.org), features forty-two gaily painted carousel horses for you and the kids to ride. The price is right, too, at $1.25 per ride for this Old-World-style musical carousel. Also at the park are an on-site artists' studio, two Oregon Trail wagons, and the carousel gift gallery.

For a comfortable overnight stay, consider **A Creekside Garden Inn Bed and Breakfast,** 333 Wyatt Court NE, Salem (503–391–0837; www.salem bandb.com), an impressive Mount Vernon colonial–style house located bankside, on Mill Creek, just a few blocks from Deepwood Estate and the Bush House rose gardens. Breakfast, a hearty affair, is served in the sunny dining room. For eateries in the area, ask about **Jonathan's Oyster Bar** and **Konditorei Cafe.** You can also ask about goings-on at the renovated ca. 1925 **Elsinore Theatre,** 170 High Street SE (503–375–3574; www.elsinoretheatre.com).

From Salem consider making another detour, this one from I–5 east to **Silver Creek Falls State Park** and **Mount Angel Abbey.** Located in the foothills of the Cascade Mountains, the park contains fourteen waterfalls interlaced with a maze of inviting trails in the cool forest—an especially good option on those ~sional ninety-degree days in late summer. In autumn a colorful Oktober- held near Mount Angel. The abbey offers modest rooms and meals for folks who may have overdosed on work or simply have had too much civilization. For information about how to retreat to this lovely place, with its wide-angle views of the Willamette Valley, call (503) 845–3030.

Or, to bed down in a cozy bed-and-breakfast in the pastoral Silverton area, try the restored ca. 1890 *Water Street Inn Bed & Breakfast,* 421 North Water Street (866–873–3344) or *The Edward Adams House Bed & Breakfast,* 729 South Water Street (503–873–8868).

For good eats in Silverton, try *The Silver Grille,* 206 East Main Street (503–873–4035); *O'Briens Cafe,* 105 North Water Street (503–873–7554); and *Silver Creek Coffee House,* 111 North Water Street (503–874–9600).

On your way south from Silverton, pause to visit the splendid *Oregon Garden,* at 879 West Main Street (503–874–8100; www.oregongarden.org), which features a botanical display garden, conifer garden, children's garden, Northwest species garden, and outdoor amphitheater. If time allows, call *Havenhill Lavender Farm* (503–873–0396; www.havenhilllavender.com) and ask about their French Harvest Festival, usually held in late June.

You can also head east into the high Cascades on Highway 22, going across 4,817-foot *Santiam Pass* and reaching central Oregon at Sisters, near the headwaters of the Metolius River. Santiam Pass, flanked by Mount Washington and Mount Jefferson, emerged as the main wagon route into the Willamette Valley from the high-desert and rangeland areas; it was scouted up the South Santiam River by Andrew Wiley in 1859. U.S. Highway 20 from Albany roughly follows the old wagon route, connecting with Highway 22 near *Hoodoo Ski Area* at the top of the pass.

From Highway 22 wind west and south of Salem via US 20 to *Albany.* Back in 1845, two enterprising Scots, Walter and Thomas Monteith, bought the Albany town site along the Willamette River, just 15 miles south of Independence, for $400 and a horse. Each of the three *Albany Historic Districts* offers fine examples of early-nineteenth-century architecture. If possible, do the walking tour—you can park your car near the Visitors' Gazebo on Eighth Street. Some 350 homes—from Georgian revival, colonial revival, and federal to classical, stick, Gothic, and Italianate—have been restored and given status on the National Register of Historic Places. Next to Astoria on the north coast, Albany has one of the most impressive collections of such vintage structures in the state.

You'll see all styles, except perhaps the more flamboyant steamboat Gothic so well known in the southern United States. Folks can also contact the State Historic Preservation Office (503–378–4168) for more information about all kinds of vintage structures open to the public at various times throughout the year—from restored homes and historic churches to vintage

# Snooping into History: Architectural Gems and Historic Sites

Although there are myriad wonderfully renovated historic homes, historic structures, and other architectural gems and historic sites throughout the state, I have many personal favorites. They just seem to wear very well. For me they conjure up romantic images of other times, other eras, other values. I want to know their stories, their secrets. I want to learn about the people who built them and who lived in these places—what were their hopes, dreams, aspirations, failures, and successes? Are there, perhaps, stories of ghosts past and present? I want to draw inspiration for plots and story lines for all those novels and mysteries I plan to write. I imagine all sorts of intriguing characters like villains, scoundrels, scamps, and rascals as well as heroines, heroes, vamps, comics, and sidekicks. There must be hundreds of stories; my imagination takes flight just thinking about all the possibilities: It was a dark and stormy night. . . .

My current list of favorite places to fuel the imagination:

**The Benson Hotel**
downtown Portland

**Elsinore Theatre**
Salem

**Flora (ghost town)**
northeastern Oregon

**Frenchglen Hotel**
Frenchglen, southeastern Oregon

**Geiser Grand Hotel**
Baker City, eastern Oregon

**Heceta Head Lighthouse**
central coast

**Historic Deepwood Estate**
Salem

**Jacksonville Pioneer Cemetery**
southern Oregon

**The Jenkins Estate**
southwest Portland-Beaverton area

**Larwood Covered Bridge**
Albany

**Majestic Theater**
downtown Corvallis

**The original Manor House**
Lewis and Clark College, southwest Portland

**Museum of Art on University of Oregon campus**
Eugene

**Oregon Caves Chateau**
Cave Junction, southern Oregon

**Oregon Electric Station**
downtown Eugene

**Pittock Mansion**
northwest Portland

**Shore Acres Gardens and Simpson Estate grounds**
Coos Bay–Charleston, south coast

**Timberline Lodge**
Mount Hood

**Union Station**
downtown Portland

For helpful information to entice you to plan your own travels into history, you can also contact the State Historic Preservation Office in Salem (503–378–4168; www .oregonstateparks.org) for a list of historic homes and structures currently open to the public.

department stores, carriage and stable companies, and early theaters. These structures are located throughout the state.

Before beginning the walking tour, linger at the gazebo to see old photos of Albany's beginnings and to enjoy a small garden graced by scented lavender, bright snapdragons, pale clematis, deep purple heliotrope, and double hollyhocks. For helpful maps and information about the historic districts and the July *Victorian House & Garden Tours,* contact the Albany Visitor Information Center, 300 Second Avenue SW (800–526–2256; www.albanyvisitors.com). Also ask for directions to visit the carving-in-progress volunteers at the *Brass Ring Carousel Project.* Don't miss it.

Good eateries to check out in Albany include *Ciddici's Pizza* at 133 Fifth Avenue SE (541–928–2536); *The Depot Restaurant* at 822 Lyon Street South (541–926–7326); *Boccherini's Coffee & Tea House* at 208 First Avenue West (541–926–6703); and *Cafe Cristo* at 831 Elm Street SW (541–926–7583), which offers early-evening gourmet dining.

For a pleasant drive into the countryside, ask about the self-guided map to ten covered bridges in the surrounding area. At *Larwood Bridge,* ca. 1939, crossing Crabtree Creek off Fish Hatchery Road, just east of Albany, enjoy a shady park near the swimming hole, along with the nostalgia of an old waterwheel just downstream that has been restored.

Visit one of the most recently renovated covered bridges, *Irish Bend Bridge,* just 14 miles west of Albany, in *Corvallis,* near the campus of Oregon State University. The bridge spans Oak Creek near Thirty-fifth Street and is now part of a popular bicycle and jogging path that meanders from here to nearby *Philomath.* The bridge, dismantled in 1988, originally spanned the Long Tom River at Irish Bend, a tiny community near Monroe, just south of Corvallis. Local bridge buffs and an army of volunteers worked several weekends to reposition the old covered bridge and give it a new roof and fresh coats of white paint. Everyone turned out for the dedication in November 1989, including the OSU president, the Corvallis mayor, and all those hearty volunteers. For additional information about the area, contact the Corvallis Visitor Information Center, 553 NW Harrison Boulevard (800–334–8118; www.visitcorvallis.com).

For a pleasant midsummer afternoon outdoors, get directions at the visitor center to *Avery Park and Rose Gardens,* located at Sixteenth Street and Allen Lane. Here you can sit amid a fine stand of towering redwoods near the extensive rose gardens while the kids somersault and play Frisbee on the enormous lawn. The roses bloom all summer and into fall.

For a comfortable place to hole up for the night in Corvallis, call the friendly bed-and-breakfast innkeepers at *Hanson Country Inn,* 795 SW Hanson Street (541–752–2919; www.hcinn.com), a five-acre, ca. 1928 estate with a gorgeous sunroom and library; *Harrison House Bed & Breakfast,* 2310 NW Harrison Boulevard (541–752–6248), a Dutch colonial–style home built in 1939 and furnished with antiques; and *Chapman House Bed & Breakfast,* 6120 SW Country Club Drive (541–929–3059), a spacious Tudor-style home that overlooks the Coast Range.

For a pleasant side trek from Corvallis, collect lunch or picnic goodies and take Highway 34, which locals call Alsea Highway, heading west toward the coast. Visit *Greengable Gardens,* located at 24690 Highway 34 (541–929–4444), open daily 10:00 A.M. to 6:00 P.M. Continuing on, in the community of Alsea, garden lovers can find *The Thyme Garden* at 20546 Alsea Highway (541–487–8671; www.thymegarden.com). Visit the half-acre English-style display gardens and browse in the nursery, which offers a large selection of herbs and flowers. It's open daily from April 15 to June 15, 10:00 A.M. to 5:00 P.M. and then Friday through Monday until the end of August. Stop at *Alsea Falls* to enjoy your picnic lunch or for a romantic twilight supper. For avid fisherfolk, the Alsea River offers excellent fly fishing for cutthroat, steelhead, and rainbow trout. You can also find a covered bridge nearby, the 1918 *Hayden Covered Bridge,* off Highway 34, which is still in use; it's located about 2 miles west of Alsea. Or you could take your picnic to a higher vantage point, 4,097-foot *Mary's Peak,* also off Highway 34, where you can enjoy panoramic views from the summit and see one of the rare alpine meadows in the Coast Range. Both Alsea Falls and Mary's Peak offer day-use picnic areas and easy walking trails.

If you'd rather eat in Corvallis than picnic, try *Sam's Station,* at 1210 NW Twenty-ninth Street (541–752–6170), for freshly baked goods, sandwiches, and homemade soups; *New Morning Bakery,* at 219 SW Second Street (541–754–0181); *Big River Restaurant & Bow Truss Bar,* at 101 NW Jackson Street (541–757–0694), for Northwest cuisine and local beers; and *The Fox & Firkin,* at 202 SW First Street (541–753–8533), a British-style pub with indoor and outdoor tables. For fine dining try *Michael's Landing,* 603 NW Second Street (541–754–6141), which offers tables with good river views.

Resuming the trail of the Calapooya Indians, continue south on old Highway 99W from Corvallis, past weathered barns, broad fields, and knolls dotted with oak, to the *William L. Finley National Wildlife Refuge Complex* (541–757–7236). A large population of Canada geese winters in the Willamette Valley and along the lower Columbia River, feeding on such winter grasses as ryegrass and fescue, as well as on the cereal grains and corn that are planted in fields near the refuge just for their use. Two additional refuges are located just north of Corvallis—*Ankeny National Wildlife Refuge* and *Baskett Slough National Wildlife Refuge.*

The 5,325-acre Finley Refuge was named for the early naturalist who persuaded President Theodore Roosevelt to create the first national wildlife refuges. Along the self-guided *Woodpecker Loop Trail,* open year-round, visitors can also see wood ducks, hooded mergansers (summer nesters), and ruffed grouse, as well as ring-necked pheasants, California and mountain quail, mourning doves, and black-tailed deer. Further information is available at the office of the refuge complex, 26208 Finley Refuge Road, Corvallis (541–757–7236). Ask about *Snagboat Bend* and about the *Ankeny Refuge Boardwalk Trail* and the gazebo overlook that offers panoramic views at Baskett Slough Refuge.

From the wildlife refuge continue south on Highway 99W through Monroe and Junction City into the southernmost portion of the Willamette Valley, which includes Oregon's second-largest metropolitan area, *Eugene-Springfield.* This region also contains portions of three national forests—Siuslaw, Willamette, and Umpqua—as well as four high Cascades wilderness areas—French Pete, Three Sisters, Diamond Peak, and Mount Washington.

Eugene, home of the University of Oregon, offers not only miles of jogging and bike paths but, especially for chocoholics, the *Euphoria Chocolate Company,* located at 6 West Seventeenth Street, just off Willamette Street (541–343–9223; www.euphoriachocolate.com). Hiding inside dark and light chocolate truffles the size of golf balls are tempting morsels of ganache or crème Parisienne, a rich creamy center that may be laced with amaretto, peppermint schnapps, pecan, toasted almond, or Grand Marnier; or try solid chocolate, milk chocolate, or coffee royal chocolate.

Then, too, you could make a pit stop at *Starbucks,* nearby at West Eighteenth near Willamette Street, for a steaming cup of the coffee of the day, foamy lattes, and pungent espresso as well as delicious scones, muffins, and cookies. Actually, you can find the now familiar green-and-white Starbucks sign in major cities and towns throughout Oregon and Washington (where the regional espresso mania began).

Other fun places to eat include *Steelhead Brewing Co.,* downtown at the corner of Fifth and Pearl Streets (541–686–2739), for a great pub menu and award-winning microbrews made on the premises; and the nearby *Fifth Street Public Market* restaurants, at 296 East Fifth Avenue, which include Eugene's most popular bakery on the lower level, coffee shops, and a number of friendly cafes as well. For lunch weekdays and fine dining daily, a choice spot in a historic train station is the *Oregon Electric Station Restaurant and Lounge,* at Fifth and Willamette Streets, not far from the Fifth Street Public Market. For reservations in one of the elegantly restored and decorated parlor or dining cars, complete with vintage electric side lamps, call (541) 485–4444.

Of course you could always jog or bicycle off the extra calories on the area's network of trails and paths, but *canoeing on the Millrace* might offer a more inviting, less strenuous alternative. Constructed in 1851 by Hilyard Shaw to generate power for the flour mills, woolen mills, and sawmills lining its banks, the narrow stream bubbles up from a pipe that diverts water from the nearby Willamette River; the Millrace then flows through the blackberry vines and ambles behind a number of motels and eateries just across Franklin Boulevard from the University of Oregon campus. For many decades it was the site of college pranks and canoe fetes—often occurring under a full moon. When the water iced over during winter, everyone skated on it, and by the end of the 1920s—when the mills switched to electricity—the Millrace had become the recreational hub of the city.

In the days of the canoe fetes, around 1915, barges and even empty oil drums were transformed into everything from water lilies to seashells. Colored lights were strung along the water, and bleachers were set up along the shore. The boys would swim alongside the floats, while the girls held court on top. Although such fetes on the Millrace are a thing of the past, you can still enjoy paddling a canoe along its lazy, 2-mile-long, backyard journey to Ferry Street, where the water rejoins the Willamette River. Park close to Franklin Boulevard and near the bridge that crosses over to the *Alton Baker Park* nature trails and enjoy sitting in the sun or picnicking on the grassy banks, in the company of friendly quacking ducks that will eagerly chase after your bread scraps. For current information about renting canoes, contact Oregon River Sports at 3400 Franklin Boulevard (541–334–0696; www.oregonriversports.com).

One of the best places to go for a stroll among masses of elegant rhododendrons is a shady, fifteen-acre garden glen, *Hendricks Park Rhododendron Garden* (541–682–4800), open daily. The main paths are wheelchair accessible. Situated at Summit Avenue and Skyline Drive, the garden had its beginnings in the early 1950s, when members of the then Eugene Men's Camellia and Rhododendron Society donated plantings of azaleas and rhododendrons from their own gardens and their individual propagations. Because of this a number of rare species and hybrids are represented in the more than 5,000 varieties. From late April to June, enjoy fine magnolias, dogwoods, viburnums, witch hazels, and hundreds of other ornamentals planted among the hardy azaleas and "rhodies." Growing around the edges of the knoll and towering over all are the familiar Douglas fir and stands of white oak. A small playground and places to picnic are located nearby. Pick up a guide to the garden at the upper parking area.

By all means, take the kids to visit the *Cascades Raptor Center,* at 32275 Fox Hollow Road (541–485–1320; www.eraptors.org), just south of Eugene's city center. You'll see many types and sizes of injured feathered friends, including, for example, golden and bald eagles, osprey, great horned owls, and peregrine falcons, as well as prairie falcons, spotted owls, and red-tailed hawks. Some injured raptors aren't able to return to the wild, so these are housed at the center and often can participate in birds of prey educational programs for school youngsters. The center is open Tuesday, Thursday, Saturday, and Sunday from 10:00 A.M. to 5:00 P.M.; nominal admission fee helps fund the rehabilitation hospital.

## Spring Wildflowers Galore

By mid-March, when most folks have pretty much had it with winter, we happily discover that spring is on its way with the arrival of not only fuzzy pussy willows and pink flowering wild currant but also the bushy Oregon grape's bright yellow flower clusters and the native purple camas, which bloom in swales and woodlands throughout the Willamette Valley.

Hidden deeper in the woodlands are the heart-shaped blossoms of bleeding heart, cream-colored fawn lilies, white trilliums, and the small lavender blossoms of trailing wax myrtle as well as red columbine, purple shooting stars, and, near ponds and streams, colonies of waxy skunk cabbages with compact yellow stamens. A bit later come waves of spiky lupine loaded with small, sweet-pea-shaped bluish lavender blossoms and, nearly everyone's favorite, the wild Nootka rose. With pale pink single blossoms, this delicate rose trails and heaps over fences and along roadsides, a sure sign of spring in the valley.

Visit these Willamette Valley sites from April through June to see waves of native wildflowers as well as migratory songbirds, geese, ducks, and other wildlife:

**Finley National Wildlife Refuge** (541–757–7236). Located 10 miles south of Corvallis on Highway 99W; go 1³⁄₁₀ miles west at Finley Road to the parking area. It's an open field, about 400 acres with rough terrain and no trail, so it's best to enjoy the spectacular wildflower displays from the road. Ask, too, about **Baskett Slough National Wildlife Refuge,** just north of Corvallis, which offers a trail up to a viewing gazebo.

**Mary's Peak.** Driving up to an elevation of about 1,200 feet in the Coast Range, about 10 miles west of Corvallis via Highway 34, you'll find a variety of blooms and picnic areas.

**Mount Pisgah Arboretum** (541–747–3817). Located just east of Lane Community College in Eugene. Follow signs to the Howard Buford Recreation Area. Enjoy picnic areas and walk a network of trails from wetlands and stream banks to the upper, drier sections with hosts of wildflowers everywhere. Stay on the trails, as there are healthy stands of poison oak here.

If you'd like to explore another delightful outdoors area, especially for springtime wildflowers, head a couple of miles east of Eugene to **Mount Pisgah Arboretum,** a 220-acre natural area nestled within the Howard Buford Recreation Area. A place of solitude far from the intrepid joggers and bicyclers, the arboretum offers shady trails and sunny paths along the flank and up the sides of 1,520-foot Mount Pisgah. In early spring you'll see fawn lilies, baby blue eyes, purple camas, and a host of other wildflowers along with more than twenty-five native tree species on the hillside and riverbank areas—this is the east bank of the Willamette River's Coast Fork. This fork, along with the McKenzie River, empties into the main Willamette River channel just north of Eugene. Autumn is a colorful time to visit the arboretum as well. The kids can spot western gray squirrels busily collecting acorns fallen from white oaks. Pocket gophers inhabit a marsh on the upper slopes, and animated frogs chorus beneath a bridge that spans the lily pond near the river. Also keep your eyes peeled for ospreys, pileated woodpeckers, and red-tailed hawks. There are picnic tables and restrooms on the grounds near the headquarters cottage. Information about the arboretum, workshops and guided hikes, the annual Spring Wildflower Show & Plant Sale, the Fall Festival & Mushroom Show, and a map can be obtained from Friends of Mount Pisgah Arboretum (541–747–3817). *NOTE:* Stay on the established trails, as there are healthy stands of poison oak in the areas away from these trails.

For classy overnight accommodations in Eugene, consider **Campbell House, A City Inn,** located on the east side of Skinner's Butte at 252 Pearl Street (800–264–2519, www.campbellhouse.com). Originally constructed in 1892, the structure has been fully restored as an elegant thirteen-room inn. We're talking deluxe here—four-poster beds, fireplaces, whirlpool tubs, telephones, TVs with VCRs, private baths, and sumptuous breakfasts.

For an eighteenth-century, European-style city inn, check with the staff at **Excelsior Inn, Restaurant, and Lounge** at 754 East Thirteenth Avenue (541–342–6963; www.excelsior.com); it once was a three-story fraternity house (ca. 1912). The refurbished inn is within close walking distance of the University of

## Camping Out, ca. 1862

Using established Indian trails, Felix Scott, John Cogswell, and John Templeman Craig chopped through the forest and up over McKenzie Pass in the fall of 1862. They had with them a party of 250 workers, more than 100 ox teams and wagons, and some 850 head of cattle and horses. Do you suppose they barbecued New York strip or filet mignon steaks for dinner?

Oregon campus and to the eclectic cafes, shops, and delis that range in a comfortable jumble along Thirteenth Avenue.

Other comfortable bed-and-breakfast accommodations in Eugene include **Oval Door Bed & Breakfast,** near downtown at 988 Lawrence Street (541–683–3160); **Pookie's Bed 'n' Breakfast,** on College Hill, 2013 Charnelton Street (541–343–0383), which features decor and furnishings from the 1920s and 1930s; and **The Secret Garden,** 1910 University Street (541–484–6755), which has luxurious rooms, some with fireplaces, and one that is wheelchair accessible.

A leisurely and pleasant drive from nearby Junction City, especially with a well-filled picnic basket, loops west along pastoral Highway 36, across Bear Creek, along Long Tom River, around **Triangle Lake,** through Deadwood and Swisshome to Mapleton and the tidewaters at the mouth of the Siuslaw River at Florence. Return to Eugene on Highway 126, through Walton, Elmira, and Veneta. Linger at Triangle Lake for your picnic or stop along the way and pick out a river-worn rock to sit on. While listening to the singing of the streams and rivers, relax into nature's setting and feel the warmth of the afternoon sun—maybe even take a snooze. Along the way are several waysides and picnic areas, some with boat landings, but there are no campgrounds on this particular route.

If you travel through the area around the third weekend in March, go north about 2 miles on Highway 99W from Junction City and turn west on Ferguson Road to enjoy some 6 miles of daffodils that bloom in profusion along the roadsides and fences during the annual **Daffodil Festival** (541–998–6154; www.junctioncity.com). Go early in the day and stop at the Long Tom Grange, also on Ferguson Road, for cinnamon rolls and sticky buns along with displays of flowers, quilts, local arts and crafts, antique cars, and farm animals. Call ahead for the current dates.

# Central Cascades

If you pass through the Eugene-Springfield area during September or October, consider taking a walking tour of the **University of Oregon** campus before heading east into the mountains. The outing provides a pleasant visual overdose of autumn hues clustered on a wide variety of well-established native and non-native tree species, and you'll find plenty of places to park in and around the campus just off Franklin Boulevard.

Then head about 70 miles farther on the trail of glorious autumn foliage by continuing east from Springfield via Highway 126, to access the **McKenzie Pass Scenic Drive.** After driving through the tiny communities of Vida, Blue

River, and McKenzie Bridge—each hugs the banks of the McKenzie River like a dedicated trout angler—turn onto Highway 242, just east of the McKenzie Ranger Station, for one of the best displays of fall colors in the region.

That characteristic nip in the air signals the return of another season in the Northwest woods, and autumn declares its arrival with leaves turned bright crimson, vibrant orange, and vivid yellow. On the quiet winding road that loops and twists about 20 miles to the top of McKenzie Pass, soft breezes whisper through dark green Douglas fir and stir the colored leaves of big-leaf maple, vine maple, alder, and mountain ash.

You're in the **Willamette National Forest** now—the largest of eighteen forests within Oregon and Washington and one of the largest in the United States. The original incentive for finding a route across the Cascades in this area was the discovery of gold in Idaho more than a century ago. In 1862 Capt. Felix Scott and a couple of colleagues, John Cogswell and John Templeman Craig, formed a party at Eugene to deliver supplies to the Idaho mining area. Under the auspices of his firm, the **McKenzie Salt Springs and Deschutes Wagon Road Company,** John Craig collected tolls at McKenzie Bridge until 1891. He lived nearby for many years and is buried at the summit.

Sometime around 1910 an automobile chugged over the summit, probably with extra fuel, water, and a supply of axes and saws to remove limbs and trees that seemed always to plague early travelers on the rutted, bumpy gravel and dirt roads. You will reach the top of 5,325-foot McKenzie Pass via the scenic and *very* winding road with relative ease, however, and can detour into the parking area to walk stone steps up to the **Dee Wright Observatory.** From this towerlike stone structure, constructed in the early 1930s by the Civilian Conservation Corps, you can peer through eleven narrow windows, each

## Favorite Places for Fall Leaf Lovers

College campuses: University of Oregon (Eugene); Oregon State University (Corvallis); Lewis and Clark College (southwest Portland); Marylhurst University (Lake Oswego–southwest Portland); Reed College (southeast Portland)

Highway 242, the old McKenzie River Highway from McKenzie Bridge to the top of McKenzie Pass

Hoyt Arboretum (southwest Portland)

Japanese Garden (southwest Portland)

The western section of the Columbia River Gorge, between Portland and Hood River

# Dee Wright and Scenic Highway 242

In the early 1930s Dee Wright supervised a crew of Civilian Conservation Corps (CCC) workers who constructed the rock observatory that sits amid the lava fields at the top of McKenzie Pass. It is said that Wright was a skilled woodsman, trailmaker, and colorful storyteller. He first lived near Oregon City among the Molalla Indians and learned their culture, folklore, and survival skills. He became a government packer and learned intimately the natural terrain of the Cascade Mountains between Mount Hood and Crater Lake. One of his most stubborn mules was named Dynamite.

Dee Wright sounds to me like a combination of Humphrey Bogart, John Wayne, and Harrison Ford; a rugged outdoorsman who thrived on adventures, a colorful character well known in the early West. I don't think he would be the type of person to sit at a desk in a corporate high-rise. He died in 1934 at the age of sixty-two, just before the CCC project at the top of McKenzie Pass was completed. The USDA Forest Service named the structure Dee Wright Observatory in his memory. I think he would have liked that.

Don't miss stopping at this incredibly scenic spot, with its wide-angle views of not only massive solidified lava flows in every direction but also of the series of beautiful snowcapped mountains in the Cascades' volcanic chain. You can also hike along a paved walkway through the lava fields. The drive up windy Highway 242 is especially lovely in mid- to late October, when the autumn colors are brightest. For additional information stop by the McKenzie Ranger Station (541–822–3381; www.fs.fed .us/r6/willamette), just above the community of McKenzie Bridge.

focused on a particular mountain peak; the peak's name and distance from the viewpoint are carved into the stone.

To the southeast are Belknap Crater, Mount Washington, the North and Middle Sister, and Mount Scott; Mount Jefferson and Mount Hood hover over lesser peaks to the north. If time allows, walk the 2-mile trail—it's part of the *Pacific Crest National Scenic Trail*—up *Little Belknap Crater* to see fissures, lava tunnels, and spatter cones. Like Lava Cast Forest near Bend, it's an intriguing, close-up encounter with those massive lava fields of the high central Cascades, which cover thousands of acres with at least three layers of the rough black stuff.

As evidenced by the recent activity from Mount Saint Helens, geologists believe the fires deep inside Oregon's Cascade crest are just napping and may someday erupt again, as did Mount Saint Helens to the north, in Washington, in May 1980. The McKenzie Ranger Station (541–822–3381), just east of McKenzie Bridge, will have current weather and road information for the area, maps of the nearby *McKenzie River National Recreation Trail,* which is especially suited to beginning hikers and families with young children, and direc-

# Tree Species Known for Fabulous Fall Colors

**Autumn blaze maple:** Shows brilliant orange-red leaves and long-lasting color in fall.

**Autumn flame maple:** Its medium-green foliage turns bright red in fall.

**Autumn purple ash:** Its textured green leaves turn a spectacular range of colors in fall, from yellow-orange to orange-red to deep purple.

**Cascade snow cherry:** Its dark-green leaves turn yellow to bronze in fall.

**Chanticleer pear:** Its glossy green leaves turn gold-red to plum in fall.

**Dawn redwood:** An ancient tree and a deciduous conifer, its needles turn rusty-orange in fall.

**Emerald Queen Norway maple:** Its deep-green leaves turn yellow in fall.

**Frontier elm:** Its glossy green leaves turn burgundy in fall.

**Japanese stewartia:** Its medium- to dark-green leaves turn dark purple in fall.

**Milky Way Kousa dogwood:** Its dark-green leaves turn bright red in fall.

**Red sunset maple:** Its glossy foliage turns a spectacular orange-red to red in fall.

**Scarlet oak:** Its glossy dark-green leaves turn deep red in fall.

**Seiryu Japanese maple:** Its lacy leaves turn golden orange to orange-red in fall.

**Tamarack or larch:** A conifer well known in central Oregon's high-desert mountains east of Prineville, its lacy needles turn brilliant yellow-green in fall.

**Vine maple:** Well known in the Cascade Mountains, its medium-green leaves turn yellow, orange, and bright red in fall.

tions to nearby Forest Service campgrounds. Located on Highway 126, the ranger station is open from 8:00 A.M. to 4:30 P.M. on weekdays. *NOTE:* Scenic McKenzie Pass and Highway 242 are closed by snow during winter months; Highway 126, however, remains open across Santiam Pass to Sisters and central Oregon.

You can also call the folks at ***Belknap Resort and Hot Springs*** (541–822–3512; www.belknaphotsprings.com) to reserve a room in their historic, refurbished lodge on the banks of the McKenzie River, a couple of miles from the ranger station. Six small cabins—bring your own bedding—and forty-two camping/recreational vehicle spaces are also available, all within walking distance of two hot mineral springs swimming pools. You can also walk to a scenic section of the McKenzie River Recreation Trail from the upper campground. Then, take the footbridge across the river, near the lodge pool, and enjoy a short walk to the new woodland gardens areas, which are simply splendid.

The many mineral springs in the area were long known to Indian peoples, who believed they held restorative and healing powers. Belknap Hot Springs, discovered by R. S. Belknap around 1869, was a longtime favorite of families living in the valley.

The lodge was built across the river from the location of the mineral springs, and by 1910 a daily motor stage from Eugene had been established—the trip on the original dirt and gravel road took a whole day. During the season of 1890, some 700 lodge guests were registered, at a cost of $15.00 per week; one could tent camp at a weekly rate of $1.50.

On your visit you'll notice billows of steam rising from the hot springs on the far side of the McKenzie River; the 130-degree mineral water is piped across the river to the lodge and pool. The mineral water is cooled to a temperature of about 102 degrees in the swimming pool and is perfect for soaking one's weary bones at the end of a day of hiking and exploring the area.

By continuing east on US 26 a few miles from Belknap Hot Springs, you can stop and see a pair of lovely waterfalls that drop over basalt ledges across the bubbling McKenzie River. Named **Koosah Falls** and **Sahalie Falls,** they are within a short walk of each other. Sahalie Falls is wheelchair accessible.

Playing hide-and-seek with Highway 126, the snow-fed **McKenzie River** has long been known by lovers of fishing. According to lively accounts from

## Recipe for Hot Springs

Most hot springs contain about two dozen different minerals—from potash and arsenic, silica and potassium, chlorine and calcium to sodium, sulfuric acid, and bicarbonic acid. The hot water, from deep underground where temperatures are scalding, rises along cracks or fissures in places where the rocks have been faulted or folded by Mother Nature. The large swimming pool at Belknap Hot Springs is especially good for a soothing swim or a lazy and relaxing float on an air mattress. It's one of my favorite places to stop along US 26 as it meanders east from Eugene and over the Santiam Pass to the central Oregon town of Sisters. Pack your swimsuits and towels and stop for a swim between the hours of 9:00 A.M. and 9:00 P.M. For overnight accommodations call at least a month in advance and try to go midweek; everyone else has discovered the place, too! Bring a picnic and enjoy. Or call the historic Log Cabin Inn Restaurant (541–822–3432) in nearby McKenzie Bridge for meal reservations; it's open year-round for dinner, open all day on Sunday, and open for lunch as well June through November.

old newspapers of the early 1900s, "wet flies were disdained by the swiftly traveling denizens of the rapids and many misses suffered before anglers acquired the knack of handling the rod properly . . . whether trout bite or not, there are times when a fisherman must stop fishing and tell fish stories." For current regulations and angler's licenses, stop at one of the grocery stores in **Leaburg, Vida, Blue River,** or **McKenzie Bridge.** You can also contact the Oregon Department of Fish and Wildlife for helpful maps, brochures, and current regulations (503–947–6000 or 800–720–6339).

For information about guided river fishing in the well-known **McKenzie River Driftboats** (800–32–TROUT), as well as about other guided rafting trips, contact the Visitors' Association of Lane County, 115 West Eighth Street, Eugene (541–484–5307; www.visitlanecounty.org).

A final detour into this section of the central Cascades is accessed via Highway 58, just south of Eugene and winding about 30 miles east up to the community of **Oakridge.** Along the way notice the Southern Pacific Railroad tracks, a historic transportation link to the upper Willamette area that has operated since 1912. In the early 1930s as many as five passenger trains passed through Oakridge each day, with stops at Fields, McCredie Springs, Cascade Summit, and Crescent Lake on the east side of the pass. Rotary snowplows, mounted on the trains, kept the Cascade line open during the winter, and the train crews stopped at a cook house at the summit for hot meals.

In good weather a popular excursion in those early days was to get off the train at Diamond Creek, hike down a trail to **Salt Creek Falls,** enjoy a picnic beneath tall firs, and then take the next train back home. Travelers can do the same using an automobile. The falls are located about 20 miles east of Oakridge via Highway 58, and there you can hike a short trail to this spectacular, frothy ribbon, which cascades some 286 feet down into a small canyon. These are the second-highest falls in the state.

Next continue east on Highway 58 to the 5,128-foot summit, **Willamette Pass,** to see one of the state's oldest ski areas. Of course the original rope tow built by Roy Temple and fellow ski enthusiasts from Oakridge in the 1940s is now gone, but in its place rises a chairlift that carries a new crop of skiers nearly a mile to the top of 6,666-foot Eagle Peak. Roy and his wife, Edna, ran the original ski area for a number of years and lived at Cascade Summit, at the west end of nearby Odell Lake. Edna remembers making and serving chili, hot dogs, cupcakes, and coffee at the ski shack, with a roaring bonfire out in front. You can enjoy seeing memorabilia about Oakridge and the ski area at the **Oakridge Pioneer Museum,** at 76433 Pine Street (541–782–2402). The museum is open Tuesday and Thursday 9:00 A.M. to noon and on Saturday from 1:00 to 4:00 P.M.

For an overnight stay just east of the summit, at a brisk elevation of 4,800 feet, check with the staff at **Odell Lake Lodge and Resort** (541–433–2540), located at the sunny southeast corner of the lake. There is moorage space at the marina, and motorboats, canoes, rowboats, and small sailboats are available to rent by the hour or day. In summer and fall anglers fish for Kokanee salmon, Mackinaw lake trout, and native rainbow trout on the 5-mile-long, 300-foot-deep lake; during winter cross-country skiers and snow bunnies flock to the area from the valley. The small restaurant in the lodge is open seasonally.

From here you can continue east on Highway 58 to connect with U.S. Highway 97 in central Oregon. Crater Lake National Park is about 60 miles south via US 97.

# Covered Bridge Country

Continuing south on I–5 from the Eugene-Springfield area, exit at **Cottage Grove** and, bearing to the east past the Village Green Inn on Row River Road, stop at the Forest Service ranger station to pick up maps and information about covered bridges and historic mining areas. From Row River Road take back roads past vintage covered bridges into the **Bohemia Mine** area, enjoying the rural countryside along the way.

With good brakes and a radiator full of water, adventurous travelers can negotiate the narrow, winding gravel road to **Fairview Peak** and **Musick Mine,** at the top of 5,933-foot Bohemia Mountain. On a clear day Mount Shasta can be seen to the south, the gossipy Three Sisters Mountains to the north, and the Coast Range to the west. Along the 70-mile loop drive are other places to stop as well.

Although some 400 miners once called the Calapooya Mountains in this area home, now gentle breezes rattle broken, rusted hinges and scuttle through a fallen-down cookhouse or blacksmith shop or remnants of an old hotel or store. The mines flourished from 1890 until 1910, with some activity after World War I, but most of the mines have given way to wind, rain, snow, and time. In the old days it took six to eight horses from eight to ten hours to pull a load of supplies and mining equipment up Hardscrabble Grade, the steep, 6-mile trail.

Today smooth country roads reach into the Bohemia mining country, wrapping around green hills and pastures where woolly sheep and multicolored cows graze peacefully in the sun. *NOTE:* Even though a shack may look long forgotten and deserted, it may actually be someone's headquarters for mining exploration or assessment work; the mines are on private land and are not to be disturbed by travelers. Check at the ranger station in Cottage Grove

Willamette Valley covered bridge

if you're interested in public gold-panning areas—there are several in the immediate area.

A wagon road was the first main route into the Row River area; it wound along the river through Culp Creek to **Currin Bridge,** a covered bridge built in 1925 over Row River. In the surrounding Cottage Grove–Eugene–Springfield area, it's possible to explore nearly twenty of the fifty-three covered bridges still standing in the state. Calling forth a bit of horse-and-buggy nostalgia or images of kids with fishing poles and cans of worms, most covered bridges are under the protection of local historical societies. Although most are no longer for public use, a few do remain open to automobile traffic and, of course, to artists, photography buffs, and folks with fishing poles. In Cottage Grove the **Covered Bridge Festival** is celebrated in mid-September.

From exposed trusses and rounded portals, to Gothic-, portal-, or louvered-style windows, to tin or shingled roofs, the covered bridges in this area are more numerous than in any other section of the state. Five are in the immediate Cottage Grove area, and four are still in active use for automobiles, bicyclers, and hikers. The longest covered bridge in the state is **Office Bridge,** spanning 180 feet across the north fork of Middle Fork of the Willamette River at Westfir, near Oakridge. The shortest, at just 39 feet, is **Lost Creek Bridge,** located in southern Oregon.

In the 1930s there were more than 300 covered bridges in the state, but by the 1950s their numbers had dwindled to fewer than 140. The ***Covered Bridge Society of Oregon*** is dedicated to preserving and restoring the remaining bridges and also promotes the study of the bridges' history and unique construction. A helpful map and brochure showing all fifty-three bridge locations

## Visiting Covered Bridges

### ALBANY-CORVALLIS AREA

For helpful maps and current information, contact

**Albany Visitors' Association**
(541) 928–0911
www.albanyvisitors.com

**Corvallis Visitors' Bureau**
(541) 757–1544
www.visitcorvallis.com

**Hoffman Bridge** (1936); spans Crabtree Creek

**Irish Bend Bridge** (1954); spans 100 feet over Oak Creek on the Oregon State University campus

**Larwood Bridge** (1939); spans 103 feet over Crabtree Creek

**Ritner Bridge** (1926); spans Ritner Creek

**Shimanek Bridge** (1966); spans 130 feet over Thomas Creek

### COTTAGE GROVE AREA

Contact the

**Cottage Grove Visitor Center**
(541) 942–2411
www.cgchamber.com

**Centennial Pedestrian Bridge** (1987)

**Chambers Bridge** (1936)

**Currin Bridge** (1925)

**Dorena Bridge** (1949)

**Mosby Creek Bridge** (1920)

### EUGENE-SPRINGFIELD-WESTFIR AREA

Contact the

**Visitors' Association of Lane County**
(541) 484–5307
www.visitlanecounty.org

Ask about the guide *Oregon's Covered Bridges: Proudly Spanning the Years.*

**Goodpasture Bridge** (1938); spans the McKenzie River

**Lowell Bridge** (1945)

**Office Bridge** (1944); spans the north fork of Middle Fork of the Willamette River

**Parvin Bridge** (1921)

**Pengra Bridge** (1928); spans 120 feet over Fall Creek

**Unity Bridge** (1936)

### HELPFUL COVERED-BRIDGE RESOURCES

**Covered Bridge Society of Oregon**
www.coveredbridges.stateoforegon.com

**Willamette Valley Visitors' Association**
(866) 548–5018
www.willamettevalley.org

in twelve different areas of the state can be obtained at the Cottage Grove Visitor Center, 700 East Gibbs Avenue (541–942–2411; www.cgchamber.com).

For easy hiking into meadows carpeted with alpine wildflowers in July and August, near Cottage Grove, try the **June Mountain Trail,** the **Adams Mountain Trail,** or the **Hardesty Trail**—maps and information are available at the ranger station on Row River Road. Keep alert, too, for some of the forty kinds of edible wild berries that grow in the region. Tiny wild blackberries ripen in August, salal berries are abundant in forested areas, and the Oregon grape berries are plentiful in late summer and fall. All make delicious jams and jellies, and all were used by the Native American peoples as well.

In early spring you can see waves of blooming purple camas that carpet the swales along I–5 between Creswell and Cottage Grove. Long ago the Indians gathered the tiny bulbs of the purple camas for winter food and steamed them in large pits lined with heated rocks and wet grass, covered over with hides to hold in the heat.

In mid-July, Cottage Grove celebrates **Bohemia Mining Days** with a tour of historic homes, a lunch barbecue at Historic Snapp House, and fiddlers' contests. The Prospector's Breakfast on Sunday at the top of Bohemia Mountain ends the three-day celebration. You can also see Bohemia mining memorabilia at the **Cottage Grove Historical Museum,** housed in the ca. 1897, octagonal, former church building located at Birch and H Streets. Call (541) 942–2411 for current hours.

By all means, plan to stay overnight in Cottage Grove's covered-bridge country, and for cozy accommodations you can check with **Lily of the Field Bed & Breakfast,** 35712 Ross Lane (541–942–2049); or with Kathe and Harry McIntire at **Apple Inn Bed & Breakfast,** 30697 Kenady Lane (541–942–2393; www.appleinnbb.com).

---

## triviaquiz: willamettevalley coveredbridges

1. Which covered bridge is a pedestrian bridge?

2. Which covered bridge is a railroad bridge?

3. Which covered bridge is one of the best places to picnic?

4. Which covered bridge has an attached pedestrian walkway and is also, at 180 feet long, the longest covered bridge in Oregon?

5. Which covered bridge is currently in most need of TLC?

Answers: 1. Centennial Bridge 2. Chambers Bridge 3. Larwood Bridge 4. Office Bridge 5. Lowell Bridge

For eateries in the Cottage Grove area, try *Cafe Sheilagh,* 616 East Main Street (541–942–5510), for gourmet natural eats, scones and pastries, and espresso; and *Stacy's Covered Bridge Restaurant & Lounge,* at 401 Main Street (541–767–0320).

# Places to Stay in the Willamette Valley

## CORVALLIS

**Chapman House Bed & Breakfast**
6120 SW Country Club Drive
(541) 929–3059

**Nutcracker Sweet Bed & Breakfast**
3407 NW Harrison
(541) 752–0702

**Ramada Inn**
1550 NW Ninth Street
(541) 753–9151

## COTTAGE GROVE

**Apple Inn Bed & Breakfast**
30697 Kenady Lane
(800) 942–2393

**Village Green Motor Inn and RV Park**
725 Row River Road
(541) 942–2491

## EUGENE

**Best Western Greentree Inn**
1759 Franklin Boulevard
(541) 485–2727

## McKENZIE BRIDGE

**Log Cabin Inn**
riverfront cabins
off Highway 126
(541) 822–3432

## McMINNVILLE

**Best Western Vineyard Inn**
2035 South Highway 99W
(503) 472–4900

**Steiger Haus Bed & Breakfast**
360 Wilson Street
(503) 472–0821

## SALEM

**Best Western Mill Creek Inn**
3125 Ryan Drive SE
(503) 585–3332

**Salem RV Park**
4490 Silverton Road NE
(503) 364–5490

## SILVERTON

**The Edward Adams House Bed & Breakfast**
729 South Water Street
(503) 873–8868

## VIDA

**The WayFarer Resort**
46725 Goodpasture Road
off Highway 126
(541) 896–3613

# WINE COUNTRY WEB SITES

**Northwest Palate**
www.nwpalate.com

**Oregon Wine Advisory Board**
www.oregonwine.org

**Willamette Valley Wineries Association**
www.willamettewine.com

## Places to Eat in the Willamette Valley

### ALBANY

**Boccherini's Coffee & Tea House**
208 First Avenue West
(541) 926–6703

**Novak's Hungarian Restaurant**
2306 Heritage Way SE
(541) 967–9488

### CORVALLIS

**The Beanery Coffee House**
500 SW Second Street
(541) 753–7442

**Jamie's Great Hamburgers**
1999 NW Circle Boulevard
(541) 758–7402

**Señor Sam's Mexican Grill & Cantina**
140 NW Third Street
(541) 754–7448

### COTTAGE GROVE

**Cafe Sheilagh**
616 East Main Street
(541) 942–5510

### EUGENE

**Full City Coffee Roasters**
842 Pearl Street
(541) 344–0475

**Oregon Electric Station Restaurant**
27 East Fifth Avenue
(541) 485–4444

**Waterfront Bar & Grill**
2210 Centennial Boulevard
(541) 465–4506

### FOREST GROVE

**Maggie's Buns Coffee House**
2007 Twenty-first Avenue
(503) 992–2231

**The Yardhouse Pub & Grill McMenamins Grand Lodge**
3505 Pacific Avenue
(877) 992–9533

### HILLSBORO

**Sweet Oregon Grill**
6393 NW Cornelius Pass Road
(503) 614–8747

### McKENZIE BRIDGE

**Log Cabin Inn Restaurant**
off Highway 126 between mileposts 50–51
(541) 822–3432

### McMINNVILLE

**Rooftop Bar, McMenamins Hotel Oregon**
310 NE Evans Street
(888) 472–8427

### NEWBERG

**The Coffee Cottage**
808 East Hancock Street
(503) 538–5126

### SALEM

**Jonathan's Oyster Bar**
445 State Street NE
(503) 362–7219

**Konditorei Cafe**
310 Kearney Street SE
(503) 585–7070

### SILVERTON

**Cafe Amica at Roth's**
918 North First Avenue
(503) 873–6311

**O'Briens Cafe**
105 North Water Street
(503) 873–7554

### VENETA

**Our Daily Bread Cafe & Bakery**
88170 Territorial Road
(541) 935–4921

## HELPFUL TELEPHONE NUMBERS AND WEB SITES FOR THE WILLAMETTE VALLEY

**Albany Convention & Visitors' Association**
(541) 928–0911
www.albanyvisitors.com

**Corvallis Visitor Information Center**
(541) 757–1544
www.visitcorvallis.com

**Cottage Grove Visitor Information Center**
(541) 942–2411
www.cgchamber.com

**Covered Bridge Society of Oregon**
www.coveredbridges
stateoforegon.com

**Eugene Convention & Visitors' Association of Lane County**
(541) 484–5307
www.visitlanecounty.org

**Forest Grove Visitor Information Center**
(503) 357–3006
www.fgchamber.org

**McKenzie Ranger Station**
McKenzie Bridge
(541) 822–3381

**McMinnville Visitors Information Center**
(503) 472–6196
www.mcminnville.org

**Middle Fork/Oakridge Ranger Station**
Oakridge
(541) 782–2291

**Newberg Area Visitor Information Center**
(503) 538–2014

**Oakridge/Westfir Visitors Information**
(541) 782–4146

**Oregon Farmers' Markets Association**
www.oregonfarmers
markets.org

**Salem Visitor Information Center**
(503) 581–4325
www.travelsalem.com

**Silverton Visitor Information Center**
(503) 873–5615

**State Historic Preservation Office**
(503) 378–4168
www.oregonstateparks.org

**Washington County Visitors' Bureau**
(503) 644–5555
www.countrysideofportland.com

**Willamette Valley Visitors' Association**
(866) 548–5018
www.willamettevalley.org

# Appendix: Travel Planning Resources

**Oregon Department of Aviation**
(flight maps, flight seeing)
(503) 378–4880
www.aviation.state.or.us

**Oregon fishing information
Oregon Department of Fish
and Wildlife**
(800) 720–6339
www.dfw.state.or.us

**Oregon Historic Cemeteries
Association**
(503) 378–4168
www.oregoncemeteries.org

**Oregon Marine Board**
(503) 378–8587
www.boatoregon.com

**Oregon road and mountain pass
conditions**
(800) 977–6368
www.tripcheck.com

**Oregon State Historic
Preservation Office**
(503) 378–4168
www.shpo.state.or.us

**Oregon state parks campground
information**
(800) 551–6949
www.oregonstateparks.org

**Oregon state parks campground
reservations**
(800) 452–5687
www.oregonstateparks.org

**Oregon Tourism Division**
775 Summer Street NE, Salem
(800) 547–7842
www.traveloregon.com

**U.S. Bureau of Land Management
(BLM)**
(503) 808–6002
www.or.blm.gov

**USDA Forest Service Recreation
Information** and **Nature of the
Northwest, Portland**
(503) 872–2750

**USDA Forest Service campground
reservations**
(877) 444–6777
TDD reservations, (877) 833–6777

# Indexes

*Entries for bed-and-breakfast inns; gardens, arboretums, and nurseries; hotels, inns, lodges, and resorts; museums and historical centers; and restaurants appear in the special indexes beginning on page 264.*

## GENERAL INDEX

## BED-AND-BREAKFAST INNS

## GARDENS, ARBORETUMS, AND NURSERIES

## HOTELS, INNS, LODGES, AND RESORTS

## MUSEUMS AND HISTORICAL CENTERS

## RESTAURANTS, CAFES, BAKERIES, COFFEE SHOPS

## About the Author

Myrna Oakley has traveled the byways of the Northwest and western British Columbia since 1970, always with a camera in hand and an inquisitive eye for natural and scenic areas, as well as for wonderful inns, gardens, and places with historical character and significance. In this process she has developed an affinity for goosedown comforters, friendly conversations by the fire, and intriguing people who generally prefer to live somewhat off the beaten path.

In addition to *Oregon Off the Beaten Path,* she has written *Washington Off the Beaten Path, Recommended Bed & Breakfasts: Pacific Northwest, Public and Private Gardens of the Northwest,* and *Bed and Breakfast Northwest.* She also teaches about the business of freelance writing, novel writing, and travel writing at Portland Community College.

## About the Illustrator

Elizabeth Neilson Walker lives in Portland and operates her own graphic arts business. She also illustrates fiction and nonfiction books for children and adults.